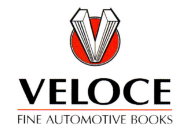

Also from Veloce Publishing

Essential Buyer's Guide series
Porsche 356 (Johnson)
Porsche 911 (964) (Streather)
Porsche 911 (991) (Streather)
Porsche 911 (993) (Streather)
Porsche 911 (996) (Streather)
Porsche 911 (997) – Model years 2004 to 2009 (Streather)
Porsche 911 (997) – Second generation models 2009 to 2012 (Streather)
Porsche 911 Carrera 3.2 (Streather)
Porsche 911SC (Streather)
Porsche 924 – All models 1976 to 1988 (Hodgkins)
Porsche 928 (Hemmings)
Porsche 930 Turbo & 911 (930) Turbo (Streather)
Porsche 944 (Higgins)
Porsche 981 Boxster & Cayman (Streather)
Porsche 986 Boxster (Streather)
Porsche 987 Boxster and Cayman 1st generation (2005-2009) (Streather)
Porsche 987 Boxster and Cayman 2nd generation (2009-2012) (Streather)

Other Porsche titles
Porsche, Cranswick on (Cranswick)
Porsche 356 (2nd Edition) (Long)
Porsche 356, The Ultimate Book of the (Long)
Porsche 911 Carrera – The Last of the Evolution (Corlett)
Porsche 911R, RS & RSR, 4th Edition (Starkey)
Porsche 911 SC (Clusker)
Porsche 911, The Book of the (Long)
Porsche 911 – The Definitive History 1963-1971 (Long)
Porsche 911 – The Definitive History 1971-1977 (Long)
Porsche 911 – The Definitive History 1977-1987 (Long)
Porsche 911 – The Definitive History 1987-1997 (Long)
Porsche 911 – The Definitive History 1997-2004 (Long)
Porsche 911 – The Definitive History 2004-2012 (Long)
Porsche – The Racing 914s (Smith)
Porsche 911SC 'Super Carrera' – The Essential Companion (Streather)
Porsche 914 & 914-6: The Definitive History of the Road & Competition Cars (Long)
Porsche 924 (Long)
The Porsche 924 Carreras – evolution to excellence (Smith)
Porsche 928 (Long)
Porsche 930 to 935: The Turbo Porsches (Starkey)
Porsche 944 (Long)
Porsche 964, 993 & 996 Data Plate Code Breaker (Streather)
Porsche 993 'King Of Porsche' – The Essential Companion (Streather)
Porsche 996 'Supreme Porsche' – The Essential Companion (Streather)
Porsche 997 2004-2012 'Porsche Excellence' – The Essential Companion (Streather)
Porsche Boxster – The 986 series 1996-2004 (Long)
Porsche Boxster & Cayman – The 987 series (2004-2013) (Long)
Porsche Racing Cars – 1953 to 1975 (Long)
Porsche Racing Cars – 1976 to 2005 (Long)
Porsche Racing Cars – 2006 to 2022 (Long)
Porsche – Silver Steeds (Smith)
Porsche – The Rally Story (Meredith)
Powered by Porsche (Smith)

www.veloce.co.uk

First published in 2024 by Veloce, an imprint of David and Charles Limited. Tel +44 (0)1305 260068 / e-mail info@veloce.co.uk / web www.veloce.co.uk.

ISBN: 978-1-787117-92-1 UPC: 6-36847-01792-7

© 2024 Brian Long and David and Charles. All rights reserved. With the exception of quoting brief passages for the purpose of review, no part of this publication may be recorded, reproduced or transmitted by any means, including photocopying, without the written permission of David and Charles Limited.
Throughout this book logos, model names and designations, etc, have been used for the purposes of identification, illustration and decoration. Such names are the property of the trademark holder as this is not an official publication. Readers with ideas for automotive books, or books on other transport or related hobby subjects, are invited to write to the editorial director of Veloce at the above address. British Library Cataloguing in Publication Data – A catalogue record for this book is available from the British Library. Design and production by Veloce. Printed in China by Asia Pacific.

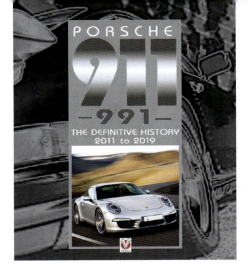

Contents

Introduction & Acknowledgements 4

Chapter 1 A new 911 generation 6
   The players 7
   The new car's styling 8
   Interior 18
   Drivetrain 24
   Chassis details 29
   Early press reaction 35
   The 991 makes its entrance 38
   991 range expansion 43

Chapter 2 The early production models 55
   The right-hand drive markets 59
   More new models 63
   Racing update 67
   The GT3 road car 69
   The 2013 MY abroad 75

Chapter 3 Expanding the range 76
   The wait is over 76
   Life goes on … 85
   2013 race review 88
   The turbocharged convertibles 89
   Export markets in the 2014 MY 90
   The Targa returns 95
   The 2014 race season 101
   The GTS models 107
   Export market news 113
   The GT3 RS 116
   The 2015 racing season 119
   The 'Black Edition' 123

Chapter 4 A major face-lift 124
   A new approach 125
   Domestic sales 132
   Early thoughts 138
   New 911 Turbos 139
   Corporate news 143
   The 911R 144
   The 2016 MY abroad 148
   The 2016 racing season 150

Chapter 5 End of the line 156
   Another new GT3 160
   More changes 165
   Yet more new 911s 169
   The 2017 Frankfurt Show 176
   Export round-up 176
   The Carrera T 178
   The 2017 racing season 181
   The GT3 RS 185
   Springtime in Stuttgart 189
   Export review 193
   Star-struck in LA 193
   Race digest 195
   The 2018-19 WEC 198
   The production Speedster 201
   The 2019 race scene 203
   The 4.2-litre 911 RSR-19 205
   The end of an era 206

Appendix I Year-by-year range details 208
Appendix II Engine specifications 212
Appendix III Chassis numbers & production figures 216
Index 223

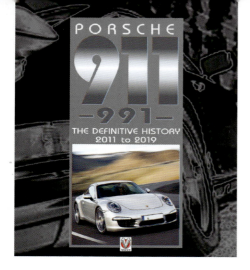

Introduction & Acknowledgements

As the third generation of water-cooled 911s, the Type 991 truly brought the Stuttgart icon into a new era. Introduced at the 2011 Frankfurt Show, it featured a fresh, lightweight body that dutifully paid homage to its ancestors, modern drivetrains (especially in 991.2 guise), and gadgets aplenty to satisfy a new breed of owner.

As before, the various grades were drip-fed onto the market, with 3.4- and 3.8-litre rear-wheel drive Carrera coupes first, then convertibles soon after, and 4WD versions of each by the time the 2013 season began. Next up was the GT3 and a line of turbocharged machines, and a welcome return for the traditional-looking Targa body at the start of 2014. Sporting GTS models and a new, very rapid GT3 RS

swelled the ranks shortly before the 991.1 morphed into the 991.2, with plenty of racers and specials along the way.

The arrival of the 'Gen II' machines brought about a new policy of using smaller displacement engines, with twin-turbos employed to bring back the expected power levels of the modern Porsches. The same thing would happen with the 981 Boxsters and Caymans as they transformed into the 718 line.

All of the old favourites were reissued in updated guise, getting ever faster and more powerful with each stage in their evolution. Some of the Model Years are a bit strange, but hopefully the text will explain how the designations were applied, and make sense of the data in the appendices ...

This volume takes the 991 story from its origins, through the prototype stages, and on to 2019 – the year that signalled the end of the series, at least officially! Taking a look at the car's competition exploits as the model matured, this book is full of contemporary factory-sourced images and detailed information on the vehicles sold in the world's major markets. Hopefully, it will provide an ideal guide for enthusiasts and historians alike, helping to serve those looking for authenticity in the future.

Acknowledgements

My first 911 book was published in 2005 as part of a five-volume set, with help coming from Klaus Parr, Jens Torner and Dieter Gross at Porsche, Family Garage and K3 Works (now Nobel Co Limited) in Chiba, Kenichi Kobayashi at Miki Press, and the Japan Motor Industry Federation library in Tokyo.

The reality is, very little has changed. Now Klaus has retired, even though we stay in touch, it is poor Jens who deals with my numerous requests – as he has done, without a single complaint, for more years than either of us would care to remember. Our shared love of photography and the Kawasaki brand keeps our relationship alive in much the same way as the one between myself and his former boss – we are friends first and foremost, and will remain so long after I've written my last book. Additional help this time around came from Adrian Streather (who kindly provided me with production numbers), and an old pal, Trevor Alder. My sincere thanks, as always, to some of the best people in the business.

Brian Long
Chiba, Japan

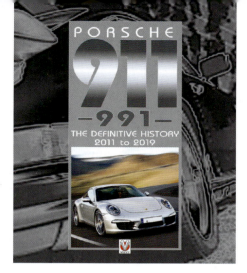

1
A new 911 generation

After the financial downturn following the 2008 Lehman Brothers crisis and the politics of the Wendelin Wiedeking era (a draining time, which almost saw Porsche take over Volkswagen, only for the situation to suddenly be reversed), the new 911 at least brought cars back into focus at Stuttgart-Zuffenhausen ...

The new 911 making its debut in Hall 3.0 at the 2011 Frankfurt Show. This is a Carrera S model shod with optional 20in Carrera Classic alloy wheels.

Launched at the 2011 Frankfurt Show (which ran from 15-25 September), the Type 991 represented the third generation of water-cooled Porsche 911s. As such, despite featuring a new platform, there was no huge jump in the technology stakes, as there had been when the last of the air-cooled machines (the Type 993) gave way to the Type 996; having a water-cooled engine in the back was now something taken for granted by enthusiasts of the marque. And, as history has taught us, any new incarnation of the 911 has to closely resemble the original

model launched way back in the early 1960s, which itself built on the lines of its predecessor, the legendary 356.

This doesn't mean that this latest Porsche was of little importance in the grand scheme of things – quite the opposite, in fact, being the first all-new 911 released with Porsche under the heavy influence of the Volkswagen Group (the latter would ultimately buy up all of the remaining shares in the Stuttgart maker in July 2012), and the car's success was all the more crucial given its special position within the increasingly complex brand structure.

While the price of crude oil was rising to rather naughty levels, at least the slow but sure global recovery from the Lehman Shock was a promising sign that the investment required for the 991 project could be recouped, even as the Porsche range expanded – proliferation is good in some ways, of course, giving buyers more choice and allowing parts sharing to reduce costs, but it also brings about a situation whereby the sales of one model line suffer at the expense of another if the division isn't clear enough. As well as the styling considerations mentioned earlier, designers also had to factor in new trends (with infotainment now seemingly just as important to some folks as how a car drove), along with the latest safety and emissions requirements, with codes getting ever stricter worldwide.

The players
It will be remembered that the new millennium was littered with politics in Stuttgart, all of which had a bearing, however subtle, on the 991's path of development, so it's worth a few lines here to set the scene.

Under the instructions of Porsche's boss at the time, Wendelin Wiedeking, Porsche had managed to gain a 42 per cent stake in Volkswagen by the autumn of 2008, and was poised for a take-over that had seemed all but impossible just a few years earlier. Then, things started to go dreadfully wrong. The financial crisis, caused largely by easy credit but symbolised by the Lehman Shock, sent shares crashing, and sales of luxury

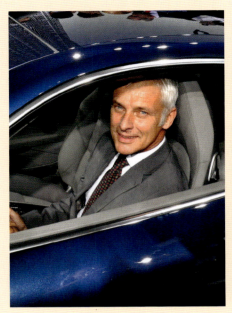

Matthias Müller, Porsche's boss at the time of the 991's release, pictured here at the 2011 IAA in the Carrera S shown at the beginning of this chapter; Wolfgang Porsche (Ferry's youngest son, born in 1943) was the head of the Supervisory Board.

August Achleitner – 'Mister 911' himself ...

Wolfgang Hatz – Porsche's R&D supremo from the early part of 2011.

Michael Mauer. Born in 1962, Mauer had a sparkling career at Mercedes-Benz before moving to Saab in 2000. He became head of styling at Porsche following the retirement of Harm Lagaay in 2004, and for this project had Tony Hatter as design leader, reporting to exterior supremo Matthias Kulla.

goods were put on hold – a situation that took a long time to turn around.

By mid-2009, Porsche was struggling to handle the debts it had chalked up in trying to take control of VW (Porsche Automobil Holding SE actually held 51 per cent of Volkswagen AG before proceedings on a fresh merger started). VW now had the upper hand, and Porsche was ultimately forced to become part of the Volkswagen Group, which by this time already included Audi, SEAT, Skoda, Bentley, Lamborghini, Bugatti and the Scania AB commercial vehicle concern.

Wiedeking's incredibly bold plan had been scuppered, and, to keep the peace, he was dismissed in July along with his finance man, Holger Haerter. This was probably the best move, as people had begun to take sides since May, and the German press corps was having a field day.

Wiedeking's place as CEO of Porsche AG was immediately taken by Michael Macht, who'd been appointed head of production in mid-1998. On the Porsche SE side, Martin Winterkorn (a respected VW man) was appointed CEO in September 2009, with Hans-Dieter Potsch as the new CFO. Following an injection of cash that secured ten per cent of Porsche SE ordinary shares for Qatar Holding LLC, and a separate investment that bought a large chunk of VW, Porsche would ultimately be merged with the Volkswagen Group.

Meanwhile, as the 991 was showing its head on the horizon, Macht moved up the Volkswagen corporate ladder, and Matthias Müller officially became the new Porsche Chairman from October 2010, only weeks after ItalDesign became yet another company to fall to VW (Karmann had recently been bought, too). Interestingly, the 57-year old Müller had been in charge of product planning at Volkswagen before his move to Stuttgart, so it was a fair assumption that shared platforms and components would become more and more common as time rolled on.

Following on from an announcement that Porsche was investing €150 million in its R&D facilities (with a new design centre and wind-tunnel accounting for most of the budget), rumours were flying in the first weeks of 2011 regarding the development of a four-cylinder engine at Porsche, perhaps earmarked for the Boxster and Cayman, as well as the forthcoming baby SUV (codenamed the Cajun at the time, but christened the Macan once it reached the showrooms).

Shortly after, Porsche appointed Wolfgang Hatz as the new head of the R&D section. Officially taking over from Wolfgang Dürheimer (who was given a fascinating new challenge in the Volkswagen-owned Bentley and Bugatti camps) in February 2011, Hatz's career had included spells at BMW, Opel, Fiat and Audi, as well as a four-year tenure at Porsche, working under Hans Mezger as a key member of staff on the V12 F1 engine project.

Ultimately, it was a hectic 2011, witnessing the opening of a huge new paint shop in Stuttgart to coincide with the launch of the new 911, and a ground-breaking ceremony to expand production facilities at the Leipzig plant at the end of the year. In the meantime, August Achleitner was busy in his role as head of 911 development – a position he'd inherited way back in 2001. Now, with that, we can at last start looking at the vehicle itself ...

The new car's styling
The 997 had brought back the true '911'

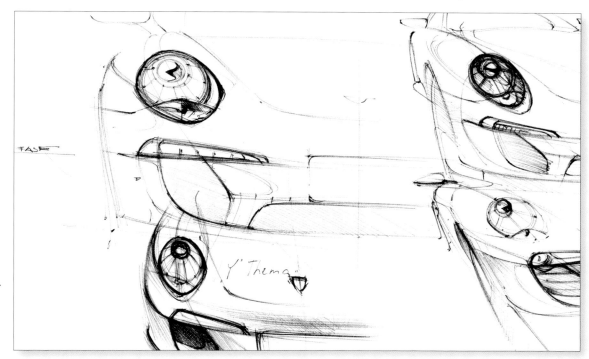

Right and opposite: Early design sketches outlining some of the styling details that would set the 991 apart from its predecessors.

look, with round headlights, even if the pods they sat in were far flatter than those of yore. It successfully blended the lines of the 993 and 996 in a way that appealed to fans of the marque, and became sharper again in facelifted guise, fitting in with design language adopted across the Stuttgart maker's range.

A longer wheelbase had been decided on from the off, to further tame the handling as the rear-engined layout could still catch out the inexperienced driver when pushing hard, even in the later cars if all the electronic gadgets were switched off. The Type 991's styling had to be revised to suit the new panelwork, but the brief handed down to design chief Michael Mauer was to retain as much of the 997's distinctive silhouette as possible – after all, it would be foolhardy to destroy a successful formula.

As Mauer stated in a promotional video: "The new 911 has to be clearly recognisable as a 911, but it also has to look fresh." Although this line of development was followed to try and win back the hearts of traditional 911 buyers in a tough marketplace for top-end sporting models, there must be few manufacturers that can afford the luxury of being able to totally re-engineer a car only to ask its designers to make it look just like its predecessor!

Mauer stated that it was important to optimise the width to height ratio, to make the car look planted to the road. Following on from that, in a bid to improve handling, the front track was increased by a significant amount, and wheelarches had to be formed to take larger wheel and tyre combinations. However, the 991's overall width remained much the same as that of the 997, keeping things practical.

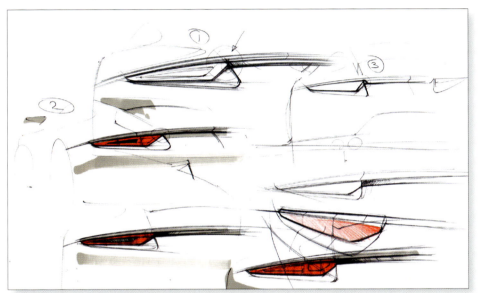

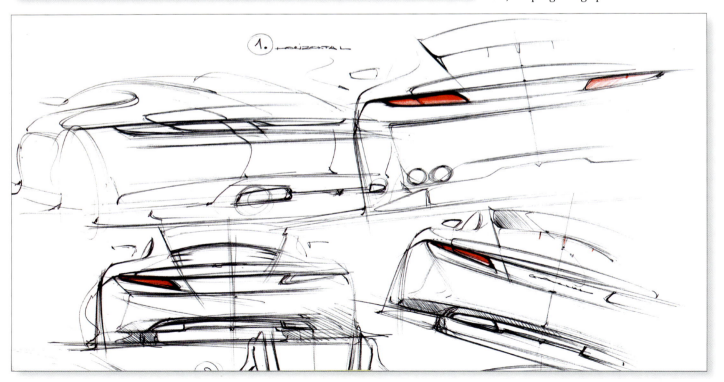

Design DNA

There was a Porsche Cars North America advert from 1992 with the headline: "Starting from a 'clean sheet of paper' is fine. If you have nothing worth keeping." This seems to sum up Porsche's way of thinking perfectly, with steady evolution having priority over revolution in the styling department.

To trace the DNA of any product emanating from the Porsche factory, one need look no further than the company's founder, Ferry Porsche (1909-1998). As a talented engineer, he was heavily influenced by his father, who gave the world cars like the VW Beetle and Auto Union racers. Ferry (left) is seen here with his eldest son, 'Butzi' (the founder of Porsche Design) alongside a rear-engined 356 – Porsche's first attempt at breaking into the sports car market. Note the slippery lines from tip to tail on this 356A coupé.

The 911 was launched in 1963 to eventually replace the 356. These early coupés are pictured outside Plant 2, and would evolve quickly after this shot was taken, with more powerful variants and a Targa body joining the line. Later models display a subtle flare in the wheelarches, and have a longer wheelbase than the original cars.

US-led safety measures brought about the 'Big Bumper' era, with the new generation introduced at the 1973 Frankfurt Show as a 1974 model. This picture shows (l-r) the flagship Carrera, a 911S coupé, and a strict 911 Targa.

Racing and rallying had always been an important part of Porsche's marketing programme, but the Turbo (launched at the 1974 Paris Salon) helped secure the company's high-performance image in the showroom with its pace, extravagant appendages and huge wheelarch flares.

While the 'Big Bumper' cars were only lightly modified for more than a decade, the 959 project, which kicked off with a 1983 concept car, was extremely modern-looking.

This 1991 911 Carrera 4 cabriolet serves as a good representative of the 964 line, which was announced in 1988, and was ultimately replaced by the 993 series.

The Type 993 in coupé guise, which inherited its front-end styling from the 959 supercar. This was ultimately destined to be the last air-cooled Porsche.

A useful reference shot, showing the water-cooled 996 in the foreground, surrounded by one of the very first 911s from 1963, a white Carrera from the 1980s, and 964 and 993 models. The 996's 'runny egg' headlights were later modified to visually distance the 911 from the less expensive mid-engined Boxster.

Front and rear views of the drophead version of the 997, pictured here at the time of its launch.

A publicity picture showing the basic 997.2 body revisions, introduced in readiness for the 2009 season, although the drivetrain was updated at the same time, with new engines and a PDK transmission option. By the end of the 991 run, the amount of 911 variants available was bewildering, even without including the racers based on this iconic model.

These renderings by Peter Varga show a car very close to the final design ...

Styling tricks like moving the headlights as far outboard as they would go, adding a little more rake and curvature into the screen, and shaving just a few millimetres off the roofline, all combined to make the car appear very low from the front, while the lighting arrangements below the headlights gave the newcomer a useful distinguishing feature.

In profile, the 997 displayed all the styling cues one would expect of this legendary machine, with the roofline falling away into the tail, and the familiar window graphics, now clearer than ever thanks to the side mirrors moving lower down onto the door panels to enhance aerodynamics. As before, the tapering of the roof section and glasshouse emphasised the powerful shoulders in the rear wing shape.

It was perhaps the tail that provided the most obvious changes, with ultra-modern, slim and sunken rear light units, sitting below a ledge that not only enhanced aerodynamics, but also made the car's stance appear wider. Ultimately, it was a case of turning technical requirements into design elements – this latest thinking being something we would see on the MR 981-series models, too, with the edge of the rear spoiler being integrated into the combination light units themselves on the mid-engined cars. The slats on the engine cover brought back some familiarity, although the panel cut line was quite different.

Although not much bigger than the Type 997 model, compared to earlier versions of the 911, the newcomer was frankly huge. We've seen this a lot of late, where new models inspired by earlier ones are much larger – think of the Fiat 500, the not-so-mini Mini, and the Range Rover, for instance (not to mention the VW Beetle). In the case of the Porsche, a lot of this gain in bulk was to do with harnessing power and improving dynamics, some of it had to do with meeting contemporary safety regulations, and a fair bit of it could be assigned to making improvements in interior comfort. The styling proportions disguised the increased dimensions to a large extent. Nonetheless, put a car from the sixties alongside a Type 991 and it's bound to raise a few eyebrows.

Leading dimensions
For reference, here are the leading dimensions of the new 991 compared with the previous generation, and the very first 911 of 1963 to highlight the differences involved. For consistency, all numbers listed here relate to European-spec base coupé models with a manual transmission, and the first of the breed.

	911 (1963)	*997 (EU)*	*991 (EU)*
Wheelbase	2211mm (87.0in)	2350mm (92.5in)	2450mm (96.5in)
Overall length	4163mm (163.9in)	4425mm (174.2in)	4491mm (176.8in)
Overall width	1610mm (63.4in)	1810mm (71.2in)	1808mm (71.2in)
Overall height	1320mm (52.0in)	1310mm (51.6in)	1303mm (51.3in)
Track (front)	1337mm (52.6in)	1485mm (58.5in)	1532mm (60.3in)
Track (rear)	1317mm (51.9in)	1525mm (60.0in)	1518mm (59.8in)
Weight (DIN)	1080kg (2376lb)	1470kg (3234lb)	1380kg (3036lb)

NB. The width quoted does not include door mirrors, and weights are German DIN figures, which tend to be on the light side compared with those posted in most other countries outside mainland Europe.

A very early narrow-bodied 911 sitting next to a 991, in this case a Carrera 4S coupé.

Looking at the front-end styling in a little more detail, compared to the last of the 997 Carrera and Carrera S coupés, it can readily be said that the changes made in creating the 991 were subtle – very subtle, in fact, to the point where the author started checking part numbers to confirm that certain items were actually new.

For starters, the shutlines on the front lid look much the same, although it is indeed a new panel, with the badge sunken into a shallow recess rather than sitting on top of the lid, as had been the case with earlier models; screen washer nozzles were cleverly hidden underneath the lid on its trailing edge. It's the same with the front wings, and headlamp shapes, even down to the washer post sitting on the small ledge ahead of them. Again, though, these were fresh items, despite the headlights continuing with the bi-xenon technology used on the previous generation on stock machines.

As such, it was the grille shapes and detailing on the bumper moulding that gave us the clearest signs of change. Actually, Porsche adopted an old trick used to separate the Boxsters and Caymans in the past, by turning the central vent section upside down (making the narrowest edge of the trapezoid feature sit at the top rather than the bottom), and then adjusting the openings either side of it to suit the new profile.

The three openings in the air dam were filled with black grilles on both the Carrera and Carrera S grades (unlike the mid-engined range, which used them as an identifying feature). The outer vents were dominated by two horizontal slats in the frame that also housed the LED light unit, with half-width blanking pieces behind them for strict Carrera models, while the central one was actually nothing more than a flat black dressing piece on most vehicles (some had the automatic distance control camera in the middle), balanced by a black insert that partially formed the lip spoiler. Incidentally, the insert was a subtly different shape on cars with a PDK transmission, having a different part number to the 7MT version.

The LED light units themselves were also revised – although they were in the same place as before, they were sharper looking for the 991, and incorporated the indicators, daytime running lights and position lights. Aft of these, and just ahead of the wheelarch, were the repeater units, which again looked familiar, just turned over so that the leading edge was at the top on the newer cars; most markets used clear lenses, although the North American regulations insisted on amber ones.

Front view of the new 991, this being a 3.4-litre Carrera coupé. Production cars had a plain, full-width black central air intake cover, by the way.

A front three-quarter shot of the same car, which we will use for reference, with a Carrera S alongside – the latter showing the fuel lid on the front wing and the S's tailpipes. The fuel filler release was in the door jamb, as per 911 tradition, while the tank was 64 litres (14.1 imperial gallons) on NA RR cars, upped to 68 litres (15 gallons) for 4WD variants.

The side view certainly paid homage to its predecessors, despite the 991 sporting a significantly longer wheelbase than earlier 911s. The alloy wheels seen here are the optional Carrera Classic rims, incidentally, which commanded €2100 (or €900 on the Carrera S).

When the first 911S came out, the 15in diameter Fuchs alloys were considered seriously big for the time. Now, 19 and 20in wheels were standard fare for the Carrera and Carrera S (an inch up from the 18 and 19in rims used, respectively, on the 997 versions), which definitely helped fill out the wheel housings and therefore make the body appear less bulky. It was an age-old trick, used not only by stylists, but enthusiasts, too, as a way to visually reduce metalwork volume without actually having to touch it. The author well remembers the first Jaguar XK8, with the back-end looking very heavy until an inch bigger wheel was adopted, and then the balance was suddenly far better. With the new 911 being significantly larger than its predecessor, this technique was ideal for hiding the extra metalwork, even if the adoption of such a wheel and tyre combination brought about different concerns, such as NVH control, and so on.

Anyway, the wheels themselves – crafted in aluminium alloy – were an open five-spoke design for the Carrera (code 411), much like the last 'Carrera S II' rim, but with the gaps on each spoke tightened. It was the opposite situation for the Carrera S (code 423), with something similar to the 'Carrera IV' wheel with more space between each spoke being adopted, almost to the point of being able to call it a ten-spoke design. As always, one could opt for Carrera S rims on the regular Carrera (but not the other way around), or there was a selection of other optional alloys available, all in the 20in diameter range.

Above the wheels, there was a truly classic 911 coupé silhouette, with short overhangs and a roof tapering back off the front screen header, and window graphics dictated by the shape of the door panel. Indeed, one could easily be forgiven for not being able to tell a 991 from the 997 before it, although careful inspection revealed some lovely detailing, from more volume in the front fender profile, to the way the door now curved to meld into the rocker panel, and the sleeker roofline, with sharper lines falling away from the rear screen; a sunroof was listed as an option. As mentioned earlier, the door mirrors were now positioned lower than before, but otherwise everything looked reassuringly familiar, even down to the door handles and the fuel filler lid shape and positioning on the offside front wing.

Around the back, the fixed rear window was a similar shape to before, albeit enlarged and almost appearing to sit in a 'flying buttress' arrangement, with a rear wiper available as an option. Aft of the screen, the engine cover design was tidied up, sitting wider with the three cooling slats

Far left: The 19in 'Carrera V' wheel (using a revival of code 411).

Left: The 20in 'Carrera S III' rim (code 423) with the standard finish. The use of 20in diameter wheels certainly gave the new 911 an athletic appearance, although a €1200 premium was required if these alloys were fitted on the 3.4-litre car, with €665 extra being asked for Platinum paint on either grade.

Tail of the strict Carrera coupé. Only the badging and exhaust pipe trim was used to distinguish this model from the 3.8-litre S version.

Detail shot of the tailpipe design on the Carrera S.

all contained on a single panel, with the uppermost one containing the high-mount rear brakelight strip in much the same way as it appeared on the 997. Further back again was the rear spoiler, which sat flat in the ledge between the lights when not deployed, but could be raised manually or automatically (speed activated) on two posts to reveal a duplicate third brakelight on its trailing edge.

Between the light units, traditional 'PORSCHE' lettering was revived, with another model badge placed below it – a chrome finish was chosen for both grades. A stronger ridge was evident in the bumper moulding above the exhaust trim panel, with additional reflector

Close-up of the rear spoiler in the deployed position. This is a Carrera S, but the arrangement was the same on the 3.4-litre machine.

Underbody panelling played an important role in the 991's aerodynamic efficiency.

for the 997s available. Neatly trimmed, boxes in the uppermost part of the sides hid the very basic toolkit and tyre sealant (there was no spare wheel), with the compressor and a warning triangle (when provided) in the trunk's rear bulkhead area, ahead of the fuel tank.

In a nod to Porsche's achievements in making the 991 fresh yet sympathetic to the iconic original, amongst several other accolades, the newcomer was given the coveted 'Red Dot Design Award' – a Germany-based international competition running since 1955, which Porsche duly won in 2012 for its product design. Not surprisingly, though, given Porsche's reputation for form following function, the 991 was not simply designed to look good – it was a slippery beast, too. Helped by an array of underbody covers, it displayed a Cd figure of 0.29.

Interior

As with the exterior, almost as much effort was made in retaining the old 911's character as providing new features. The main change was applied to the centre console, with the latest version being much like that first seen on the Panamera and second generation Cayenne (introduced as an early 2011 model) thanks to the decision to opt for an electronically-controlled handbrake. Ultimately, the new console sloped gently

strips added either side of the number plate cut-out to break it up – something not found on the 997s. Rounding things off, as had become the norm in recent years, the regular Carrera had a pair of oblong-type stainless steel tailpipes, while the S model inherited two round exhaust pipe finishers on either side.

As for luggage space, the front trunk continued to provide the bulk of it, with the same 135 litres (4.8ft^3) as quoted

Michael Mauer (holding the door mirror) surrounded by the Porsche styling team. The 991 won a number of important trophies for its looks, such as the 'Red Dot Design Award' and the 'Golden Steering Wheel Award.'

Weight is the enemy

One of the key factors in the creation of a fast, good handling car is low weight. Engineers have known this since the dawn of motoring, drilling chassis rails and honing individual parts to rid them of excess poundage, while the birth of the Silver Arrows didn't come about thanks to a colour co-ordination specialist – Alfred Neubauer, who was running the Mercedes-Benz racing team in the 1930s, stripped the cars of their traditional white paint in order to save a kilo or two! A lower kerb weight can also help improve fuel efficiency, and that's an increasingly important thing to consider, too, in this modern era.

One could opt for an aluminium body, but a monocoque shell using this material throughout tends to be expensive – fine for certain machines that are less price sensitive, and more suited to closed vehicles if truth be told. Instead, with a convertible always in the picture, Porsche decided to go down a sensible path of using super high-strength steel for much of the A-post area and the outer sills, as well as some of the structure around the engine bay, with boron-alloyed 22MnB5 steel for the upper part of the windscreen pillar back to the tail, B-post and crossmembers in the floor. The boron-alloyed steel ultimately offered exceptional forming accuracy combined with the ability to downgauge, while retaining the strength associated with more conventional HSLA grades, thus saving weight. This, combined with its high resistance to flexing and fatigue damage, made it an ideal option for parts that bore a lot of stress.

Multi-phase steel (easy to work with and offering excellent crash energy absorption, as well as reasonable cost) was added on the inner side of the rocker panels, roof crossmembers, and the door beams required for side impact regulations, while deep-drawn steel pressings were employed for the dash mount and the rear wheel housing area. All other components, including the front and rear lids, and doors, were executed in aluminium.

Using the latest CAD/CAM techniques to balance strength versus material usage and aid the placement of structural parts, the end result was a body-in-white that weighed significantly less than the 997 version. Crucially, it also attained a 25 per cent increase in overall rigidity, which is ideal for accurate chassis component response, while the use of magnesium alloys in areas like the convertible's hood frame ensured further weight reduction. Using this ultra-lightweight material in the hood also helped lower the vehicle's centre of gravity – another requirement in enhancing the handling of a top sports car, along with weight distribution, that generally has engineers trying to balance the car front and rear, and keep as much bulk as possible within the wheelbase. Generally is the operative word in Porsche's case, of course, for the 911 boldly breaks all the accepted rules of design!

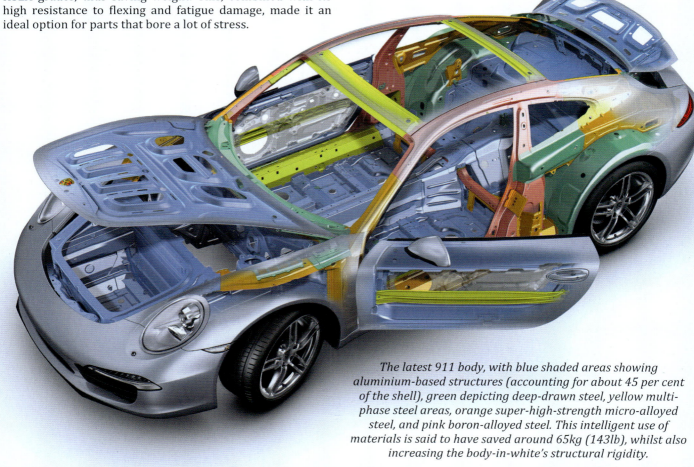

The latest 911 body, with blue shaded areas showing aluminium-based structures (accounting for about 45 per cent of the shell), green depicting deep-drawn steel, yellow multi-phase steel areas, orange super-high-strength micro-alloyed steel, and pink boron-alloyed steel. This intelligent use of materials is said to have saved around 65kg (143lb), whilst also increasing the body-in-white's structural rigidity.

A design sketch for the new interior.

upwards from between the seats and blended perfectly into the centre stack, making the interior appear less bitty and altogether more attractive, cleaning up some of the switchgear along the way, and giving passengers the sportier impression of sitting lower in the car, even though they weren't in reality.

From a driver's point of view, everything was more integrated, with a huge step forward in perceived quality thanks to some clever colouring and material usage. Naturally, five main gauges were retained in the instrument pack, with red needles on black faces and the tachometer placed in the centre, where it belongs. There was a touch more curvature in the array compared to before, but the biggest change was the adoption of a TFT display in place of the dial to the right of the rev-counter. This screen, shaped like a traditional gauge, gave all onboard computer data, a range of alerts (like a drop in tyre pressure), and things like navigation and audio displays, outside temperature, an oil level check, and so on.

Now there was an engine oil temperature and oil pressure gauge on the left of the instrument cluster, a rheostat between it and the speedometer (with a digital odometer and trip meter in the latter's base, along with a selection of warning lights), and the big tachometer in the centre, with more warning lights and a digital speedo read-out in the lower part of the meter. This had a silvered finish rather than a black one on the Carrera S model, incidentally; there was also a gear indicator for cars equipped with a PDK transmission. Moving further right, there was the TFT screen, and then a combination meter for engine coolant temperature and fuel level.

There were no real surprises in the steering wheel designs, as they were actually quite similar to those with a round centre boss from the previous 911 generation – a regular three-spoke wheel, a SportDesign version with polished spokes (with or without hefty shift paddles behind), and a multi-function wheel, which came in manual or PDK guise; cars with the optional Sport Chrono package also gained a mode indicator display above the airbag module.

Above: Driver's view of the new 911 Carrera, this one with a PDK transmission, the Sport Chrono package, and a multi-function steering wheel. Note the hefty dead pedal for the left foot, and the fuse boxes in both footwells; there was a 12V socket on the passenger's side of the transmission tunnel. As always with early press pictures, we have to be careful, and the trap on this one is the tachometer, which should be black (the silvered face seen here was a Carrera S feature, although black was offered as a no-cost option on the 3.8-litre model).

Left: The same interior viewed from a different angle, affording a glimpse of the standard seats, the door furniture, and the various items mounted in the roof area.

Aft of the steering wheel, the upper left-hand column stalk looked after the indicators, main beam and parking light selection, as well as voice command activation when fitted, while the right-hand one opposite had the various wiper settings and screen washer activation on it, along with headlight washers if specified. Interestingly, a lower right-hand stalk controlled the menu and other features associated with the TFT screen in the main instrument pack, although it wasn't fitted if the car had a multi-function steering wheel. Some cars had another stalk, below the indicators, for the cruise control, known as Tempostat in Porsche lingo. Manual or power steering column adjustment controls were found on the lower part of the column surround.

Like the 997, the instrument binnacle formed an integral part of the top roll, although the detailing around it provided quite a different impression, despite the similarities when the design was taken as a whole. For starters, the vents in the fascia were in the same positions (one at each end and a pair in the centre), but the shapes were fresher, the centre vents were now in a slightly higher plane, and the switches between the central thumbwheels in the old car were abandoned, simplifying the build process. The optional Sport Chrono clock was also sunken into a new central speaker grille rather than sitting high and a little awkwardly, as it had in the past.

Breaking up the top roll and lower parts of the dashboard was a heavy 'Galvanosilber' trim strip, which matched the air vent frames and did an excellent job of hiding the cup holders on the passenger side, and also provided a plinth for the main light switch and ignition barrel on the driver's side (to the left of the wheel on lhd machines in keeping with tradition). In a new arrangement, the huge transponder key body locked into the barrel to become the starter switch. The key continued to carry the remote control central locking functions on it, and also contained an integrated immobiliser, which was duly hooked into the alarm system when fitted. Also new

A Carrera S coupé with a PDK transmission, the Sport Chrono package, a SportDesign steering wheel, leather interior package, and a sportier seat option than the one seen in the earlier interior pictures.

was the electronic handbrake, with the small lever-type switch associated with it placed below the light switch.

The glovebox was a touch wider than before, but basically the same, with a heavy silver-coloured release, but, as mentioned earlier, the centre console area was completely different. Dominating the area below the central air vents was a CDR31 audio system, which included a CD/radio unit and a 7in touchscreen that could be used for all manner of functions. The optional PCM unit, with easier access to more advanced features, looked surprisingly similar in its latest guise, and both came with a top class nine-speaker setup as standard.

Between the AV head unit and gearbox was a band of buttons and levers controlling the air-conditioning. This dual-zone HVAC system was fitted as standard on the new 911s, complete with a stepless fan, defrost and circulating air functions, and an active charcoal filter. Switches for seat heating and the like were batched in with the HVAC controls, along with necessities like the rear screen heater, making it all very logical in terms of layout, as well as attractive to look at.

A heavy 'Galvanosilber' frame was added at the foot of the heating and ventilation section, stretching all the way back to the centre armrest, and acting as a surround for the leather-clad gearlever and another batch of switches. The hazard warning lights and door lock switches were now placed aft of the gearbox rather than high up in the top roll, and beyond these were an array of matching switches placed either side of a stand-alone section that was either blanked off or looked a bit like a sunken keyfob for sunroof or soft top activation. The other switches included a 'Sport' button that changed the engine mapping and throttle response for those wanting to enjoy an open road (as well as a bit more engine noise wafting into the cockpit thanks to a so-called sound symposer kicking in), a PASM mode switch (if fitted), a 'Sport Plus' button associated with the optional Sport Chrono package, the rear

Sports seat

Fully electric sports seat

Sports seat Plus

Adaptive sports seat Plus

The original front seat choices, with (clockwise from top left) the regular chair, the P06 option, the P07 option, and the P05 option.

duly extended to the door armrests as well. The driver had power window and power mirror controls within the switch panel (both standard on the 991s, with integral heater elements on the mirrors), and occasionally a set of seat position memory buttons above these, while the passenger had to make do with a single window lift. Below the door handle was a speaker enclosure and storage bin, while a second storage bin was located underneath the door armrest and above the courtesy light that warned oncoming traffic that the door was ajar.

As if there weren't enough switches to contend with already, there were more in the console that played host to the rear view mirror, but only really for the LED interior lighting and HomeLink buttons, whenever the latter was fitted, as well as a parking sensor kill switch and a warning lamp to show the passenger-side airbag had been disabled; both sunvisors came with an illuminated courtesy mirror, incidentally.

Regarding the seating, the regular front Sports seats had partial leather trim, an integrated headrest, power backrest and height control (with the switches on the seat base), and manual fore/aft adjustment. The Sports Seats

spoiler position, sports exhaust (when fitted), and 'off' switches for the PSM traction control system and the engine's automatic stop function.

Aft of these was a small oddments tray that could be converted via the smoker's package into a covered ashtray and lighter, while the leather-trimmed central armrest acted as a lid for another storage compartment, the latter containing another 12V power socket (there was already one in the glovebox, next to a USB/audio AUX port, and one in the passenger-side footwell).

The door furniture was definitely more stylish than that of the earlier 911s. The door releases were lower down than before, making them less of a stretch to get to, matched up with a 'Galvanosilber' capping strip on occasion, while the door handles were incorporated into the angled switch panel. Leather trim was used on the latter to add a sense of luxury,

Below: Rear seating in the new coupé. Note the backrest release lever on the front seat – fitted to both sides of the headrest for ease of use.

23

Safety

The strength of the bodyshell naturally played a key role in the safety of passengers, with front and rear crumple zones built into the design, and door beams to reduce cockpit intrusion from a side impact.

Numerous areas within the cockpit were padded to reduce injury, and naturally the seatbelts used all the latest technology available, such as pre-tensioners and force limiters. In more serious collisions, folks could rely on two-stage full-size dual airbags up front, and Porsche's POSIP side impact system, which incorporated a small airbag in the outer side-frame of each seat and a larger curtain one in the door cappings that deployed upwards in order to protect an occupant's head.

Accident avoidance is by far the best policy, of course. Lighter weight meant that the car was endowed with a nimble chassis, and combined with superb brakes (with an ABS and EBD system as standard), electronic traction and stability aids, decent lights and the power to make a positive move, Porsche made sure that drivers were given the foremost chance of going down this more desirable route long before other safety features needed to be called upon.

In addition to the car's nimble reactions and strong body, safety was enhanced via door beams and an array of airbags, with advanced electronics adding another layer of driver protection.

Plus option (P05) added heavier side bolsters into the equation, with a silver-grey shell on the back. Next up was a P06 seat, which had 14-way power adjustment, including lumbar support, and was matched up with a memory feature. And finally, the P07 seat was basically the P05 version with 18-way power adjustment and a memory facility; seat heating and ventilation packages were available separately, and a full bucket seat would be listed soon after the launch as well.

Porsche 911 owners have always appreciated the model's 2+2 seating facility. The front seatbacks tilted forward to give access to the rear of the cabin, with occasional seating provided for two by way of some very deep and shapely chairs, their form being dictated by a heavy tunnel that extended back from the central armrest and tapering of the tail. They were certainly useful for short journeys or for those with small kids, though, while folding down the back of the rear seats helped increase the coupé's luggage capacity from 135 litres (4.8ft^3) to 260 litres (9.2ft^3).

Finishing off the cockpit area for the time being (standard specs and the multitude of options will be covered in detail later on), there were black treadplates with a metal model-specific logo insert. There were also front and rear lid releases via switches in the driver's-side sill, handed for left- and right-hand drive cars.

Drivetrain

The flat-six engine design was basically carried over from the 997, but with several changes applied in order to release more power, and enhance fuel consumption and emissions by around 15 per cent whilst still avoiding a hybrid setup. As such, the 3.8-litre powerplant morphed from the MA1/01 unit into the MA1/03 version, while the 3.6-litre MA1/02 lump was given a smaller 3.4-litre capacity in its latest MA1/04 form.

To recap, compared with the older M96 and M97 units, the design of these normally-aspirated all-alloy water-cooled 24v engines was completely overhauled, with significantly fewer moving parts (including the dismissal of the IMS shaft, which had been known to cause problems in service on early M96 sixes), and seven per cent less rotational mass for quicker response to the electronic throttle. New, stiffer cylinder blocks were prepared, with a different bore and stroke relationship, and the lubrication system was changed, with an oil scavenge system that included four pick-up points and the use of an electronically-controlled oil pump, hooked into the ECU to react to loading better, thus improving oil consumption and giving a slight power gain into the bargain.

At the top end, direct fuel-injection was employed for the first time by Porsche on the MA1s, introduced on the 911s in 2008. Combined with a higher compression ratio, the DFI system boosted power, and also reduced fuel

The internal workings of the award-winning MA1 engine, this being the 3.8-litre MA1/03 version.

A more conventional view of the Carrera S boxer six.

Thermal management was vastly improved to enhance economy via quicker warming up times.

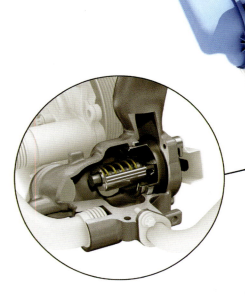

Engine bay of the Carrera S. The 3.4-litre power-unit looked similar, with 'Carrera' on the left-hand silver panel, and the engine size on the right.

consumption and emissions compared to earlier port injection setups thanks to the use of leaner air/fuel mixtures. This naturally led to the adoption of a new air filter housing and intake manifolds, but there were also lighter tappets for the double overhead camshafts on each bank, as well as a new water pump and a new exhaust system. As before, individual coils were adopted for the sparkplugs, which sat between the four valves in the middle of the combustion chamber roof.

Ultimately, both sixes were about 5kg (11lb) lighter than before, more refined, and capable of delivering better mid-range punch thanks to a resonance-effect intake manifold arrangement (further improved via the addition of a switchable valve in the S) and the innovative Variocam Plus variable valve timing mechanism. In addition, the engine height was reduced, lowering the car's centre of gravity, and it was quieter, too – a point not always appreciated by petrolheads, but the flat-six still sounded nice approaching the red-line, and an optional sports exhaust (retaining a three-way catalytic converter for emissions) was duly made available in any case; that sounded real sweet!

As mentioned earlier, while the 3.8-litre capacity was retained for the S grade on the 991, it was decided that the base car should use a smaller 3.4-litre lump, as employed in the early days of the 996 series. This gave a stronger defining line between the two models, and also helped Porsche in the fight against emissions through lower fuel consumption. Ultimately, a higher compression ratio on the strict Carrera (upped to the same value as that specified for the S model) and tuning tweaks via the Siemens SDI 9.1 black box used on the 991 machines allowed an on-paper gain in power anyway, thus creating a win-win situation on all fronts.

Looking in more detail, the 3.4-litre MA1/04 unit kept the 97mm bore of the old 3.6-litre engine and combined it with the shorter 77.5mm stroke of the 3.8-litre six to give a new cubic capacity of 3436cc. With a 12.5:1 c/r, it produced 350bhp DIN at 7400rpm and 288lbft of torque at 5600rpm when used in the Carrera. While the torque figure was the same as that posted by the previous model, it should be noted that the torque curve was flat from around 4500rpm until 6500rpm, and power had increased by 5bhp despite the smaller capacity. In any case, a specific output of 101bhp per litre was outstanding for a road car from any era, let alone one having to push its 'green' credentials, which it did through delivering significantly better fuel economy figures than those recorded against the old 3.6-litre engine.

Meanwhile, the 3.8-litre MA1/03 powerplant kept its 102mm bore and 77.5mm stroke, thus resulting in a 3799cc displacement. Sporting the same 12.5:1 compression ratio as before, power increased by 15bhp, nonetheless, compared to the old Carrera S, now being quoted at 400bhp DIN at 7400rpm (both 991 models red-lined at 7600rpm on the tachometer, by the way), whilst peak torque was increased by 14lbft to 324lbft, developed at 5600rpm. At 105bhp/litre on 98 RON unleaded, the specific output was every bit as eye-watering as that posted by the smaller engine – add in the improvement in fuel consumption, and it was all the more remarkable. As with the strict Carrera, the 'Sport' button on the centre console gave more dynamic engine response, while the Sport Chrono package took things a stage further, typically cutting 0-60 times by 0.2 seconds.

Integrated dry sump lubrication helped with packaging, eliminating the need for an external oil tank, and better thermal management translated into quicker warming up times to improve economy. An interesting development was the intelligent electrical system recuperation setup, which focused battery recharging windows on braking periods, thus reducing engine loads when power was called for, while at the other end of the scale, an auto stop feature shut down the power-unit when certain situations arose (such as sitting at traffic lights) to save fuel, automatically starting it again as soon as the driver was ready to move off, either by putting the vehicle back in gear on manual vehicles, or releasing the brake on PDK-equipped machines.

On the subject of transmissions, the lightweight seven-speed PDK gearbox had established itself as the weapon of choice for two-pedal Porsche drivers ever since its introduction on the 997.2 models. Having its roots in the race environment gave it kudos, while its ease of use and smooth, fast changes in the hands of regular enthusiasts made it a firm favourite, seemingly gaining market share from manual cars with every passing season. After all, in city work, it could be used as a relaxed automatic machine, and then provided everything a manual vehicle had to offer except a clutch pedal as soon as the road cleared, with changes executed via the selector or shifters/paddles on the steering wheel.

The original dual-clutch Type CG1/00 PDK unit was duly refined into the CG1/05 transmission as an option for the normally-aspirated RR (rear engine, rear-wheel drive) 991 range, which now came with a 'sailing' feature to cut drive, and therefore save fuel, when the driver backed off the throttle for a predetermined amount of time. Notwithstanding, the internal ratios were carried over, with 3.91 on first, 2.29 on second, 1.65 on third, 1.30 on fourth, 1.08 on fifth, 0.88 on sixth, and 0.62 on

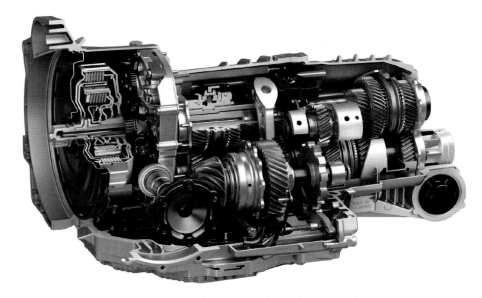

The PDK transmission, which was "quicker and punchier" than before according to Evo. The 0-60 sprint was 0.2 seconds faster with the PDK gearbox than a 7MT unit, showing how far automatic transmissions had come since the slushboxes of yore.

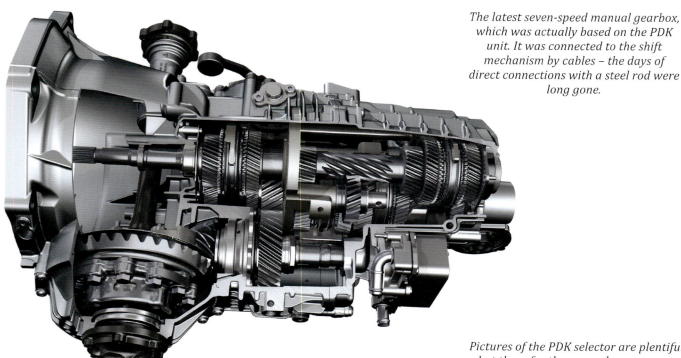

The latest seven-speed manual gearbox, which was actually based on the PDK unit. It was connected to the shift mechanism by cables – the days of direct connections with a steel rod were long gone.

Pictures of the PDK selector are plentiful, but those for the manual car are rare. This shot shows a rhd machine with the 7MT gearbox.

seventh; the final-drive ratio was also the same, listed at 3.44:1.

The biggest change was the replacement of the traditional 6MT manual gearbox with an all-new G91/00 transmission. This was basically a PDK transaxle adapted to work with a clutch pedal to provide a seven-speed manual gearbox, and would share as many parts as possible, despite having a single input shaft compared to the two of the PDK unit.

Anyway, developed in conjunction with ZF (as per the original PDK box) and hooked up to a 240mm (9.4in.) diameter clutch, it had all the same ratios as the PDK transmission (including the 3.44:1 final-drive) except for 1.55 on third and 0.71 on the top gear. The shift pattern was that of a 'double-H' for first through sixth, with seventh up and to the right of it; reverse was selected by moving the gearlever to the left of first. Not surprisingly, given the extra cog and a five-plane selector layout, weight increased a touch, making the 7MT unit only 20kg (44lb) lighter than the automatic PDK transmission (the manual gearbox had posted a 30kg/66lb

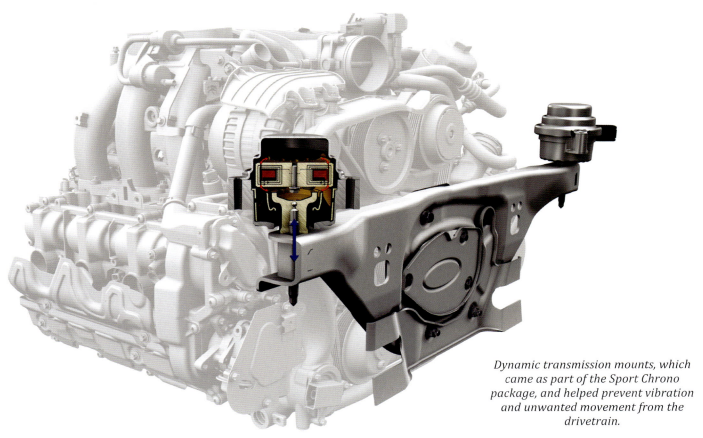

Dynamic transmission mounts, which came as part of the Sport Chrono package, and helped prevent vibration and unwanted movement from the drivetrain.

advantage in 997.2 days), although the gain in bulk was readily offset by the taller gearing in the higher ratios.

Not surprisingly, given the layout of the 991 series, power was taken from the side of the transmission (or transaxle, to be totally correct in this case) to the back wheels via traditional CV-jointed driveshafts.

Incidentally, a mechanical limited-slip differential was included in the PTV system, which we'll come to later. It was classed as standard on the Carrera S, but was not deemed necessary for 3.4-litre cars in standard trim.

Before leaving this section, one should also be aware of the dynamic gearbox mounts included in the optional Sport Chrono package, which used sensors to instruct the pair of active mounts to counter the inertia we experience when driving. Their stiffness and damping could be controlled to suit tastes and conditions via the 'Sport' or 'Sport Plus' switches on the centre console, but ultimately they were a traction aid with the added bonus of being able to help cancel out drivetrain vibration.

Chassis details

Sharing its basic concept with the 997, the chassis components would have been familiar enough to any long-standing Porsche enthusiasts, with, in the main, only minor tweaks being applied to existing designs. One of the biggest changes was in the power-assisted steering system, which went from traditional hydraulic assistance to electrical assistance (EPS) to improve economy and packaging.

Generally speaking, having vintage leanings, the author is no fan of these systems, but in the modern era, the fuel saving they provide by cutting out a drain on engine power is all too often given priority over ultimate steering feel and feedback. There's also less maintenance involved compared to a traditional rack with hydraulic assistance, which is another plus point to be considered, of course.

Anyway, this electro-mechanical system employed an electric motor attached to the rack, using sensors to gather information on driver input and data from the road wheels to judge the amount of assistance necessary (with variable ratios ranging between 16.6:1 and 12.2:1) according to the calculations made by the black box's software. As such, it was programmed to give a more agile response at higher speeds, and greater assistance at lower speeds. An optional Power Steering Plus setup brought a speed-sensitive element into the equation, which was particularly useful for urbanites constantly having to make parking manoeuvres.

As was becoming the norm in the modern era, the catalogue wasn't much use when it came to describing the make-up of the all-round independent suspension – more space was dedicated to gadgets, and marketing types seemed to conclude that all we needed to know was that the car did indeed have one, and that it worked efficiently.

As we stated at the beginning of this section, it was similar to previous

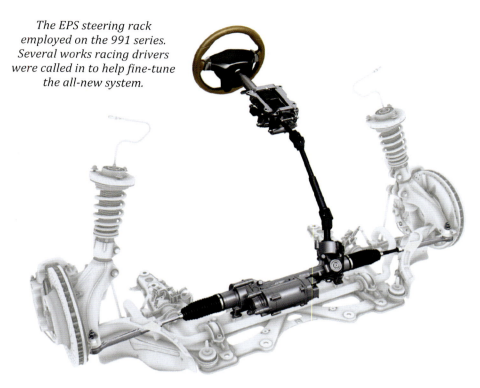

The EPS steering rack employed on the 991 series. Several works racing drivers were called in to help fine-tune the all-new system.

Porsche sports car designs, with a wider track up front to help minimise roll (and bring the wheels flusher to the body sides to deliver a sportier impression whilst the car was stationary), geometry changes, and the honing of certain components to improve things further, such as the adoption of a new front crossmember structure to optimise location and enhance the precision of parts as they moved in reaction to driver input and road conditions.

The suspension system at the front-end consisted of a modified MacPherson strut secured at the top and placed into a hub carrier, with a pair of lower links attached to the bottom of the strut to form a wishbone of sorts. This 'wishbone' was then bolted to the alloy front subframe, which also carried the anti-roll bar mounts; as before, the sway bar and steering rack were placed ahead of the front axle centreline, while dedicated spoilers helped guide air around the various arms.

The suspension at the back was much the same as before, and not dissimilar to that at the front in many respects, mounted on an elaborate subframe. The spring and damper unit bolted to the body at the top once more, and again sat in a hub carrier. This time, though, the latter was shaped so that the pair of lower links were widely spaced, with a trailing arm added for location; the anti-roll bar ran aft of the axle centreline in this case.

While the regular Carrera suspension used traditional gas-filled shocks, the Carrera S employed the advanced PASM active suspension setup. Secured via option code 475 on the 3.4-litre car, the PASM system had different electro-magnetically controlled dampers hooked up to a black box to provide an active suspension with 'Normal' and 'Sport' mode selection, giving the driver a choice in whether to go for ride comfort or a range of sportier settings. PASM lowered the car by 10mm (0.39in), while other options (code 030 or 031) lowered the vehicle by 20mm (0.79in) thanks to stiffer springs, shocks and anti-roll bars; the latter options came with a different lip spoiler and greater extension on the rear wing, incidentally.

As mentioned earlier in the chapter, base cars now came with a 19in wheel and tyre combination, while the S had a 20in one. The 3.4-litre model came with 8.5J wheels shod with 235/40 ZR-rated rubber at the front, combined with 11J rims and 285/35 ZR19s at the rear; the 3.8-litre car employed the same rim widths, but 245/35 ZR20s up front, and 295/30 tyres at the back. Not surprisingly, numerous alternatives were made available, from changing the 411 rim for the bigger 423 one, or

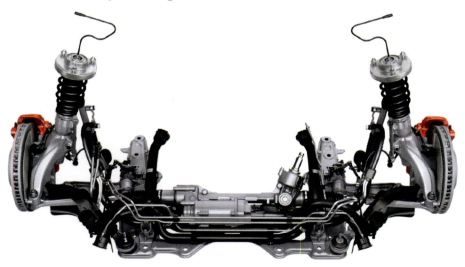

The front suspension, steering and braking setup of the Carrera S. This illustration includes the PDCC and PASM systems, with the latter standard on the 3.8-litre car; the active Porsche Dynamic Chassis Control (PDCC) system was a costly option, aiding roll stability for faster cornering, and only available on the S grade.

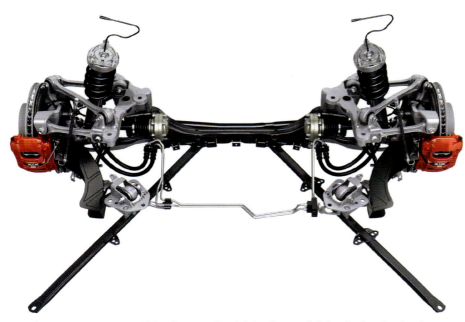

The rear suspension of the Carrera S, with brakes and driveshafts also in place.

selecting one of the distinctive 20in alloy wheels offered as pure (and costly) options.

Braking was via discs all-round. All four were vented and cross-drilled, served by four-pot aluminium alloy monobloc calipers up front on the strict Carrera and six-piston versions on the Carrera S; four-pot calipers were used at the rear on both models. The 3.4-litre car came with 330mm (13.0in) diameter discs at the front, which were 28mm (1.1in) thick, while the larger S version was 340mm (13.4in) across and a touch thicker; both had the same 330mm (13.0in) x 28mm (1.1in) discs at the rear.

In addition to the disc size difference, the brake calipers were black on the strict Carrera, and painted red on the 3.8-litre models – one of the few reliable distinguishing features when looking at a vehicle from the side. Notwithstanding, some cars had yellow calipers, signifying the fitment of the optional PCCB braking system. This included 350mm (13.8in) diameter ceramic discs all-round, which weighed about half as much as regular rotors, along with six-pot front and four-pot rear calipers. Incidentally, calipers were always mounted at the trailing edge of the front discs and the leading edge at the rear, thus keeping as much weight as possible within the wheelbase to improve handling through a reduction in yaw moment.

In all cases, a four-channel anti-lock braking system via the Bosch ABS 9.0 setup ensured weight reduction and optimised brake force distribution (EBD), with servo-assistance taken as read. Further use of the latest electronic advances was evident in the adoption of the electric parking brake (EPB) we mentioned in the interior section, which employed a dash-mounted switch to apply and release the handbrake rather than a traditional lever or pedal, although it also had an automatic deactivation

The inner workings of the PASM active suspension.

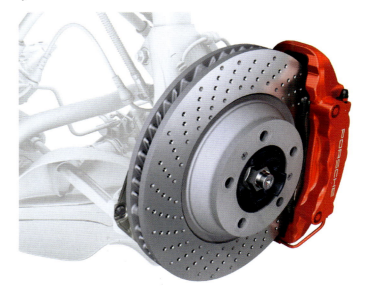

The front brakes on a Carrera S, with racing spec six-pot calipers fitted as standard.

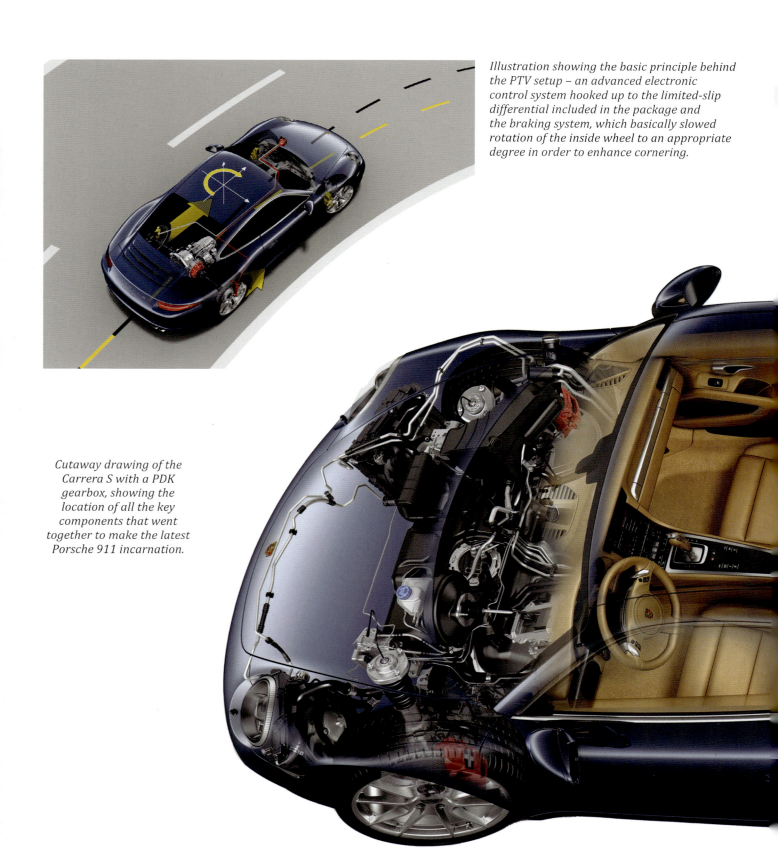

Illustration showing the basic principle behind the PTV setup – an advanced electronic control system hooked up to the limited-slip differential included in the package and the braking system, which basically slowed rotation of the inside wheel to an appropriate degree in order to enhance cornering.

Cutaway drawing of the Carrera S with a PDK gearbox, showing the location of all the key components that went together to make the latest Porsche 911 incarnation.

setting that doubled as a hill-start assistance feature. In simple terms, the EPB worked via a small electric actuator motor attached to the rear brakes, with shoes employed to give a good handbrake, acting on the inner surface of the elongated rear brake disc centres.

The Porsche Stability Management system (PSM) was a standard fitment, using the electronics in the brakes to monitor the car's direction, speed, yaw velocity and lateral acceleration, so that it could control extreme oversteer and understeer situations via selective braking on individual wheels (and cutting power if necessary) in order to rein in those that push a little too hard for their own good. The system included ABD and ASR functions, helping maintain traction and stability, as well as MSR throttle control, although it could be switched off when desired.

Porsche Torque Vectoring (PTV) took things a stage further, working in tandem with the electronics of the PSM system and adding a limited-slip differential into the equation to further enhance stability during high-speed cornering, and improve traction coming out of bends. Standard on the S and optional on the 3.4-litre model, for sure, one could reduce lap times if that way inclined, but the purity of direct car control was slowly being eroded with each and every 'advance' demanded by the newer generations. One cannot blame today's makers, of course, and sales of the Porsche brand have never been so high – it just seems that the

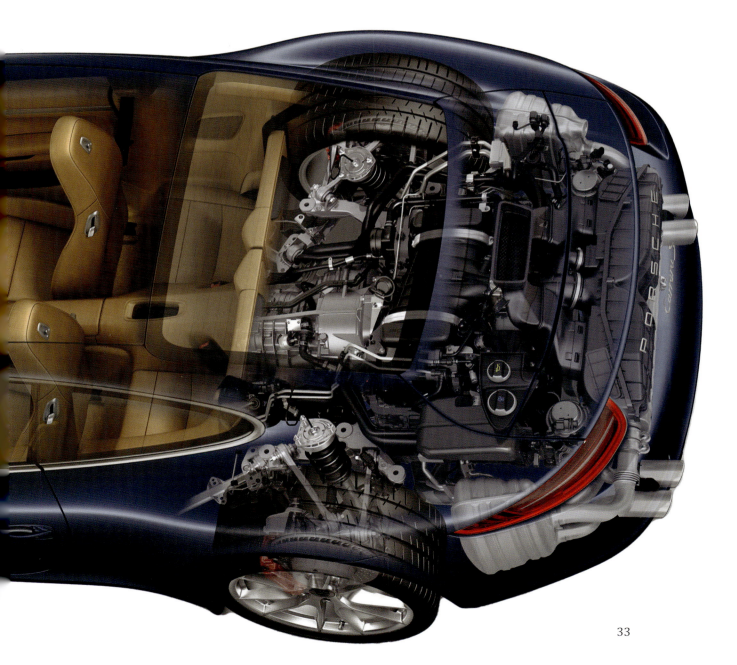

Naturally, the new 911 was subjected to an extensive testing programme in various environments before being rubber-stamped for production status. These pictures show it on test in South Africa, although a few spy shots were leaked during runs in Germany as early as August 2010. Back then, some magazines were calling the newcomer the 998 (which makes sense), although 991 was ultimately used for the project number.

While other vehicle lines were built in different facilities, owned either by Porsche or Volkswagen, the new 911 was produced exclusively at the famous Zuffenhausen plant, situated in the northern part of Stuttgart. This is what the sprawling site looked like in 2018.

Stuttgart company is catering for a rather different clientele to the one that would have considered nothing but a Porsche only a couple of decades earlier.

Early press reaction
As if following on from the last paragraph, *Car & Driver* made an interesting statement after its first drive: "Longer, lower, wider, faster, more efficient, and – amazingly – slightly lighter, the new Porsche 911 Carrera is a better car in every way. Which means it's less like a 911 than ever, because let's face it, much of what made the model an icon had been its eccentricities."

However, having got used to the steering, the UK's *Car* magazine summed up the newcomer with the following prose: "It's more refined, more comfortable, and more economical than ever before, but what really matters is that it still has that unique 911 feel and character. The outgoing Carrera GTS is more interactive and involving, but this new Porsche 911 isn't far behind, while offering up a much broader range of talents to a bigger audience."

Motor Trend noted that the EPS was every bit as linear as the old steering setup, the brakes were said to be "excellent" both in terms of their performance and feel, and the PDK transmission – already good – was even better than before. The interior was also praised, calling it "a handsome blend of 911 heritage and Panamera innovation."

Regarding the handling, *Road & Track* wrote: "The new 991 is hard to fault dynamically. You really have to make a gross driving error to get the chassis to break a sweat, and even then the stability nannies intervene in the gentlest, least intrusive way. Forget any past wicked tendencies toward lift-throttle oversteer; the 991 exhibits easily catchable, controlled breakaway, and circles our skidpan at an impressive 0.99g. The new electric-assist steering is nicely direct and communicative, filtering out the most obnoxious bumps and nibbles, but still letting you feel every crack and surface nuance. If there's any doubt of the 991's handling prowess and controllability, consider that its Nordschleife lap time of seven minutes 40 seconds is a full 14 seconds quicker than its predecessor's."

The final words go to Greg Kable of *Autocar*: "The 991 is not only more capable than the 997, its handling also hints at greatness. In Carrera S form, it is faster, more neutral at the limit, considerably more stable, incredibly comfortable, a lot quieter at motorway speeds, and amazingly frugal. At the end of the day, I'd even come to terms with the new steering, accepting that it lacks the ultimate precision and sensitivity of the old hydraulic arrangement. The question I'm asking myself now is how can Porsche possibly top it? For

(Continues on page 38)

Some of the pictures released at the time of the 991's launch. This selection features a bevy of German/EU-spec Carrera S models, with the red car fitted with optional SportDesign alloys.

the moment, the original supercar has reached a new zenith – both in ability and desirability."

With plenty of compliments on the styling, and even the forthright folks at *Auto, Motor und Sport* declaring themselves happy that absolutely nothing had been lost in the transformation from 997 to 991, after a lengthy gestation period, the scene was finally set for the new 911 to go on sale, with orders being taken from September 2011 in Germany, and the first domestic deliveries expected in the first week of December …

The 991 makes its entrance
The 2011 Frankfurt Show witnessed the debut of several interesting concept cars, such as the Jaguar C-X16 coupé and Mercedes F125 fuel cell model, but for Porsche fans, even though the diesel Panamera was also taking a bow, naturally all eyes were on the new 911.

A domestic price list had already been prepared in time for the IAA, with the basic tin-top 3.4-litre coupé commanding a very reasonable €73,800 plus taxes (German VAT stood at 19 per cent at time of launch, incidentally), while the Carrera S version was listed at €85,900 before about €180 of German necessities, taxes and options, and there were certainly plenty of those available to tempt customers into parting with their hard-earned cash, despite the newcomers having an enhanced level of standard equipment.

Ultimately, the days of a handful of options being a small footnote at the end of a catalogue were long gone. Now, one almost needed a separate publication to list them all, and a glance at an official contemporary price list hints that people tackling restorations in the future are going to be navigating their way through a minefield. Still, by taking things in chronological order and noting changes as they happened, we should be able to build up a clear picture of what was (and what wasn't) standard for any given year.

Starting with the standard equipment on domestic cars, we had alloy wheels, bi-xenon headlights (with a washer system included), ABS, PSM, power-assisted steering, central locking, tinted glass, power windows and mirrors, a seven-speaker audio unit with an integral CD player, dual-zone air-conditioning, power seats with partial

The moment the new 911 broke cover in Frankfurt …

A 3.4-litre 911 Carrera pictured outside the Porsche Museum in mid-October 2011. This car is fitted with optional 'SportDesign' (428) alloy wheels.

An early Carrera S pictured at the factory, equipped with standard wheels and a sunroof.

leather upholstery, a leather-trimmed steering wheel and gearshift, a high-spec alarm system, and a choice of four exterior and four interior colours.

Paintwork options included the four standard solid hues (FOC), metallic paint (€990 plus tax), shades termed as special colours (€2230) and, for the princely sum of €3500, the option of unique coachwork as per the customer's sample, if they were willing to wait an extra six months.

The standard partial leather trim included hide on the seat facings and upper side bolsters (including the headrest area), the door and central armrests, and the inner door handle. Adding €1135 brought extra leather trim on the regular and P06 seats, while €2720 provided full leather upholstery in a series colour (including the top roll and a 'Galvanosilber' strip on the doors); another €500 allowed the owner to choose a two-tone interior or a special grey hide shade, or a €1200 premium brought the 'natural' red or brown hues into play. Colour matching to a customer's sample was also available for those willing to pay over €4000 for the privilege.

Mechanical options included the seven-speed PDK transmission (option code 250, priced at €2950 plus tax), cruise control (454), a sports exhaust system (176), the Sport Chrono package (639 if specified without the PCM setup, or 640 with it), the €7150 PCCB brake upgrade (450), the PASM active suspension package for the base Carrera (475), a lowered suspension with PASM (030), Porsche Dynamic Chassis Control (PDCC) for the Carrera S (352, or 031 if combined with the lowered suspension), the PTV system for the 3.4-litre car (220, or 221 on PDK-equipped vehicles), and speed-sensitive power steering (658).

Base car owners could have the 20in 'Carrera S' alloy wheels fitted (with a regular finish only initially, although a darker Platinum satin option became available from January 2012), while either 911 could be shod with 'Carrera Classic' (427) rims. The latter, sporting a ten-spoke design, had an 8.5J x 20 front and 11J x 20 rear combination on the 911s (wider than wheels specified for the 981 range), coming with 245/35 and 295/30 ZR-rated rubber, respectively. Another alternative was the more intricate but slightly cheaper 'SportDesign' alloy wheel (428), with the same rim sizes and tyres as the 427 option. Coloured wheel centre crests, a tyre pressure monitor, and 5mm/0.2in wheel spacers rounded things off in this area.

Upgrading the headlights was

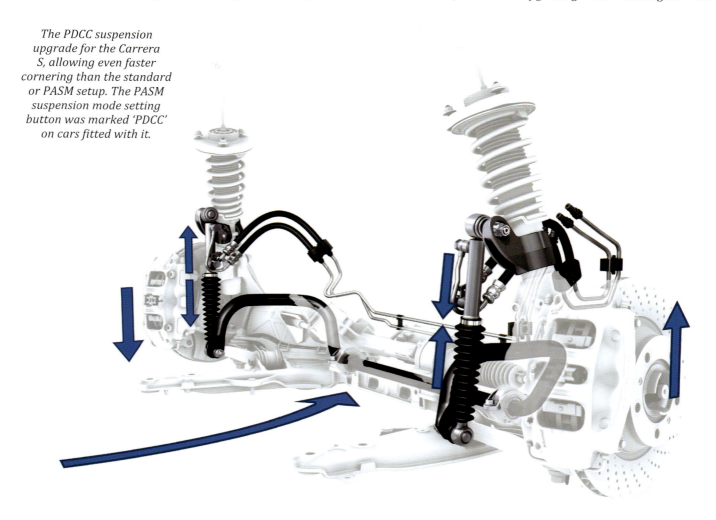

The PDCC suspension upgrade for the Carrera S, allowing even faster cornering than the standard or PASM setup. The PASM suspension mode setting button was marked 'PDCC' on cars fitted with it.

possible via option 603, which brought a bi-xenon setup complete with the Porsche Dynamic Light System (PDLS). PDLS was basically an evolution of the idea first seen on the innovative Citroën DS, with the main headlamps moving in relation to the steering angle to illuminate more of the road entering a turn. In addition, sensors controlled the range of the dipped beam in relation to speed, while turning on the rear foglight fine-tuned the headlight pattern to reduce reflection in poor conditions; headlight washer nozzles could be finished in body colour on request.

Other options included deletion of the model badge, a '911' badge for the tail (dropping the Carrera or Carrera S reference), a grey-tinted band on the windscreen, a rear wiper, automatic dimming interior and exterior mirrors combined with a rain sensor, electrically-operated folding door mirrors with courtesy lighting, a metal power sunroof, a roof rack foundation package, a parking assistant system using ultrasonic sensors hooked up to an audible warning and visual guidance setup (code 635 for the rear only, or 636 for both the front and rear of the car), the Porsche Entry & Drive system (enhanced keyless entry features and keyless engine starting), a HomeLink garage door opener, fire extinguisher (509), and the PVTS tracking system.

Interior options were plentiful, to say the least, with items like floormats (including special versions), a multi-function steering wheel, a SportDesign steering wheel (with shift paddles on the PDK version), a contrast leather colour or Alcantara trim on the steering wheel, steering wheel heating (with the switch located on the back of the lower spoke), Alcantara trim on the PDK selector, the 630 lighting package (with additional LED lights overhead, in the door panels, and footwells), childseat preparation, a leather key pouch, and a smoker's package. A black tachometer face (standard on the 3.4-litre car) was available for Carrera S owners as well, free of charge, while either white-, red-, yellow- or beige-painted instruments (including the Sport Chrono dial) could be specified as another option, albeit a

The original tilt/slide power sunroof option.

rather costly one in this case – almost €800 if the Sport Chrono meter face was added into the equation.

A variety of extended trim parts were also listed, mainly in the Exclusive catalogue. For those who opted for leather trim, the interior package was available with a colour-coded painted finish (EER for the dashboard dressing piece and door capping insert at the same height, or XDM for the dash piece only, albeit changed to an EET code in 2013), with other painted parts including the dashboard air vent slats (CDN), air vent surrounds (CTR), the centre console aft of the audio unit and ending at the point where the central armrest begins (XYG), and the car key body.

The same options listed in the previous paragraph were available in leather, rather than painted, using the EEA code for the bundle (the door capping trim was hide in this case), with XVP (later EES) being the dashboard dressing piece only option; the CDN equivalent was CZV, CTR was CTK, and XYG was XHB. The dashboard trim package (CZW) included the outer edges on both sides, the area butting up to the windscreen and speaker covers being trimmed, while CXM was the equivalent for the doors, albeit not dropping as low as the loudspeaker grille; fusebox lids could also be specified with leather trim.

The wood interior package used mahogany trim pieces, EEB being the dashboard, door capping trim and gearknob for manual cars, while EEC was the fascia sections and gearknob only; EED and EEF were the equivalent parts for cars with a PDK transmission. XHF was a multi-function steering wheel with a wooden rim to match, and XHG was the frame in the extension of the centre console.

The carbon interior package was much the same, with EEG being the same in make-up as the EEB wood equivalent, EEH corresponded to EEC, EEJ to EED, and EEK to EEF. XHL was a multi-function steering wheel with a carbonfibre rim, and XHM the part that trimmed the centre console aft of the HVAC and audio controls. It was a similar story with the brushed aluminium package, with EEL, EEM, EEN and EEP making up the gear selector and trim pieces, while XYE was the console section; XYA was a special alloy head for the PDK selector.

Meanwhile, seating could be upgraded via the P05 option (Sports Seats Plus, trimmed in smooth leather), the P06 option known as Power Sports Seats (complete with a memory feature), or the P07 option (Adaptive Sports Seats Plus, which were shaped like the P05 model but built on the Power Sports Seats spec with additional adjustment on the side bolsters). Heating was available for all seats, including the

The PCM package, with the navigation screen on display in this picture.

The Exclusive page found at the back of the very first 991 price list. Strangely, even though the items were all listed in September 2011, hardly anything illustrated could be provided straight away, but it's still useful for reference as it shows the painted grilles and spoiler option up front, the XDA wheels, embossed headrest and centre console lid designs, and an aluminium PDK selector.

Two stereo system upgrades were listed – one from Bose of America, and the other from Burmester of Germany. Bose was already well known in the automotive sector, while the slightly younger Burmester concern was just starting to make inroads there, building on its reputation for high-end home audio equipment.

standard items, along with a ventilation package, although the two couldn't be combined.

As for audio items, the P23 Porsche Communication Management (PCM) package was the main one, for although it had the same touchscreen size as the standard CD/radio unit, it contained a navigation system module and was easy to upgrade. For instance, option code 671 brought in voice control, 666 was a telephone module (669 being the cordless handset to go with it), 676 a TV tuner, and 641 an electronic logbook. Meanwhile, the Bose surround sound system took things a stage further than the standard Sound Package Plus setup, with 12 speakers and a stronger amplifier, with the 12-speaker 820W Burmester option being there as well for true audiophiles at €3690 – a hefty €2500 more than the 445W Bose SSS. A six-CD changer was listed for the standard stereo (692) and PCM unit (693), and there was also a mobile phone preparation service for those without PCM.

Many of these items were available via the Tequipment catalogue, meaning dealers could add them at the time of purchase or as a retro-fit. Winter tyres on standard rims were a useful accessory for those wishing to keep a car for a decent length of time, although snowchains were also offered as an alternative. Locking wheel bolts, wheel spacers, crested tyre valve caps, rubber floormats, a luggage compartment liner, childseats, car covers (indoor and outdoor types), cleaning materials and a dedicated 12V trickle charger covered all the practical angles of ownership.

So, as the 2012 season began, the domestic market listed the new Carrera (€88,037 on the road – only a little more than the 2011 equivalent) and Carrera S (priced at €102,436) alongside an extensive range of older 997-based 911s, which included the €104,935 Carrera GTS coupé, three fhc Carrera 4 variants (base, S and GTS), six cabriolets to cover the same grades as the coupés just mentioned, a Targa 4 and Targa 4S, the €178,596 four-litre GT3 RS, and the 911 Turbo and Turbo S in open and closed guise (with prices from €148,727 to €184,546). To put these prices into perspective, the cheapest Porsche at the time was the basic Boxster, at €46,982, while the most expensive model outside the 911 range was the Panamera Turbo S, which had a €167,291 sticker price.

The new Carrera Cabriolet.

991 range expansion

Followers of Porsche lore thus far would not have been surprised in the slightest to find the Carrera and Carrera S coupés joined by a pair of equivalent convertibles soon after their launch – it had become something of an established pattern by this time. Although the 911 Carrera Cabriolet and 911 Carrera S Cabriolet were officially launched at the 2012 Detroit Show in January, details were released at the end of November 2011, and indeed, one was able to start placing orders as soon as the first day of December 2011 in the car's native Germany – a full three months before the domestic launch was scheduled in the press release.

Mechanically identical to their tin-top stablemates, for the €12,500 premium (if one uses the domestic OTR price including VAT), the cabriolets were given a new one-touch power hood that retained the coupé's lines when up, and sat flush with the tail section under an integral tonneau cover when stored away behind the rear seats. Made extensively from magnesium alloy, the fabric-covered top (available in four colours) was particularly light, and practical, too, being taut, fully lined, and equipped with a heated glass rear screen. Operated via buttons in the switch group aft of the gear selector or the key remote, it could be raised or lowered in around 13 seconds, and either while the car was stationary or on the move at speeds of up to 31mph (50km/h).

The rear quarter windows operated in tandem with the front side glass whenever the hood was moved, and while the folding function was deleted on the rear seats (taking away one of the luggage options), this was because the space behind them was required for the pair of hefty automatic pop-up bars to provide protection in a roll-over situation.

A further refinement was the fitting of an electrically-controlled windblocker as standard – a fixed item now, and put into position by a switch that sat in the middle of the two hood buttons. While the windblocker cut drafts, reduced wind noise, and took only a couple of seconds

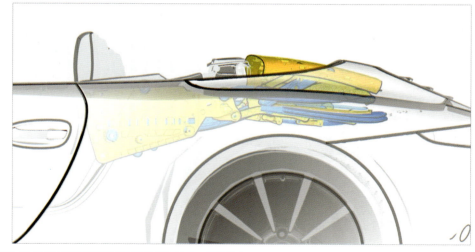

The elegant hood operation, and a drawing showing what the packaging looked like when the hood was dropped. A lot of thought had gone into the three-part design, even down to the fitting of rain channels to help prevent folks getting wet when opening the doors. Another nice touch was the provision of rear-end parking assistance on the convertibles, as rearward visibility was not so good compared to the coupés if the hood was up.

to operate (it could even be raised at motorway speeds), it should be noted that once up, the windblocker ruled out the use of the rear seats for virtually anyone other than a leprechaun.

The additional bracing around the B-pillars, sill areas and windscreen frame came together to keep the bodyshell virtually as rigid as that of the coupé, and pleasingly free of scuttle shake. According to the German DIN method of measurement, the convertibles were some 70kg (154lb) heavier than their fhc counterparts, but it's worth noting that a new 991 Carrera Cabriolet nonetheless weighed the same as a 997 Carrera coupé. As such, the official performance figures were still very impressive, with the 0-60 time quoted as five seconds dead for the manual Carrera Cabriolet (without Sport Chrono activated), or 4.7 for the manual

The roof and windblocker switches. This picture also brings into focus a lot of the buttons mentioned earlier in the chapter.

An illustration showing a convertible with airbags and the rear pop-up bars deployed. The latter was basically the same safety system as that employed on the 996s and 997s.

The new windblocker design.

Carrera S version; the PDK shaved 0.2 seconds off these times, which brought the dropheads perfectly in line with the manual coupés.

Other than the items already mentioned, standard equipment levels and options were basically the same in the coupés and convertibles, apart from body kits and lowered suspensions. As if there weren't enough options already, more were made available for the 991s from January 2012 ...

One could now specify painted wheel spokes and centres in body colour (XD9) or black (XDA), or a Platinum finish on the 423 'Carrera S' wheel (a full gloss black finish would also be listed in due course). Seatbelts could be ordered in silver grey, beige, red, yellow or blue, while a body-colour finish was made possible for the back shell of the P05 and P07 seats; a Porsche crest on the seat headrests provided a nice finishing touch. Leather trim could now surround the main instruments, and could also be ordered for the inner door sill guards.

Although listed from the start, high-gloss anodised aluminium side window trim (559) didn't officially become available until February 2012. In the following month, buyers could have body-coloured front intake grilles, a body-coloured lower section on the front spoiler, a body-coloured rear apron, and painted model badging on the tail. Decals for the doors (with the model grade) were listed at the same time, with the script in grey and decorative lines in black, red, yellow or silver.

Also new for March were the five-spoke XRT 'SportTechno' alloys (€2235, or €1035 on the Carrera S), which were a fraction wider than the other 20in rims, and had beefier 305/30 rubber on the back. The P05 and P07 seats were given a leather-trimmed back shell option from this time, and the transmission tunnel between the rear seats, as well as the seatbelt receivers and guide covers, could also be given the leather treatment. Leather trim was now available on the steering column surround, and the rear view mirror also, while customers could have the central armrest upgraded with a Porsche crest

(Continues on page 48)

A selection of press images from the time of the convertible's launch. The silver car is a 3.4-litre model, and the red one a 911 Carrera S Cabriolet.

(XPT) or model designation script (XUV).

The classic Cup aero bodykit for coupés (XAA), a SportDesign package including a front and rear spoiler setup (XAT), and the option of the SportDesign front apron and spoiler only (XAS) were made available in April. These particular kits and appendages could also be bought through the Tequipment catalogue, by the way. Sports tailpipes (XLT), which looked vaguely similar to those of the Carrera S, were another new item. Wheel spokes and centres could be painted in a contrast colour from the following month, and in June 2012, a glass sunroof (653) was put on the lists to augment the existing metal one.

Other items that became available at this time (having been announced a little earlier) included the X51 power kit

The Aerokit Cup (XAA) fitted to a Carrera S coupé with the XDA alloy wheel option.

Standard colour & trim guide

These colour variations were listed from the start of 991 production until June 2013 on mainstream 911 Carreras. Please see the text for variations applied to other model lines and specials.

Solid coachwork colours
Black (041), Carrara White (B9A), Guards Red (80K), and Racing Yellow (1S1). Carrara White replaced by White (C9A) from June 2012.

Metallic coachwork colours
Basalt Black Metallic (C9Z), Agate Grey Metallic (M7S), Platinum Silver Metallic (M7T), Ruby Red Metallic (M3X), Dark Blue Metallic (M5X), Aqua Blue Metallic (M5R), and Anthracite Brown Metallic (M8S). Ruby Red Metallic (M3X) replaced by Mahogany Metallic (M8Y) from June 2012 onwards; Amaranth Red Metallic (8L1) became available from January 2013.

Special coachwork colours
GT Silver Metallic (M7Z), Lime Gold Metallic (5P1), and Cognac Metallic (M8Z). A 'colour to sample' option was also available.

Hood (convertible top) colours
Black, Red, Blue, and Brown. Hood always lined in black.

Leatherette (vinyl) and leather trim
Black, Platinum Grey, Yachting Blue, and Luxor Beige. Carpeting and floormats came in matching hues; the headlining came in black on the black and blue options, or grey and beige to match the trim.

Regular two-tone leather trim
Agate Grey with Pebble Grey, and Black with Platinum Grey. Black with Luxor Beige became available from January 2013. Carpeting and floormats came in the lighter shade, with the roofliner in the darker one.

Special leather colours and natural leather trim
Agate Grey, Carrera Red and Espresso. Umber became available from June 2012 onwards. Carpeting and floormats came in matching hues; the roofliner was black on the red option, or grey and brown to match the trim. A 'colour to sample' option was also available.

The SportDesign aerodynamic appendages on a Carrera S Cabriolet. The front spoiler, which was similar to the Cup one, albeit a little less dramatic, could be bought on its own, or in conjunction with a ducktail spoiler. The wheels are the XRT 'SportTechno' rims, by the way, and the car also has the XLT sports tailpipes, which had a brighter finish than stock Carrera S items.

A strict Carrera coupé with a glass sunroof and 'Carrera S' alloys.

Glass tilt/slide sunroof

for the Carrera S. Sporting the same 12.5:1 c/r as the regular 3.8-litre six, thanks to modified cylinder heads, hotter camshafts, a new intake system, a sports exhaust and a number of other tweaks, this took power up from 400bhp to 430bhp (at 7500rpm). Incidentally, although maximum torque was the same as that of the stock Carrera S engine, it came in a fraction further up the rev-range. We should also note that the Sport Chrono package came with the X51 upgrade, along with a third cooling radiator, calling for a new insert in the central mouth of the front air dam.

Also new was the option of fully-painted mirrors, the ability to have painted

Another Exclusive promotion page, this one showing a cabriolet with wheels in a Platinum finish hiding PCCB brakes, and a selection of mahogany interior parts.

Porsche Exclusive

A distinctive identity is another form of exclusivity.

With the range of options featured in this catalogue, you can make your Porsche even more special. Introducing Porsche Exclusive. Have your vehicle individually and exclusively tailored to your wishes even before it leaves the factory. Aesthetically and technically, inside and outside, using fine materials and with customary Porsche quality.

Our overriding principle? That your car is uniquely handcrafted to your taste. You will find a wide range of design options in the separate Porsche Exclusive 911 catalogue.

Either your Porsche Centre or the customer centre in Zuffenhausen (tel. +49 (0)711 911-25977, email: customercentre-exclusive@porsche.com) will be happy to answer any questions about Porsche Exclusive that you may have. Please note that delivery times may be extended for certain Porsche Exclusive equipment.

In keeping with tradition, an Exclusive power kit (X51) was announced for the Carrera S just before the first round of colour changes. Although it took power output up to 430bhp, at €11,600 plus tax (or €360 more if combined with a PDK gearbox), it was certainly a costly option, so it's no wonder that some effort went into making it look a little different to the standard power-unit.

Drawing highlighting the main changes applied to the Exclusive engine. Additional cooling was provided by a third radiator up front, mounted between the existing pair ahead of the wheels.

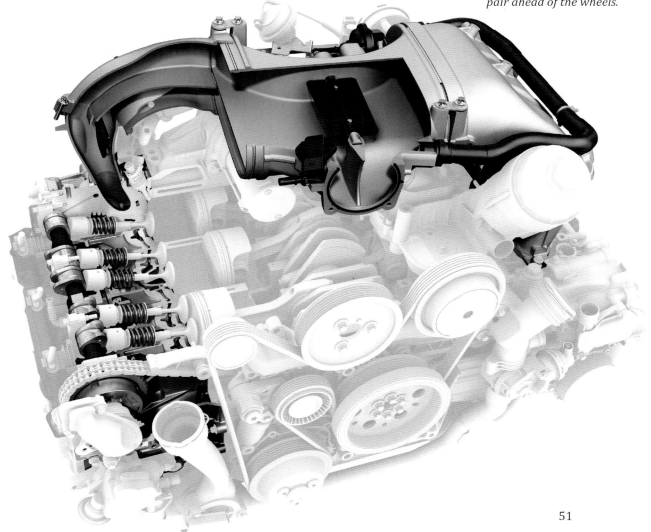

A picture from the 'Identity 911' exhibition, held at the Porsche Museum during the spring of 2012.

exterior parts bundled together as a package (DAR), privacy glass (XPL), P03 bucket seats (with or without painted seatbelt guides), a painted finish or leather trim for the PCM unit, and rear footwell lighting.

It should be noted that there were a few changes to the colour palette by this time. June 2012 saw Carrara White replaced by plain ol' White and Ruby Red Metallic superseded by Mahogany Metallic, while Amaranth Red Metallic duly joined the fray as an additional paintwork hue at the start of 2013. Although Emerald Green was on the cards for the early 991s at one point, this particular colour failed to make it into the 2013 MY catalogues. As for trim, Umber (classed as a special leather) became available from June 2012 onwards, while Black with Luxor Beige two-tone leather trim was listed from January 2013. While the latter entry (and the Amaranth Red one) might be jumping the gun somewhat, it has been mentioned here to fit in with the data in the sidebar on page 49.

While all these changes were taking place, Porsche announced the limited edition 911 Club Coupé model in May 2012. Priced at €142,831 and restricted to just 13 cars (with one kept by the factory) in acknowledgement of the first Porsche owners' club being started 60 years earlier by 13 German enthusiasts, this Carrera S-based machine featured Brewster Green paintwork, the full SportDesign bodykit, the Sport Chrono package combined with the X51 engine upgrade, SportTecho wheels with body-coloured highlights covering PCCB brakes, an Espresso leather interior with beige contrast stitching, special badging, and a number of other items one would usually find on the option list.

Looking at the big picture, with record sales in 2011, and the new Macan waiting in the wings to augment a fresh range of mid-engined machines (the 981 Boxster, which had been launched at

53

The delivery hall in Stuttgart, with a US-spec 911 Club Coupé stealing the limelight. The nose of an Acid Green convertible can also be seen in the foreground (the colour being available through the Exclusive programme), while the Speedster given to Ferry Porsche for his 60th birthday sits quietly in the background.

the 2012 Geneva Show and would duly be followed by the Cayman later in the year), it was perhaps ironic that in the summer of 2012, as expected for some time, it was announced that Porsche Automobil Holding SE and Volkswagen AG would form an integrated automotive empire, with Porsche AG duly becoming part of the Volkswagen Group. Given the intertwined histories of these German giants, it could easily be said that what comes around, goes around …

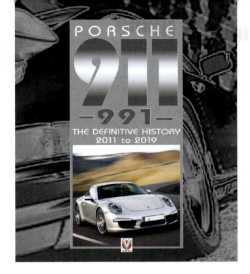

2

The early production models

The 991 was already pretty well established in Germany by the end of 2011 – most interested parties had seen one in the flesh, and many people had placed Christmas present orders for this latest 911 generation, either in fhc or dhc guise, with the two engine options for each body. This chapter will bring us up-to-date with the export markets, and then take the convoluted story on to the 2014 MY ...

The new 911 officially went on sale in America in the first week of February 2012. Before then, though, there had been a long-winded build-up that had started back in mid-October, with a couple of cars on display at the Porsche Rennsport Reunion meeting at Laguna Seca. As Bernd Harling of PCNA stated: "As the 911 race car and street car histories are completely intertwined, it is fitting to show our latest 911 at a motor racing extravaganza. Everyone will see that this newborn is truly a member of the family."

A few weeks later, the cars headed south on Route 5, with the 911 Carrera and Carrera S coupés making their official North American debut at the 2011 Los Angeles Show, which opened to the public on 18 November. The Panamera GTS was another debutante, and Porsche's commitment to the LA area (ultimately, this part of California accounts for one in five US Porsche sales) was confirmed with the announcement of plans for the Los Angeles Performance Centre – a spot, like that already in place

The new 911 on display at the Rennsport Reunion IV bash. Note the number plate housing for this European-spec car, which was then shipped to the LA Show. Unfortunately, most of the press material showed EU vehicles with different plates and nothing more, making them virtually useless for reference. (Courtesy Curt Smith from Bellevue, WA, USA/Wikimedia Commons)

This bright red 911 Carrera Cabriolet was driven onto the Porsche stand at the 2012 Detroit Show following a tasteful promotion video. Fortunately, this vehicle, being ably described by Matthias Müller, has the correct lighting and number plate arrangement for a US-spec car. (Courtesy Autoviva/Wikimedia Commons)

in several other locations across the world, where Porsche fans could polish their skills and experience their cars in a safe environment.

The next milestone was a little odd, for the cabriolet made its 'world debut' at the NAIAS in Detroit on 9 January 2012, naturally accompanied by the tin-top version at the Cobo Centre. The reason for saying it's odd, is because you could already put your money down for one in Europe, but this was definitely the first international show for the new convertible line (chosen because the US had always provided the biggest 911 Cabriolet outlet in the past), so perhaps the term is right, after all ...

Due to the 'world car' era (with even advertising, brochures and press pictures largely shared across markets), differences between the domestic cars and those sold in the States were very few by design. The most obvious things were the speedometer calibrations (in mph rather than km/h) and the side repeater on the front wing, which had an amber lens on US-spec machines rather than a clear one; a close look also revealed a tighter alcove for the rear number plate to sit in, with US plates being far smaller than their European counterparts.

Another difference of sorts was the offering of option packages – bundles being a long-established thing in America, but rare elsewhere. The Premium Package included PDLS lights, auto-dimming mirrors, and either P06 or P07 seats with heating; the Premium Package Plus built on this by adding Porsche Entry & Drive, the interior light design option and ventilated seats into the equation. In addition, the stereo upgrades could be bought with a CD-changer and satellite radio included in the deal.

Going through reams of US road tests, it's interesting to note the differences in opinion. Most were quick to point out that the 991 was a good car overall, although several people noted that the interior was very tight considering the size of the latest exterior, described by one witty journalist as looking like a "bright yellow Hindenburg when parked next to my 1984 Carrera."

Other comments that kept cropping up noted that the new 911 was much softer than before – pandering to the tastes of buyers that are getting progressively older than those that used to buy the air-cooled Porsches. Less noise, less communication, more comfort features, and an abundance of 'nanny' systems was just something one had to accept as the eras changed. Fortunately, it wouldn't be long before diehard enthusiasts were given something more in keeping with their image of 911s, although modern road conditions probably meant you were better off with the mainstream cars, which, despite the gripes of the old school brigade, were selling in numbers previously unheard of. Porsche was obviously doing something right. And ultimately, history has taught

Below and next page: Some of the shots from the first US press releases, although the cars themselves are actually European specification. Still, the images are too attractive not to use, and also serve as a reminder to be careful when researching, even with official publicity images.

us all too often that catering for the few – and even fewer having the wherewithal to stump up a wheelbarrow full of cash – simply doesn't pay the bills ...

Amid a flurry of fresh awards and media attention (most articles were appreciative and complimentary, it has to be said, and winning the '2012 World Performance Car' title along with *Motor Trend*'s coveted 'Best Drivers' Car' trophy seemingly sealed the argument in favour of the 991 concept), the basic 911 Carrera coupé went on sale at America's 196 dealers at $82,100 (plus a $950 delivery charge), with the S badge adding a further $14,300 to the invoice.

Generally sold as 2012.5 MY cars rather than early 2013 models, the pricing was a little up on before, but the marginal increase (just $3100 in the case of the strict Carrera) deserved to be applauded at the end of the day.

Sales of the new convertible started a few months later, in time for the warmer spring temperatures. The 3.4-litre model cost $93,700, while the 911 Carrera S Cabriolet commanded $103,800 plus delivery charges. To put these prices into perspective, the contemporary Boxster was $48,100, while the cheapest of the Cayennes was only $100 more than that – no wonder it was selling so well, given such a reasonable price-tag and an SUV boom in full swing.

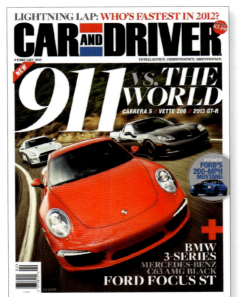

The new 911 gracing the cover of Car & Driver.

More realistically, there were still no less than 25 997-type 911s to choose from. Of those, the 911 Carrera GTS coupé was $103,100, a sporting 911 GT3 would have been $115,700, and the flagship GT2RS was well over twice that amount, assuming you could get one.

The right-hand drive markets

Most of the cars sold in the EU were basically the same as those sold in Germany, although Britain's insistence on driving on the left (hence the use of rhd) meant that special vehicles were needed for this niche – but nonetheless important – market. Some of the switchgear, such as the main headlight control and the ignition barrel next to it, had to be reversed to suit the steering location; speedometers were calibrated in miles per hour, too, to suit the local regulations (but then so were those for Stateside clients, of course). Otherwise, there was little difference between the UK cars and their counterparts in the European mainland.

The coupés went on sale in Britain in mid-December, with the 3.4-litre car priced at £71,449, and the S grade listed at £81,242 – similar money to a Nissan GT-R, as it happens. These prices were carried over as the convertible versions joined them in the spring, commanding £79,947 and £89,740, respectively. Bearing in mind that one could buy a 2.7-litre 981 Boxster and a 2.9-litre 987 Cayman as a pair for about 77K at the time, these purchases were definitely not for the faint-hearted. It still didn't stop folks forming a queue for them, though, or the selection of older 997 models that were still available for that matter ...

In the Antipodes, sales of both the tin-top and drophead cars started in

Studio shots of a 3.4-litre Carrera for the UK market. This example has the standard wheels, but is fitted with a sports exhaust.

Interior and exterior of a UK-spec Carrera S coupé. Thanks to the contemporary British registration system, the '61' number plate helps to confirm that this car is indeed the earliest of the 991 breed, just as the '12' confirms the convertible pictures in this section are the first to be released.

A manual 911 Carrera Cabriolet model for the British Isles.

A UK-spec Carrera S drophead fitted with a PDK transmission, the Sport Chrono package, and a SportDesign steering wheel. The welcome screen in the TFT display next to the tachometer was a nice touch, showing a convertible rather than a coupé.

March 2012 in Australia, with prices ranging from $229,900 to $288,300; a PDK transmission added almost $6000 to the invoice. As it happens, there was a pretty significant drop in pricing for the 2013 season proper, but we can look at that as the story unfolds further.

Heading north of Oz, Porsche's sales arm in Japan made an all-out effort to promote the new car, placing full-page adverts in the national press and double-page spreads in a number of automobile-related magazines.

Coupés were listed in the Land of the Rising Sun from November 2011, with the new Carrera commanding 11,170,000 yen in manual guise, while the PDK version added 750,000 yen and the chance to opt for right-hand drive (7MT cars came in lhd only at this stage). The same was true of the steering options on the Carrera S, although the prices were 13,810,000 and 14,560,000 yen in this case. As in other countries, the cost was a little higher than before for the 991. Meanwhile, the Cabriolets were listed with a PDK transmission only on their arrival in the early part of spring, with the convertible top commanding a premium of around 1,800,000 yen – enough to secure a basic Suzuki Swift Sport in the JDM arena.

Whilst in Asia, we should mention China, not least because by the time the 991 series came along, it had already become a very important market for the Stuttgart maker, moving up to be second in the league table of Porsche

Japanese advertising for the new 911, which was much the same as elsewhere by this time. Ultimately, even the lighting is correct for Japan, and lhd cars are quite common, despite the country officially being right-hand drive.

Opening pages from the 2011 Tokyo Motor Show catalogue, which used the advert image for the cover. The Panamera and Cayenne pictures on the right show that Porsche was creating a 'family' look across the range, with the Boxster and Cayman very similar to the 911 in appearance.

outlets. Unlike Japan, with a long history attached to the marque, this lhd country is a newcomer to the joys of Porsche motoring. But, as with parts of the Middle East, this is somewhere we will have to acknowledge as a major market sooner or later, assuming the current pace of growth keeps up. The fact that the first Porsche Performance Centre in Asia was established in Shanghai would seem to point to the folks in Stuttgart believing it will ...

More new models

New 991s were coming thick and fast to take the place of existing grades in the 997 range, which still ran alongside each other at this stage in the proceedings. Just a year after the newcomer first broke cover, there were already 911 Carrera and 911 Carrera S models in open and closed form, and the 2012 Paris Salon (which opened to the public on 29 September that particular year) witnessed the debut of four-wheel drive versions of each, taking the 991 line-up to eight vehicles.

As before, the provision of 4WD was not to allow owners to go mud-plugging, but to give an additional degree of traction and stability in bad weather and/or on poor road surfaces. This translated into better all-round performance, of course, helping to justify the extra weight, complication and cost.

Porsche Traction Management (PTM), which was the name given to the improved active and rear-biased 4WD system as a whole, was the main difference when comparing the rear-wheel drive cars to their four-wheel drive counterparts.

A very elegant Getrag casting (like that on the contemporary 997-type Turbos) was used to take power to the front axle, acting as a carrier for the differential and front section of the two-piece propshaft, connecting it to the gearbox at the back of the vehicle, but also helping to keep the drivetrain stiff at the same time. And, as before, the front hubs were modified to take driveshafts that sprouted from the diff at the car's bow. According to Ulrich Morbitzer, the man in charge of chassis development, it was electronics that played an important role in the advances made in Porsche's 4WD system, allowing precise amounts of torque to be sent to the front axle rather than a rough quota. For those interested, a new menu in the instrument cluster informed the driver of the torque flow.

A 911 Carrera 4 Cabriolet and 911 Carrera 4S coupé on display at the 2012 Paris Salon. Note the active cruise control (ACC) camera on the front of both of these Aqua Blue cars, as well as the 4WD-type outer front grille designs and side dressing pieces under the sill.

Cutaway drawing showing the main components that make up the 4WD drivetrain, and a detail shot of the Porsche Traction Management system, located at the front-end of the car.

Tail of a 911 Carrera 4 Cabriolet, with this angle showing off the vehicle's extra width and illuminated red strip between the rear combination lights.

Beyond that, however, a lot of the specifications were familiar. The engines were identical to those employed by the RR (or C2, if you prefer) machines, with the same codes, too (indeed, the MA1/03 and MA1/04 were used all the way through the 991.1 run on the numerous 911 Carrera variants).

As for the gearboxes, naturally these were revised in order to take drive to the front wheels, so the CG1/05 PDK unit morphed into the CG1/35, while the 7MT G91/00 became the G91/30. The gearing and 3.44:1 final-drive ratio at the rear-end were carried over, though, with a 3.33:1 f/d specified up front. All four transmission variants continued throughout the 991.1 run.

Chassis items were also the same except for the rear tyre width (mounted on familiar rims, nonetheless): the C2's 285/35 size went to 295/35 on the C4, and C2S's 295/30 to 305/30 on the C4S. This fatter rubber and wider rear track led to beefier rear wheelarches being employed, adding 44mm (1.7in) to the overall width.

The extra width blunted the car's aerodynamic efficiency a little, and with 50kg (110lb) extra to lug around compared to the equivalent RR car, this resulted in a small loss of performance – 0.1 seconds in the 0-60 dash, and 2.5mph (4km/h) less at the top end, which is next to nothing in the real world. Fuel consumption, whilst vastly improved over that of 997 versions thanks to a successful diet and improved engine efficiency, was about three per cent higher than the 991 RR cars, though, prompting Porsche to fit a 68-litre (15 imperial gallons) fuel tank in place of the usual 64-litre (14.1 gallon) one used in the C2 and C2S variants.

Apart from the badging on the tail and treadplates, the other visual differences were quite subtle. The outer pair of front air intakes had a slightly different look to them (the two slats being joined at the ends), a new black trim piece was added to the lower edge of the rocker panels, and a red strip connected the two taillights, continuing C4/C4S tradition.

Otherwise, styling features and standard specifications were shared across the Carrera range. The vast majority of option prices were carried over, too, with only a handful increasing in cost since their introduction. Even then, it was only by a token amount, although following the arrival of the four-wheel drive models, a few more options were added to the already extensive list.

Firstly, the CMX door decals were replaced by new, more tasteful black (CAS) and silver (CAT) versions, and an Alcantara gearshift for manual cars was added (CLB). From November, when the 981 Cayman made its debut, these items were joined by dark PDLS headlamp surrounds (XEX), rear lamp units with a clear glass appearance (XXG), a selection of aluminium or carbonfibre treadplates (regular, illuminated or personalised), an aluminium alloy pedal set, and the Porsche Active Safe (or PAS for short) package – a radar system that combined adaptive cruise control (ACC) with emergency braking assistance.

It should also be noted that the Sport Chrono package was adjusted on manual 2013 MY cars to provide automatic double-declutching on downshifts in the Sport Plus mode. And finally, as mentioned in the previous chapter, Amaranth Red Metallic paintwork was listed from January 2013, along with Black with Luxor Beige two-tone leather trim.

Sticker prices on the RR coupés and convertibles were carried over, meaning a range of €88,037 to €114,931 OTR in the domestic market. The 3.4-litre Carrera 4 coupé was launched at €97,557 including German taxes, with the Carrera 4S coupé commanding €112,313; the C4 Cabriolet was listed at €110,290, while the C4S version was €14,756 more.

However, a new price list was released on the first day of 2013, with the base price (excluding VAT) increasing by €2000 and €2200 on the rear-wheel drive 3.4-litre cars, and an average of €2400 on the RR S grades; prices were retained on the recently-introduced 4WD range, and the cost of options was the same as before, as was the selection available.

By the spring, LED headlights (incorporating the PDLS system) had become available as a new option (code 602, priced at €2380 plus VAT), offered as an alternative to the 603 bi-xenon lights. An alloy fuel cap was another newcomer

A 911 Carrera 4S coupé on the move. Introduction of the four-wheel drive models put the final nail in the 997's coffin – all 911 road cars were now 991-based machines.

Picture showing a 4WD model in unfamiliar territory for most 911 owners – drifting on snow at a Porsche Driving Experience event in Finland at the end of 2012. Other winter training camps were held in Canada, Italy and Switzerland, with plenty of options open to enthusiastic owners during the summer months as well.

(XYB), along with a carbonfibre-trimmed PDK selector (XHJ), a storage net in the passenger footwell, and a speed limit indicator and/or digital radio for those with the P23 PCM unit. One was also able to specify interior packages with or without the door capping dressing piece from this time, a SportDesign steering wheel trimmed in Alcantara, seatbelt exit covers on the B-post in the same exotic material, and an upgraded audio unit (the P25 option) that was basically the original CDR31 stereo combined with the UN1 online services package, which continued as a separate item.

Incidentally, domestic sales had increased by around 16 per cent in 2012 thanks to the new 911 variants and other debutantes – about the same as the worldwide figure (which was actually a

An Austrian-registered Carrera 4S coupé built for Ursula Piech (the wife of Ferdinand Piech – the nephew of Ferdinand Porsche, and a man who did a great deal of work enhancing the Audi and VW brands after his spell in Stuttgart-Zuffenhausen), captured on film at the Porsche Museum in May 2013.

fraction higher due to an exceptionally strong Chinese market), and in line with those in North America.

Racing update

Naturally, given the introduction dates involved with the 991 series, the 2011 season was campaigned exclusively by 997 variants in top class events. The same was true in 2012, in reality, with the GT3 Cup, GT3R and RSR models helping to keep the Porsche name in the spotlight. Even the one-make races had continued using the 997-type GT3 Cup during 2012, but new track warriors were waiting in the wings – the first of them to take a bow, unsurprisingly, being the latest incarnation of the GT3 Cup line.

Introduced on 8 December 2012 at the annual 'Night of Champions' event at Weissach (well ahead of the GT3 road car), this enabled the new GT3 Cup to be used in the Carrera Cup and Supercup series' – promotional tools that needed to be in step with what was on display in the showrooms.

The latest GT3 Cup being introduced at the 'Night of Champions' event at the end of 2012. Ultimately, if one includes the GT America in the run, 643 would be built.

The new RSR taking part in some pre-season testing, with the lack of paintwork showing up the carbonfibre body panels nicely.

The works cars and their drivers due to compete in the GTE-Pro category of the 2013 WEC. From left to right, we have Jorg Bergmeister, Patrick Pilet, Timo Bernhard, Romain Dumas, Richard Lietz, and Marc Lieb.

The standard 3.8-litre Carrera S was now packing 400bhp, of course, so obviously one would expect more power in the racers. Indeed, the NA flat-six in the new GT3 Cup developed 460bhp at 7500rpm, while the six-speed gearbox adopted steering wheel-mounted shift paddles like those seen on the GT3R and RSR (a first for a Cup car), delivering drive to the rear wheels. The design of the centre-lock wheels was revised, shod with fatter Michelin racing rubber, and hiding a new braking system using six-pot calipers up front, with four-pot versions at the rear. Safety was also improved via a new seat, roll cage, and a small rescue hatch integrated into the roof. Available exclusively in white, prices started at €181,200.

While the GT3R was simply updated in its existing form, there was another 991-based newcomer in the shape of the 911 RSR (the GT3 reference being dropped, incidentally), characterised by its light weight and superior aerodynamics. As per the 991 road car, there was a significant increase in the length of the wheelbase, and a new 'wishbone' front suspension was adopted, replacing the more conventional MacPherson strut setup of the past. There was also a lighter gearbox, with steering wheel paddles carried over to manipulate the 460bhp flat-six it was hooked up to, and huge steel brake discs working in conjunction with alloy calipers.

In fact, the normally-aspirated 3996cc water-cooled engine was one of the least altered elements of the vehicle, being optimised only in detail compared to the 2012 version, with

the cooling system getting the most attention. Virtually the entire body was constructed using carbonfibre to reduce weight, while the windows were made of a thin and lightweight polycarbonate material; the use of a lithium-ion battery also helped shed a few pounds.

Two works RSR machines would be run under the Porsche AG Team Manthey banner for 2013, taking part in the FIA World Endurance Championship (WEC) only at this stage in the proceedings, whilst being careful not to tread on the toes of private teams. An LMP1 car was on the way, too, so Porsche's racing programme was definitely moving up a gear ...

The GT3 road car

Making its debut at the 2013 Geneva Show (which opened on 7 March that year), the 991-type 911 GT3 was basically an all-new machine, with a fresh body, engine, transmission, and chassis, including the adoption of active rear-wheel steering – a first for a production Porsche.

Sporting roughly the same dimensions as the Carrera 4 (the GT3 was ultimately a fraction longer and lower), the longer wheelbase and wider track would aid stability, while the 991's construction and regular RR fuel tank helped reduce the vehicle's weight to 1430kg (3146lb) DIN.

Available in all of the coachwork colours listed from June 2013 onwards (which puts initial deliveries into perspective), the front air dam looked a lot like a hybrid version of those supplied in the two optional body kits, but with an air outlet cut into the moulding just ahead of the luggage compartment lid, and a

Front and rear views of the new GT3, which was announced at €137,303 (including VAT) in Germany. The wheels shown in the stationary shot are the 'correct' design for the GT3 (code 431), requiring special hubs.

heavier lip spoiler that extended up the leading edge of the front wheelarches. These changes combined to increase downforce over the front axle, with the openings protected by titanium-coloured grilles.

New ten-spoke centre-lock wheels added to the drama, with subtly revised SportDesign door mirrors (duly made available for other cars via option code 529), and the Carrera 4's sill trim and wider fenders at the back. The large, fixed rear wing had a modified ram air collector in its base, while cut-outs above the black badging (which could be deleted, as always) and in the corners of the rear bumper moulding added another distinguishing feature.

Lower down, the central tailpipes (finished in black) were surrounded by a new diffuser, aiming to make the most of the modified panels running underneath the car. The aerodynamic package as a whole was not quite as slippery as that of a regular coupé, but the compromise on downforce meant that a Cd of 0.33 was still very respectable.

The normally-aspirated MA1/75 engine was based on the Carrera S unit, but with the moving parts extensively modified. For instance, there was a new crankshaft, freshly forged pistons attached to titanium con-rods, and a number of changes made to the valve gear to allow a heady 9000rpm red-line. In production form, with a third radiator added, a 12.9:1 compression ratio and a new ECU (although only a 'GT3' logo to show any differences externally when in situ), the 24v 3799cc flat-six delivered 475bhp at 8250rpm, along with 325lbft of torque 2000rpm lower down the rev-range.

The PDK dual-clutch transmission was also familiar, yet quite different to the regular NA 911s, hence its CG1/90 designation. With characteristics close to those of a sequential gearbox, the gear ratios were brought closer together (3.75, 2.38, 1.72, 1.34, 1.11, 0.96 and 0.84, combined with a revised 3.97:1 final-drive), the shift speeds were made faster, and the shift paddle action improved, with better feel and shorter travel. In addition, neutral could now be selected simply by pulling on both paddles at the same time.

PTV Plus (the name given to the PTV system for PDK cars – ie, the 221 option rather than the 220 one for 7MT machines) was fitted as standard, meaning a limited-slip differential was included on the spec sheet, although no manual option was offered this time

around. This move initially raised a few eyebrows, but it's fair to say that most protesters were silenced after trying the latest setup, which worked in perfect harmony with the dynamic engine mounts and numerous chassis changes.

Regarding the latter, there was an active suspension (lowered by 30mm/1.18in, with adjustment possible on the toe and camber settings, as well as the anti-roll bars), a revised steering ratio, forged 20in alloys with a Platinum finish (9J at the front, shod with 245/35 ZRs, while a 12J width was employed at the back, complete with 305/30 rubber), and huge 380mm (15in) diameter brakes at both ends, operated by red six-pot calipers up front, and four-pot versions at the back; naturally, the PSM stability package (taking in traction control and the ABS system) was included. The

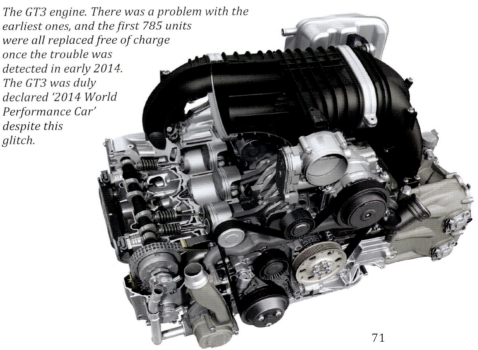

The GT3 engine. There was a problem with the earliest ones, and the first 785 units were all replaced free of charge once the trouble was detected in early 2014. The GT3 was duly declared '2014 World Performance Car' despite this glitch.

The innovative rear-wheel steering system employed on the GT3. Although not a new idea, it was foolish to doubt its worth, and not just on the track – parking manoeuvres were made easier, too.

Interior of the GT3 model, this car having the optional Sport Chrono package.

The Clubsport package (option 003).

biggest change, though, was the adoption of a novel electro-mechanical rear-wheel steering system, replacing the leading control arm with an actuator that moved the wheels in the same or opposite direction to those at the front in order to improve stability or agility, depending on the vehicle speed.

As for the interior, most of it looked familiar to 991 owners with black trim, and indeed, most of the equipment was the same, too. However, the GT3 came with sporting P05 seats as standard, trimmed in black leather with Alcantara inserts and the 'GT3' logo embroidered on the headrests; the adaptive P07 version could be ordered for those wanting a little more comfort for long journeys, or there were P03 seats for race enthusiasts. Alcantara, as well as being used for the rooflining, also graced the rim on the special SportDesign steering wheel, gear selector, door handles, and

A stunning catalogue image showing the GT3's elegant curves

the door and centre armrests. The 'GT3' logo also appeared on the titanium-coloured tachometer face, gear selector surround, treadplates, and on the transmission tunnel just ahead of the simplified rear seats (more like shelves than seats, in reality).

Of the more interesting options, it was possible to specify a 90-litre (19.8 imperial gallon) fuel tank without cost, and a front-end lift system (code 474) for tackling awkward slopes in parking areas. There was also the Clubsport package (003), which had to be bought with bucket seats, and included a rear roll cage, red six-point seatbelts for the driver, a fire extinguisher, and battery kill switch. For the less adventurous, there was always a special version of the aluminium interior package (P1A and P1B), and the chance to have extended leather trim (still in black only), a regular leather steering wheel rim, and red contrast stitching.

For extra pennies there was a host of regular options, such as the Sport Chrono package, PCCB brakes (larger than usual), cruise control, a silver or black finish for the wheels, an alloy fuel cap, PDLS or LED lighting, painted headlight washer nozzles, darker headlights and/or clear rear light units, a grey band on the windscreen, privacy glass, automatic dimming mirrors, carbonfibre interior trim parts, coloured instrument dials, P03 seats (with or without red six-point seatbelts), P07 seats, seat heating, coloured seatbelts, the interior lighting package, a PCM unit and various upgrades, the P25 audio system and a sound package upgrade (to take the car back to seven speakers, as per the other 991 models, rather than the four the standard GT3 came with), a CD-changer, various telephone options,

The 911 GT3 pictured at the 2013 New York Auto Show, which opened at the end of March and ran into the first week of April. (Courtesy zombieite/Wikimedia Commons)

floormats, a passenger-side net, special treadplates, a fire extinguisher, tracking system, painted car key, and a smoker's package.

On the Nürburgring, the new car was capable of covering the challenging Nordschleife (or North Loop) in only seven-and-a-half minutes dead, while the 0-60 sprint took just 3.3 seconds. Top speed was listed at 196mph (315km/h), although, at the end of the day, these are simply numbers on a spec sheet. *Evo* did an interesting test, putting the latest GT3 up against the Nissan GT-R on fast, winding public roads – a more realistic environment than a track. It was noted how agile and informative the Porsche felt compared to its Japanese rival, and how easy it would be to use as a daily driver. While the latest GT3 lost just a little in low-down torque and ultimate steering feel compared to its predecessors, it was "still very much a GT3," which was good news for enthusiasts.

In a similar vein, Steve Sutcliffe went a stage further, saying after his test of the rear-wheel drive newcomer: "I think this is the best sports car I've ever driven." From an *Autocar* veteran like Sutcliffe, that really is a compliment worth taking on board ...

The 2013 MY abroad

The US market continued to be the biggest outlet for Porsche at this time, and, in reality, would doubtless remain the most important – sales in China were simply numbers as far as the author is concerned, based more on a hoarding or 'look what I've bought, neighbour' mentality than enthusiasm for the brand, or even motoring in general. On saying that, the rapidly growing sales (up 30 per cent in 2012) in the Asian powerhouse were certainly useful at balancing the books back in Stuttgart, and the handful of Chinese petrolheads buying 911s for the right reason will always have my full support in following their dream ...

Anyway, the 4WD Carrera range made its US entrance at the 2012 LA Show (where the 981 Cayman made its official world debut), and went on sale there in early 2013, with prices ranging from $91,030 plus delivery charges. The cheapest 911 for 2013 was the 3.4-litre Carrera coupé, listed at $82,100, followed by the four-wheel drive version, and the drophead, which cost $93,700 in RR guise, and $102,930 with 4WD; adding an S badge on the tail put about $14,000 extra onto the invoice.

Although the $130,400 GT3 was announced at the 2013 New York Show in March, it was classed as a 2014 model due to its later sales date in the States, and the Turbos – which came after the GT3 – naturally followed suit.

In the UK, the four C2 grades were carried over for the 2013 season (with pricing unchanged), duly augmented by the four C4 models, which ranged in price from £77,924 to £96,619 at the start of the 2013 MY. As it happens, apart from the cheapest convertible, which had a small increase applied to it in the spring, Britain's pricing then remained unchanged until the 2014 season rolled along, with the introduction of some fresh exotica.

Apart from the 4WD range, starting at $261,350, things were quiet in Australia, too, with the GT3 and other new models coming online in September 2013. The same was true in Japan, for although the lhd-only GT3 was announced in March (priced at 18,590,000 yen – more than a Jaguar XKR-S, and running close to Aston DB9 money), it was simply not available until the end of the year. It was the same situation with the Turbos, with details released in May, but the 2014 Model Year certainly promised to be something special ...

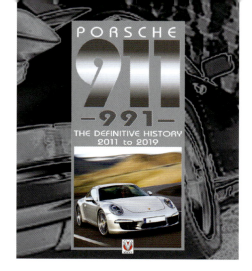

3
Expanding the range

Introduced at the 1973 IAA in prototype form, when the first Porsche 911 Turbo (the legendary 3-litre Type 930) at last hit the road in the spring of 1975, a 0-60 time of 5.5 seconds was simply phenomenal. Now, even the entry-level Carrera was able to eclipse this rarefied level of performance, and with a lot more comfort and safety in hand, too. Inevitably, the new Turbo would have to be something very special indeed ...

The attributes of the exhaust-driven turbocharger had charmed Ferry Porsche long before the 930 came about, for he realised it could double as a fuel-saving device as well as a power booster; superchargers have a romance attached to them, sound wonderful and deliver their advantage immediately (there's no lost time spooling up), but cannot beat a turbo on the economy front in a conventional application. As such, it allowed increased performance balanced with the need to show 'green' credentials, and also kept alive a proud tradition. For sure, the word 'Turbo' didn't have the same wow factor as it did in 1973 (most turbocharged cars don't even advertise the fact they have one nowadays), but to Porsche fans, the details of each 911 Turbo generation that followed on from the 930 are always awaited with bated breath.

The wait is over
The 997-type Turbo and Turbo S models had been selling in reasonable numbers throughout the early days of the 991 series. However, when word of their replacement arrived via a press

The Porsche Turbo certainly had a lot of history attached to it, with the 930 at one end of this esteemed line, and the newcomer at the other. As such, it had something of a reputation to live up to ...

A design sketch for the new Turbo by Peter Varga.

release dated 3 May 2013, it came as no surprise – it had been on the cards from the moment the new generation of 911s had been released back in 2011. The only real shocker, given the 40th birthday of the machine and the fact it was such a technical tour de force, is that more wasn't made of the announcement – the GT3 had taken centre stage at Geneva, the 50th anniversary of the 911 was celebrated in New York, while the hybrid version of the Panamera was being pushed in Shanghai.

Anyway, many of the 997 Turbo's significant features (notably the use of a twin-turbo engine and four-wheel drive) were carried over, albeit with each salient element refined in almost every detail. There were also lots of new innovations, allowing the latest Turbo and Turbo S coupés (the cabriolet versions would follow for the 2014 season proper) to retain their position as the flagships of the 911 line.

Being the Turbo, we should start with the flat-six engine. This was ultimately one of the least changed items, with the MA1/70 morphing into the MA1/71. The 3.8-litre capacity (102 x 77.5mm) was retained, along with DFI, VarioCam Plus variable valve timing, a trick intake manifold, and the use of two variable turbine geometry (VTG) turbochargers – one for each bank, with each having its own intercooler.

While the 9.8:1 compression ratio of the MA1/70 unit was kept, power still increased by 20bhp, the peak now being listed at 520bhp at 6000rpm. Maximum torque was also up a fraction, with 487lbft developed anywhere between 1950 and

The engine of the mighty Turbo. Installed, it looked much like a Carrera lump, with just the nameplates changed – the left hand nameplate has the model designation, while the right-hand one has the familiar '3.8' script.

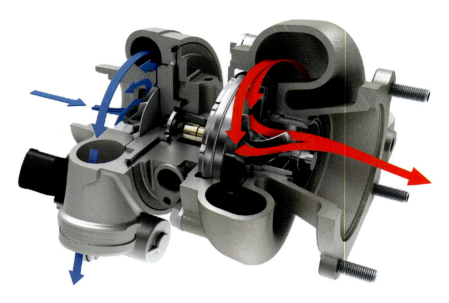

Inner workings of a VTG turbocharger.

5000rpm; significantly more would be released in an overboost situation.

With the car's lighter weight, an automatic stop-start system, improvements in thermal management and other tweaks (including the coasting facility incorporated into the transmission), fuel economy was said to be up to 16 per cent better, despite the increase in power.

The Turbo S was much the same, powered by the bi-turbo MA1/71S lump, which was tuned to give 560bhp at 6500bhp, and a minimum peak torque figure of 516lbft (about the same as a standard Turbo engine with overboost). Interestingly, the same economy gains were quoted for this boxer unit, too, which is quite remarkable given the 40bhp jump in output.

The manual option was no longer listed, so the choices were a seven-speed PDK or nothing at all. As before, the diameter of the paired-up clutches was increased for the CG1/55 PDK unit to handle the Turbo's strapping torque, and the internal ratios were revised. In the case of the new Turbo and Turbo S, the cogs chosen gave ratios of 3.91, 2.29, 1.58, 1.18, 0.94, 0.79 and 0.62, combined with a 3.44:1 final-drive at the rear, and a 3.33:1 ratio on the front axle.

The PTM active four-wheel drive system was borrowed from the latest C4 models, suitably uprated (the electro-hydraulic system even featured dedicated cooling for the front axle's final-drive), and, in view of the copious torque available in the tail, adjusted so that more torque could be sent to the front wheels to transfer as much power as possible to the road. As a result, the 0-60 time was cut to just over three seconds, while the top speed was listed as 197mph (315km/h) for the Turbo, and a heady 199mph (318km/h) for the Turbo S.

Naturally, the turbocharged pairing featured all the latest suspension goodies, being active (including the PDCC system up front on the S grade), and also coming with the rear-wheel steering mechanism introduced on the GT3. Add in a revised steering ratio, the PTV Plus system, PSM, and GT3 brakes (uprated to the GT3's optional 410mm/16.1in front and 390mm/15.3in rear PCCB braking system on the Turbo S), and one had a car that was able to take corners as fast as anyone in their right mind would want to. Indeed, the latest 1605kg (3531lb) 911 Turbo S could circulate the Nürburgring even faster than a new 911 GT3.

While the 997-series turbocharged cars had shared their bodywork with the C4, the newer versions were made even wider at the back – a fact that would

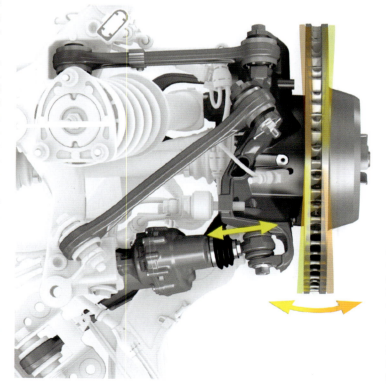

Details of the rear-wheel steering mechanism, with an actuator replacing the regular control arm in front of the axle line.

Dramatic front end of the new Turbo. This car has the standard bi-xenon headlights (the LED versions looked quite similar, with different upper and lower light housings under the glass), and an optional radar camera mounted in the central aperture of the bumper moulding.

have gone against the grain for some enthusiasts used to the practical size of the earlier machines, but somehow accepted today, despite roads and parking spaces that have remained the same width for decades.

Apart from the increased 1590mm (62.6in) rear track, though, which translated to a 1880mm (74.0in) overall width (or 1978mm/77.9in with mirrors included), dimensions were otherwise similar to the regular 3.4- and 3.8-litre coupés, with the Turbos sitting between the Carreras and GT3 in overall length.

However, those massive rear wings (with air intakes cut into them, like those of their predecessors) were not the only changes to the 991 body. At the front, there were bigger outer intakes, meaning new LED light units to share the opening with the two horizontal black slats. Careful inspection revealed different intake trim for the S, the insert being termed an 'air blade' on this model. The two-part lip spoiler was also new, while more subtle lines were sculpted in above the central mouth, rather like the GT3.

SportDesign mirrors graced the doors of the Turbo S (an option on the regular Turbo), while both cars had wheelarches filled by new 20in forged alloys. The 520bhp machine came with a sharp ten-spoke design using a traditional bolt fixing (code 429), and the S had a new interpretation of the 'RS Spyder' wheel (with ten 'spokes' instead of seven), complete with a centre-lock system. The 'Turbo III' wheel could be specified FOC on the S, incidentally, as could the new 'Sport Classic' rim; available from November, the latter was a cost option on the strict Turbo, as was the 'Turbo S' wheel.

Tyre sizes were the same as those specified on the GT3, by the way, with the 429 'Turbo III' alloy coming in 8.5J front and 11J rear widths; the 435 'Turbo S' and pseudo Fuchs-style five-spoke XRU 'Sport Classic' wheels were a half-inch wider at both ends.

Side view of the strict Turbo model, fitted with the 'correct' 'Turbo III' alloy wheels and door mirrors. Despite the heavy rear wing profile, the Cd figure was still listed at a very reasonable 0.31.

One could also see the large 959-esque cut-out in the rear corners and the new rear spoiler profile from the side. Actually, apart from the holes, the rear bumper moulding wasn't all that different to that of a C2 model, only wider, and sporting novel tailpipes underneath, with squared-off twin exhausts on both sides of the car. To distinguish the grades, there was the badging, and a black-chrome finish on the S's exhaust pipes.

Meanwhile, the rear spoiler was similar to that of the outgoing Turbo, in shape at least, with the engine cover ahead of it featuring different ridges to

The centre-lock 'Turbo S' wheels and SportDesign mirrors, as well as the larger PCCB braking system employed on these particular turbocharged cars.

Tail of the strict Turbo. Note the louvre pattern in the engine cover.

Catalogue page showing the innovative PAA system.

Porsche Active Aerodynamics (PAA)
For the first time in a Porsche road car, the new 911 Turbo models use active aerodynamics. Derived from similar systems used on Porsche race cars, the new Porsche Active Aerodynamics (PAA) meets two critical objectives: to make the drag coefficient as low as possible, and to set a new standard for downforce.

PAA is a combination of multistage adjustable front and rear spoilers. The front spoiler—which is made from a flexible, pneumatic elastomer—and the rear spoiler will extend and retract synchronously in three positions.

In Stage 1 (Start), the front and rear spoilers are completely retracted. It's intended for everyday use—there's less risk of getting the front spoiler caught on ramps, speed bumps, or curbs. The spoiler lip is well-protected.

In Stage 2 (Speed), after 74 mph, the front and rear spoilers are partially extended. This ensures a high level of stability and a low drag coefficient.

Stage 3 (Performance) is activated by the press of a button, with the spoiler button or—in conjunction with the Sport Chrono Package—the Sport Plus button.

The front and rear spoilers are now completely extended. The "turbo" or "turbo S" logo can be seen on the front spoiler lip. Also, in Stage 3, the rear spoiler is tilted by up to 15 degrees. Thanks to the high level of downforce on the front and rear axles, in this setting the new 911 Turbo can release its full performance potential—for example, on the racetrack. The downforce also provides advantages when braking at high speeds.

Porsche Active Aerodynamics (PAA). A system that combines everyday use, efficiency, and driving performance. And reaches its objectives in the 911 Turbo way.

1 Rear spoiler in Start position | 2 Front spoiler in Start position | 3 Rear spoiler in Speed position | 4 Front spoiler in Speed position | 5 Rear spoiler in Performance position | 6 Front spoiler in Performance position

Despite the supercar performance, the Turbo models remained practical, with plenty of luggage space up front, and 2+2 seating, with the rear seats able to fold down to create a parcel shelf as per the Carrera coupés.

the other 991s. The spoiler itself was now part of an active aerodynamics package (PAA), linked in with a rubber-type appendage below the fixed part of the lip spoiler up front. Both components had a three-stage setting: retracted, an automatic semi-extended deployment reacting to speed, and a wilder button-activated mode, mainly for track work. More than a gadget, the PAA system could shave a full two seconds off a lap of the Nürburgring.

Driver's-eye view of the regular 520bhp Turbo.

Interior of the Turbo S, with carbonfibre trim pieces fitted as standard, and a close-up of the same car's dashboard.

Auto-dimming mirrors, parking sensors (rear only on the 520bhp car) and a top alarm system were fitted as standard, and metallic paint was classed as standard fare. However, the four solid hues were available as a no-cost option (NCO), with the colour choices being the same as those offered on the Carreras from June 2013 onwards.

Naturally, the interior was updated to match that of the other 991-type 911s. Again, the June 2013 colour palette was applied, with the Turbo S having the special option Black with Carrera Red two-tone trim, which was classed as an NCO.

As one would expect, the standard specification was luxurious. There was a SportDesign steering wheel with shift paddles, power adjustment on the steering column (hooked into the seat memory feature), leather upholstery, P06 seats on the Turbo and 18-way adaptive P07s with full leather trim on the Turbo S (the 14-way P06 seats were offered as a NCO on the latter), black gauges with chrome outer rings and 'Turbo' and 'Turbo S' logos, the PCM unit, the Bose sound system, and dedicated treadplates.

Although announced early, the first deliveries were not expected until late September 2013, which explained the colour options. The regular 911 Turbo was listed at €162,055 in Germany (including taxes), while the S version commanded €195,256. Considering the more powerful Turbo S added things like the Sport Chrono package with dynamic engine mounts, centre-lock wheels over PCCB ceramic brakes, the PDCC suspension upgrade, and LED headlights (not to mention a whole host of little extras, such as cruise control, a windscreen with a grey band, an alloy fuel cap, and carbonfibre trim to replace the 'Galvanosilber' interior parts), the jump in price would appear to be easily justified.

Some rather nice pictures of the Turbo S with a glass sunroof on the move, taken at the time of the car's launch. Note the internal layout of the LED headlights compared to the bi-xenon units.

Of course, even with the high level of standard equipment, there were plenty of options still available to tempt potential buyers into parting with a lot more cash than the prices quoted in the previous paragraph. As well as the items mentioned earlier, there was Power Steering Plus, special sports exhaust tailpipes (code 138), a sunroof (steel or glass), clear rear light units, the PAS safety system, painted exterior parts, a black finish on the 429 or XRU wheels, model-specific door decals in black or silver, bucket seats, a Burmester stereo, and the various Exclusive interior upgrades soon had the invoice ballooning faster than the author at an Italian food extravaganza.

What did the press think? Most of the comments were positive, often verging on euphoric. Toning things down, the UK's *What Car?* tried a regular Turbo, and decided that it made "a persuasive case for itself. It's an absurdly capable yet remarkably forgiving thing to drive quickly, and by comparison to exotica such as the Ferrari 458 Italia or McLaren MP4-12C, it's pretty good value, too, even though the price has risen substantially over the older model.

"However, although the new 911 Turbo offers similar performance to both of its aforementioned supercar rivals, it doesn't quite have the same presence or sense of occasion. Even bigger issues abound in the form of the rest of the 911 range, because a Carrera 4S is [a lot cheaper] and on any public road will deliver just as much fun, if slightly less ballistic acceleration. If you want something that will double as a track car, the GT3 is a better bet ..."

As it happens, *Motor Trend* gave the Carrera 4S its 'Best Drivers' Car' trophy for 2013, so the *What Car?* people were certainly onto something. Ultimately, though, a real Turbo customer was probably interested in little else, and there was absolutely no doubt that it was

a fantastic machine by any standards. Testing the S grade, Greg Kable wrote in his summary at the time of the launch: "Arguably better looking, a good deal roomier, more powerful, faster over any given road, infinitely more stable at speed, and more engagingly agile than ever before, the new Porsche 911 Turbo S is everything that we expected ... It is arguably today's most proficient everyday, all-season supercar."

Life goes on ...

In the background, changes were being made to the existing line-up. Compared with the early colour options, one of each of the silver and blue metallic shades was replaced by fresh versions of a similar hue, and Cognac Metallic was dropped. In addition, the shortlived Umber trim was replaced by a new two-tone upholstery option.

About the same time as the colour changes took effect, the limited run '911 50th Anniversary Edition' model was announced in Stuttgart. Limited to 1963 units to commemorate the 911's original debut (as the Type 901), and available from the end of September, this Carrera S coupé-based special featured the wider C4 body painted in either Geyser Grey Metallic, Graphite Grey or Black, a sports exhaust, a lowered active suspension, and the 'Sport Classic' wheels mentioned in the Turbo section, finished in matt black with machine-polished spokes and rim edges like the iconic Fuchs alloys they were designed to represent.

Other details included bi-xenon lights with PDLS, high-gloss window frames, chrome accents on the front outer intake blades, engine cover grille and the dressing piece between the rear lights, SportDesign door mirrors, and special badging on the tail.

Moving inside, the leather trim options were Agate Grey with Geyser Grey fabric seat inserts, or Black with Dark Silver inserts, while the Exclusive trim pieces and gearlever were in brushed aluminium rather than 'Galvanosilber.' The tail badge was repeated as a coloured logo on the P06 seat headrests, glovebox trim piece (with the car's limited edition number), treadplates, and even the tachometer face. A nice touch was the green calibrations on the gauges, with white pointers mounted on chrome centres, harking back to Porsche's earlier days.

With buoyant sales, the option list was still growing for the run-of-the-mill cars, too. From the first day of July 2013, Porsche had offered a special '50 years of 911' upgrade for European customers – a bundle including the Sport Chrono package, PCM with a navi and telephone module, front and rear parking sensors, and seat heating. Priced at under €5000, it represented quite a saving, but wasn't around for long. Later, in early 2014, it evolved into the P9S Comfort Package, which lost the Sport Chrono element, but added a camera to the parking sensors, and also gained cruise control and auto-dimming mirrors.

There was also a P01 seat, which, although it was listed earlier, wasn't actually available until October 2013. It was basically the P03 bucket seat option combined with a memory function. In the following month, one could specify a personalised PDK selector or 7MT gearknob, along with a back-up camera to match the PCM unit and parking sensor system.

Standard colour & trim guide

These colour variations were available on mainstream Carreras from June 2013 until March 2014. Please see the text for variations applied to other model lines and specials.

Solid coachwork colours
Black (041), White (C9A), Guards Red (80K), and Racing Yellow (1S1).

Metallic coachwork colours
Basalt Black Metallic (C9Z), Agate Grey Metallic (M7S), Rhodium Silver Metallic (M7U), Dark Blue Metallic (M5X), Sapphire Blue Metallic (M5J), Amaranth Red Metallic (8L1), Mahogany Metallic (M8Y), and Anthracite Brown Metallic (M8S).

Special coachwork colours
GT Silver Metallic (M7Z), and Lime Gold Metallic (5P1). A 'colour to sample' option was also available.

Hood (convertible top) colours
Black, Red, Blue, and Brown. Hood always lined in black.

Leatherette (vinyl) and leather trim
Black, Platinum Grey, Yachting Blue, and Luxor Beige. Carpeting and floormats came in matching hues; the headlining came in black on the black and blue options, or grey and beige to match the trim.

Regular two-tone leather trim
Agate Grey with Pebble Grey, Black with Platinum Grey, and Black with Luxor Beige. Carpeting and floormats came in the lighter shade, with the roofliner in the darker one.

Special leather colours and natural leather trim
Agate Grey, Carrera Red, Espresso, and two-tone Espresso with Cognac. Carpeting and floormats came in matching hues; the roofliner was black on the red option, or grey and brown to match the trim. A 'colour to sample' option was also available.

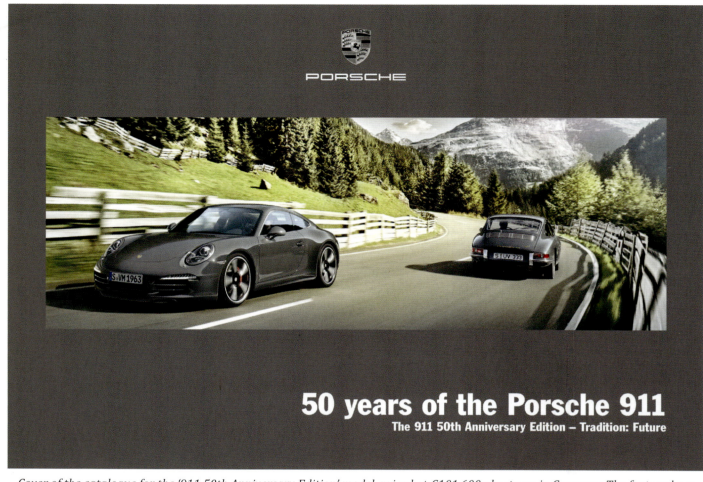

Cover of the catalogue for the '911 50th Anniversary Edition' model, priced at €101,600 plus taxes in Germany. The featured car has Graphite Grey paintwork, incidentally.

Close-up of the rear-end detailing on the '50th Anniversary' car. The tail of the early car in the brochure cover shot clearly shows where the inspiration came from.

Interior of the '50th Anniversary' model, this car having a PDK transmission, though it could be ordered with a manual gearbox and extended leather trim parts. For performance-minded types, one was also able to specify the X51 power kit, Sport Chrono package, the PCCB brakes, PDCC front suspension upgrade, and LED lighting system.

The '911 50th Anniversary Edition' model pictured at the Porsche Museum with some of its predecessors. This shot of a Geyser Grey car clearly shows the 'correct' intake trim and wheels for this limited run vehicle. Incidentally, according to factory-supplied numbers, a total of 1968 were built rather than 1963.

2013 race review

The opening round of the World Endurance Championship (WEC) marked the debut of the new 911 RSR. The 470bhp works machines would compete in the GTE-Pro category, leaving the door open for private teams in the lower GTE-Am Class using 997-type GT3 RSRs.

The Porsches were unfortunately kept off the podium by Aston Martin and Ferrari drivers, but there were no major problems, at least. Spa wasn't much better, though, and the GTE-Am guys were also stuck in a groove. Then came the breakthrough, and at Le Mans, too, where everyone was watching: Marc Lieb, Richard Lietz and Romain Dumas won their Class in style, followed home by the sister car to make it a Porsche one-two, with another 911 taking GTE-Am honours. That was ultimately the highlight of the season, but the RSR had at least shown a lot of potential, and would come back in 2014 as a better machine, running alongside the new 919 Hybrid in the LMP1 category.

Outside the WEC, it was a disappointing season in most of the European GT series, but the teams were running 997s in the main, so for this book, we can leave it at that. Older machines were also being campaigned in the States, but a new works campaign was promised for 2014 in the revamped IMSA TUSC championship, following a merger of the ALMS and Grand-Am calendars.

In the Porsche Mobil 1 Supercup championship, 2013 was the first year with the 991-series models. After nine well-supported races, Nicki Thiim was declared the champion on 140 points, although the untimely death of Sean Edwards meant he missed the final two heats in Abu Dhabi, which might well have given the Englishman the title (Thiim scored a maximum 40 points at the Yas Marina circuit). As it was, he was second on 118 points, with Michael Ammermüller third on 115.

Still covered in dirt from Le Mans, this is the GTE-Pro Class winner pictured back at the factory, with the second-placed sister car seen behind.

The turbocharged convertibles

Running from 12 to 22 September, visitors to the 2013 Frankfurt Show were able to see the production version of the 918 Spyder for the first time, but Porsche decided to keep the Turbo Cabriolet and Turbo S Cabriolet under wraps until the day after the IAA closed its doors. A price list was duly issued, dated 23 September, and a press release sent out on the same day noted that the world première was scheduled for the Los Angeles Show in the second half of November. Remember, too, that the price list for the Type 991 turbocharged coupés was released in May, a good four months before it was due to land in dealerships. All very confusing ...

Anyway, with a base price of just over €10,000 more than the equivalent coupés in Germany (not surprisingly, prices were carried over on these models, as they were on all the other 911s), this meant the top drophead broke the €200,000 barrier once taxes were applied, which is a serious amount of dough – enough to buy all members of both a home and away football team a basic Peugeot 207! Indeed, ignoring the 918 Spyder, only the GT3 Cup was more expensive in the Porsche line-up.

For the extra money, one got a power hood and windblocker borrowed from the Carreras, and frankly not much else – apart from a grey band on the windscreen of the 520bhp convertible (usually a Turbo S feature), technical specifications, standard equipment levels and optional extras were the same as those listed for the equivalent coupé. An alloy pedal set was added to the option list, but otherwise everything was the same as it had been in May.

Domestic dealers were told to expect the initial batch of turbocharged DHC deliveries in December. This meant that the only mainstream 911 grades that hadn't been replaced from the old 997 line-up so far were the GTS and Targa variants, but one of those was just around the corner, and the other would duly follow not long after.

For the record, Porsche also launched the Macan at the 2013 LA Show; it was on display at the Tokyo Show, too, but with a lot less fanfare. The important point, though, is that this smaller SUV really opened up the brand to a whole new set of clients – folks that probably wouldn't have considered a Porsche before, as they needed something a tad more practical, but for whom the Cayenne was simply too big. Indeed, official numbers cited that three out of four buyers were moving across to the Porsche marque for the first time. These conquest sales meant that the Macan quickly became a bestseller, and whilst the 918 Spyder may have caught

Nicki Thiim on his way to victory in Abu Dhabi, and (right) the Dane celebrating winning the Supercup title.

the attention of enthusiasts, the exotic hybrid had only a brief life (the last car being built in June 2015) and very limited production. The 918 Spyder may have been a great promotion tool, but to survive, with acres of factory space (plus further expansion at Leipzig) and a growing workforce, Porsche really needed volume ...

Export markets in the 2014 MY
Things were going well in America, with 42,323 units sold in 2013 to create an all-time sales record for the US (the previous record, set in 2012, was just over 35,000 vehicles), and the GT3 and four Turbo variants coming on line in December to give dealers another bite of

Dr Wolfgang Porsche

Born in May 1943, Wolfgang Porsche is the youngest of Ferry Porsche's four sons, and has been on the Porsche Supervisory Board since 1978. He became its Chairman in 2007, and joined the VW Supervisory Board the following year, adding an Audi string to his bow in 2012. Although he has always regarded his main role as that of continuing the work of his father (and grandfather, for that matter), balancing the interests of family members, as Oliver Blume said recently: "He is not only the bearer of our brand name, he is also the personable figure with whom people identify our company. He has always been there when needed, and, for this, we admire him."

Wolfgang Porsche pictured in early 2014 with a Carrera Cabriolet outside the family home where the first VW prototypes were built.

Exterior and interior of the Turbo Cabriolet.

Tennis superstar Maria Sharapova was on hand to promote the new Macan in LA.

the Porsche line-up as a whole had the £38,237 2.7-litre Boxster at one end of the scale, and the £657,400 918 Spyder at the other – a staggering three times the cost of a Rolls-Royce Ghost!

Down Under, the cost of Porsche motoring dropped just a little, with the basic manual 911 Carrera coupé now down to $206,500. Only 17 customers went for the '911 50th Anniversary Edition,' which was listed at $270,100, but Porsche Australia gave enthusiasts plenty of choice at the supercar end of the spectrum. Released in September 2013, there was the $294,100 GT3, or there were always the four turbocharged models, ranging from $359,800 to $463,100.

In Japan, the '911 50th Anniversary Edition' was the same as the UK and Aussie one, with 400bhp. Priced at 16,370,000 yen in manual guise (lhd only) or 17,120,000 yen with a PDK transmission with a choice of left- or right-hand drive steering, the latter was only 1,470,000 yen cheaper than a GT3 when it was announced. However, prices increased in the spring as VAT jumped from five to eight per cent, so the entry-level 911 Carrera coupé now commanded 11,780,000 yen; the C4

the sporting section of market share. The fact that the Cayenne SUV was the top seller, with 18,500 units sold, bode well for the Macan, too.

911 prices started at $84,300 for 2014, and, apart from the usual market-specific changes and the vast array of packages on offer, the cars were generally the same specification as those sold in Europe. There were a few differences, though, with a metal sunroof classed as standard on the Turbo coupés, for instance, and the $124,100 '911 50th Anniversary Edition' came fitted with the X51 power kit as standard.

There were no real surprises in the UK market, with everything following Germany's lead. Pricing started at £73,413 on the 911s, with the newcomers naturally costing a lot more: The Turbos ranged from £118,349 to £149,511, while the GT3 commanded just over £100,000. To put this into perspective,

The Turbo S Cabriolet featured on the cover of a US catalogue of the time.

For those who are never satisfied, the tuning business was as strong as ever when it came to offering something different. This is the RUF RT-35S, reported to have 650bhp on tap.

Cover from a contemporary Japanese model range catalogue, showing how the Porsche range had grown. From left to right, we have the Boxster, the Cayman, the 911, the new Macan, the Panamera, and the Cayenne.

Greg Larson's design sketch for the new Targa.

range started at 13,010,000 yen, while the cheapest cabriolet was listed at 14,340,000 yen. The S grades ranged from 14,560,000 yen all the way up to 18,250,000 yen, which was terribly close to GT3 money. The Turbos, meanwhile, started at 21,280,000 yen, and hit just over a million yen shy of the 30,000,000 yen mark at the top end – a Turbo S Cabriolet. Incidentally, while the GT3 was available in left-hand drive only, the Turbos all came with a lhd/rhd option.

The Targa returns

Around long before the Cabriolet variant, Porsche had first introduced the production Targa body as an open alternative to the coupé back in 1966, with the zip-in rear window soon being changed for a more practical glass one. The silver bar that replaced the B-posts and the roof structure aft of them became an iconic symbol of the Stuttgart marque, and apart from the colouring, didn't change much throughout the air-cooled 911 run. And then it disappeared …

When it finally returned on the 996.2 model, in reality it was a Targa in name only, sporting a large glass sunroof and a hatchback arrangement, which continued on the 997 models. For the 991, though, the roof would look and work like a traditional Targa one, albeit with a modern twist, for where one would have removed the panel between the windscreen header and the Targa bar by hand in the old days (and then stowed it away somewhere), the new design was basically an evolution of the Cabriolet top – everything folded away or put itself back in place at the touch of a button.

Announced at the 2014 Detroit Show (NAIAS) on 13 January, there was no advance notice in Germany this time around – the first dealer price list carries the same date, and the 84th Geneva Show would be used to give the newcomer its European debut in early March. At last, some sense and tradition was returning to the camp, with the first domestic deliveries expected in May.

Now used to seeing 991s with a huge glass sunroof, the Targa needed to be an interesting design if it was to have any value in the line-up, and even the most ardent fans of classic 911s must have been pleased. Those present at the Cobo Centre could see that the distinctive Targa bar had returned in the B-post area (complete with a familiar finish, badging and fins), with a movable panel ahead of it, and a classic wraparound rear window aft of it to replace the C-pillars.

In effect, the Targa was a four-wheel drive Cabriolet, sporting that model's wide bodyshell and drivetrain (in C4 and C4S guise), modified to take a new roof system. The innovative bit came in the way it transformed from a closed car to one with an open roof section above the seats or back, all in a fully automatic manner, in just 20 seconds.

For the new Targa, first the rear window and bodywork surrounding it (much the same as the 'tonneau' cover on the convertible) moved up and back, allowing the fabric centre section (kept taut by a pair of magnesium elements)

Matthias Müller (left) with Wolfgang Hatz (R&D boss) (middle), and Bernhard Maier (Porsche's sales and marketing guru) at the launch of the Targa in Detroit.

to be raised and dropped into a position behind the rear seats after the top corners of the bar flipped inwards to allow some clearance. Once the corners popped back, the rear window section then returned to its original position, sealed up against the Targa bar. To close it again, as long as the car was stationary, one simply pressed the buttons on the centre console (the same as those found on the convertibles), and the process reversed.

With a steel structure underneath the Targa bar, the safety and added torsional rigidity was there, and with the Cabriolet's windblocker not required, the rear seats – whilst not as welcoming as those of the coupé – could be used regardless of whether the car was running in open or closed mode, or the backs could be folded down for extra luggage space. The only downside was wind noise, which was quite marked compared to the conventional DHC, although a small hand-operated deflector was fitted above the sunvisors to help reduce it.

The clever roof mechanism of the new Targa.

The Targa 4, seen here equipped with optional 'Carrera S' alloys. Note the wind deflector in the raised position at the top of the windscreen, the detailing on the Targa bar, and the red strip between the rear lights – a feature on all the normally-aspirated four-wheel drive cars.

The Targa 4S, with its different exhausts and badging compared to the 350bhp model, as per the other Carreras. This car is fitted with 'Carrera Classic' wheels.

Weighing only 90kg (198lb) more than a Carrera 4 coupé and just 20kg (44lb) more than the equivalent drophead, with the same engines and gearing as the other normally-aspirated 4WD machines (a seven-speed manual gearbox was standard), performance was naturally not much different to that of the other models. Ex-racer Tiff Needell commented that the Targa 4S had the same 0-60 time as a 3.4-litre coupé, but in the real world, as Rolls-Royce would have put it in the good ol' days, acceleration was "adequate" – more than adequate, in fact.

With the standard equipment levels and options aping those of the equivalent Carrera Cabriolet, ruling out body kits, the 911 Targa 4 cost €109,338 in Germany (including VAT), while the Targa 4S version was priced at €124,094.

The cost of options, incidentally, was basically the same as it was at the time of the 991 model's launch. The tyre pressure monitor (or RDK) fell off the list, as it became a standard fitment in the spring of 2014, while the 429 alloys off the Turbo augmented the other 20in rims already on offer.

Incidentally, the Targa was

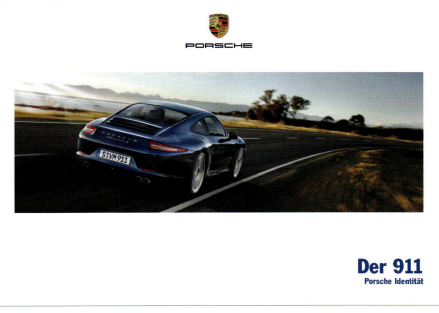

Cover of the German 911 Carrera catalogue from the spring of 2014.

launched at a time when the colour palette was revised once more. Compared with the early colour options, Carrara White Metallic was new, taking the place of Amaranth Red Metallic on the palette, and Basalt Black morphed into a Jet Black shade. In addition, the Carrera Red natural leather upholstery was replaced by a new Garnet Red shade, which was duly made available as a mono- or two-tone trim. This move meant that the Turbos could adopt exactly the same colour and trim guide as the Carreras.

Standard colour & trim guide
These colour variations were available on mainstream Carreras from March 2014 until the end of 991.1 production. Please see the text for variations applied to other model lines and specials.

Solid coachwork colours
Black (041), White (C9A), Guards Red (80K), and Racing Yellow (1S1).

Metallic coachwork colours
Jet Black Metallic (C9X), Agate Grey Metallic (M7S), Rhodium Silver Metallic (M7U), Carrara White Metallic (S9R), Dark Blue Metallic (M5X), Sapphire Blue Metallic (M5J), Mahogany Metallic (M8Y), and Anthracite Brown Metallic (M8S). Anthracite Brown Metallic was dropped in June 2015.

Special coachwork colours
GT Silver Metallic (M7Z), and Lime Gold Metallic (5P1). Lime Gold Metallic replaced by Lava Orange (M2A) from June 2015. A 'colour to sample' option was also available.

Hood (convertible top) colours
Black, Red, Blue, and Brown. Hood always lined in black.

Leatherette (vinyl) and leather trim
Black, Platinum Grey, Yachting Blue, and Luxor Beige. Carpeting and floormats came in matching hues; the headlining came in black on the black and blue options, or grey and beige to match the trim.

Regular two-tone leather trim
Agate Grey with Pebble Grey, Black with Platinum Grey, Black with Garnet Red, and Black with Luxor Beige. Carpeting and floormats came in the lighter shade, with the roofliner in the darker one.

Special leather colours and natural leather trim
Agate Grey, Garnet Red, Espresso, and two-tone Espresso with Cognac. Carpeting and floormats came in matching hues; the roofliner was black on the red option, or grey and brown to match the trim. A 'colour to sample' option was also available.

A pair of 'Martini Racing Edition' cars with one of the vehicles that provided the inspiration for them.

The delivery hall at Zuffenhausen, photographed in October 2014. This is a useful reference shot, as it's very rare to find pictures released by the factory showing the Targa with its centre roof section in place.

Although options were largely unaffected, the base cost increased on many of the 911s on the first day of June 2014. The C4s were left untouched, but the rear-wheel drive Carreras were now between €2000 and €2500 more expensive; the Turbos averaged a €2750 hit, while the Turbo S pairing went up by €1500.

A few more options were added at this time, incidentally: Carreras were given the option of an Alcantara centre box lid with 'Porsche' script or a Porsche crest on it, as most parts were now available trimmed in this pseudo-suede. In addition, painted rocker panel trim (XAJ) was added for the Carrera 4s and Turbos, while the latter also gained the option of a painted lower rear apron insert (XUE).

Mention should also be made of the 'Martini Racing Edition' – an Exclusive model based on the 911 Carrera S coupé with an Aerokit, announced just before the 2014 Le Mans 24-hour Race. Limited to just 80 cars (in white or black, with a high-spec interior and the Sport Chrono package as standard), this model was only available in a limited number of countries (the UK, Japan, China, Holland, Italy, Spain, Poland, Ukraine, the Czech Republic, Finland, Cyprus and parts of Latin America), although the decal kit was later made available through the Tequipment catalogue.

Meanwhile, naturally, the Targas filtered through to export markets during the summer, with the new variant making its US debut at the New York Show in April; the Targa 4 was priced at $101,600, while the Targa 4S was about $15k more. Australia called cars in the new colours an early 2015 model, incidentally, as they were released in June 2014.

The 2014 race season

Naturally, the big news in the Porsche camp for 2014 was the arrival of its LMP1 challenger – the 919 Hybrid. Combining two different energy recovery systems with a two-litre turbocharged V4, the company described the vehicle as a "technological front-runner for production cars."

The RSR for the 2014 season (see also next page, top).

The 911 GT America in profile.

This almost overshadowed the fact that the GT programme was also in an expansion phase, with a two-car works team running alongside two LMP1 machines in the WEC, and a second pair of 911 RSRs to be handled by Porsche Motorsport North America (in conjunction with CORE Autosport) as a works entry in the newly-configured IMSA Tudor United SportsCar Championship (or TUSC, for short).

As for the cars themselves, the 911 RSR received a revised front air dam, and a new rear wing design to enhance stability. The front suspension was tweaked to improve handling at lower speeds, wider rear rims improved it at higher velocities, and the body was made stiffer to give superior steering response. Other detail changes for the RSR included a new air filter arrangement, a fresh fuel tank offering a lower centre of gravity, and the fitting of a live telemetry system. These were useful advances, as the 911 RSR was now starting to filter through to customer teams.

While the GT3R and strict GT3 Cup

Patrick Pilet showing his delight in Shanghai. It was only the second win for the RSR that year, and would prove to be the last, too.

models were carried over, the so-called 911 GT America was introduced to contest the GTD category in the TUSC series in the States. This was basically a Type 991 GT3 Cup car but featuring a larger 4-litre engine (kicking out 470bhp, and hooked up to a six-speed gearbox with paddle shifts), a few aerodynamic revisions, uprated brakes, and the availability of a special endurance race package.

Following its merger with Raeder Automotive, Porsche also bought a majority share in Manthey Racing GmbH – a business with many years of collaboration with Porsche thanks to the efforts of Olaf Manthey, and with no less than 20 drivers under contract for 2014, this was going to be a busy season for Porsche.

As far as the RSRs were concerned, the WEC season started well, with a one-two in Class, but Porsche fans had to wait another five rounds before an RSR took the chequered flag again, and that would ultimately prove to be the last win of 2014. Finishing second to Ferrari in the championship, the LMP1 programme also gave a mixed bag of results, but with such a complex car, no-one could have expected miracles straight out of the box.

The 911 GT America of Dempsey Racing at Daytona.

It was perhaps ironic that the 'failure' of two major Stateside championships and the subsequent formation of an amalgamated series (the TUSC) made it that much easier for Porsche Cars North America to throw its support behind it. Four Classes were prepared for the TUSC, with GT Le Mans (GTLM) for the equivalent of ALMS GT models, and GT Daytona (GTD) for Grand-Am GT and GX cars, plus ALMS GTC models, being the ones that interested the Porsche guys. The 470bhp GTLM works cars were the same as the 911 RSRs used in the WEC, while the bigger private teams used the $279,000 911 GT America described earlier, which was designed to make the most of the GTD rules.

The IMSA Tudor United SportsCar Championship kicked off with the Daytona 24-hour Race. The number 912 works machine had a problem with the engine after 489 laps, but its stablemate (number 911) had a trouble-free run to claim a magnificent sixth overall, securing GTLM Class honours along the way; the 911 GT America of Snow Racing was second in the GTD category.

Together on the calendar once more, the TUSC circus moved to Sebring for the 12-hour classic. The Daytona-winning trio were involved in an accident, costing them valuable time, but the sister car of Long/Bergmeister/Christensen held off a strong threat from Dodge, BMW and Ferrari drivers to take a Class win, while the Team Falken Tire RSR (the first of the models to reach a customer team) finished fifth in GTLM, and Magnus Racing provided the 911 GT America with what would hopefully be its first of many Class victories.

A pitstop cost the works RSRs dearly at Long Beach, while a penalty for 'on-track contact' robbed them at Laguna Seca. The GTLM cars skipped the next two rounds, so Watkins Glen was next. However, domestic machinery dominated the six-hour event, and a third in Class in GTD was the best the Porsche runners could muster amongst them; the 911s struggled in Ontario, too.

Indianapolis was a little kinder, providing PCNA with a podium finish. With a new front splitter and rear wing allowed by the rules, as well as a larger restrictor for the engine, hopes were higher at Road America, but it was ultimately something of a learning curve experience. The Team Falken Tire RSR was second in GTLM at Virginia, making up for a poor works display, while Patrick Dempsey and Andrew Davis got onto the GTD podium, finishing on the same lap as the Class winners.

Desperate to make an impression, PCNA entered a third works car for the Circuit of the Americas race in Texas (wearing number 910), which

Opposite: Some frantic pitwork in Texas during the TUSC event.

Wolf Henzler and Bryan Sellers guiding the Team Falken Tire 911 RSR at Long Beach.

Patrick Long (left), a proper Porsche stalwart, and Michael Christensen were crowned North American Endurance Cup champions at the end of the TUSC season.

coincided with the WEC round. Porsche was unlucky, but a third place for Long and Christensen kept the German company in with a shout at claiming the manufacturers' silverware as the final round at Road Atlanta loomed.

The Petit Le Mans race was an epic battle, which ultimately saw the Team Falken Tire RSR claim GTLM honours, followed home by works cars in second and fifth. Porsche finished second, third and fifth in GTD as well, narrowly handing the Stuttgart marque the title in both categories.

For the record, the Daytona, Sebring, Watkins Glen and Road Atlanta meetings counted towards the North American Endurance Cup, and the GTLM Class ultimately went to Porsche, with Patrick Long and Michael Christensen being named as top drivers in the category.

There was little Porsche interest in the two Blancpain championships (one

A 3.4-litre Carrera in a VLN endurance event at the Nürburgring in the summer of 2014. The Nürburgring 24-hour Race (sometimes held as part of the VLN championship, sometimes a stand-alone competition) always attracted 911 racers in droves.

Earl Bamber after winning the Supercup title.

being a rebranded FIA GT Series), and there were no wins in the European Le Mans Series, despite some strong representation for the Stuttgart marque. There wasn't much to report in the SCCA World Challenge or Japanese Super GT series either, and even the Nürburgring 24-hour classic failed to produce any silverware.

At the end of the day, there's one big series a Porsche driver is always guaranteed to win – the Supercup! With its position as an F1 support race approved for another three years, the 2014 Porsche Supercup series took in ten rounds at nine tracks, with the last race being a double-header at the new circuit at Sochi in Russia.

Earl Bamber eventually came out on top after a season-long tussle with Kuba Giermaziak, and Michael Ammermüller overcame some bad luck to take the third place spot. Mention should also be made of Nicki Thiim, who missed a few races, but turned on the style later in the season, justifying last year's Supercup title.

As it happens, Bamber was having quite a season, coming eighth overall and winning the Class B category in the Australian Bathurst 12-hour Race with a 997-type GT3 Cup model (ably assisted by Ben Barker and Stephen Grove), and the Kiwi was about to make quite an impression in the States, too …

The GTS models

Bridging the gap between the Carrera S and the GT3, 8 October 2014 witnessed the rebirth of the 911 Carrera GTS grade. Although most of the bits that make the GTS what it is were available through the options list, this off-the-shelf package had always proved popular.

Based on the wider C4 body, the four GTS models (offered in either open or closed form, with rear-wheel drive or 4WD options on each) were powered by the Carrera S unit with a power kit and the Sport Chrono setup, and were available with a 7MT or PDK gearbox. With 430bhp on tap, only a small increase in weight, PTV and the same gearing as the base cars, the fastest of the bunch was able to break through the magic 300km/h barrier (equivalent to 187mph) with ease.

The front-end was distinguished by a colour-keyed SportDesign front apron, smoked bi-xenon headlights with black surrounds (and PDLS as standard), and SportDesign mirrors. The sporting theme continued with a matt black paint finish on 20in centre-lock 'Turbo S' alloys, and although the regular Carrera S braking system behind them was considered adequate for the job, the GTS came with a PASM active suspension lowered by 10mm (0.4in).

Around the back, one was greeted by traditional-looking black engine cover louvres, with the trim strip between the rear lights gaining matching contours and the same gloss black treatment on C2-based machines; 4WD cars continued with the customary red lighting strip. There was black badging on the tail (with the 'GTS' logo repeated on the doors, if wanted, and even the engine ID plate for the owners who lifted the cover), and the tailpipes of the sports exhaust system were finished in black chrome.

Inside, there was the familiar GTS (I011/I019) treatment, with Alcantara dominating the cockpit on the regular GTS interior. Black leather-trimmed P05 sports seats with Alcantara inserts and a 'GTS' logo embossed in the headrests were considered the norm, with the logo found again on the black tachometer face and treadplates.

Alcantara could also be found on the door handles and armrests, the SportDesign steering wheel rim, gearlever, and centre box lid; the B- and C-posts, lower section of the door cards, glovebox lid, and sunvisors could be added as new individual options, along with a Porsche crest embossed on the central cubby lid. The dashboard and centre console used black anodised trim pieces to add some weight to the car's sporting image.

For those who preferred it, the mainstream grey, beige and blue trim was available, as well as the two-tone trim and special leathers. Other major options included the PDK transmission, SportDesign rear spoiler, LED headlights, 'Carrera S' wheels with a number of finishes, PDCC, ceramic brakes, upgraded steering for all cars, painted intake grilles, painted sill trim, a painted rear apron, clear rear light units, automatic dimming mirrors, folding mirrors, gloss black arms on the SportDesign mirrors, P06, P07 and P03/P01 seats, an alloy pedal set, the Comfort Package, cruise control, the PAS safety package, various parking assistant items, Porsche Entry & Drive, a leather or multi-function steering wheel, extended leather trim items, extended Alcantara trim, a special GTS package (with carbonfibre trim parts and red or silver contrast stitching, plus a red tachometer face), various separate pieces of carbonfibre or brushed aluminium trim, coloured seatbelts, a painted finish for interior components, the PCM unit and stereo upgrades, and an alloy fuel cap.

There was also a larger fuel tank, a 20mm (0.8in) lower suspension, a metal or glass sunroof, privacy glass, and a rear wiper for the coupés. The Cup bodykit was also listed for the tin-top models, albeit with the standard engine cover panel, while the rear seats could be deleted via option 713.

These pictures of a 911 Carrera 4 GTS coupé rather nicely show off the various styling changes applied to the GTS grade. Note the long-winded badging on the tail, aft of the new engine cover grille. Incidentally, C2-based GTSs had a black strip between the rear lights, whereas the C4-based models had the lighting band seen here.

A GTS Cabriolet with the 'correct' wheels for the grade, although other options were available. Hood colour choices remained at four, incidentally.

A GTS coupé with the regular GTS interior.

A car with the GTS package, bringing carbonfibre trim elements, contrast stitching, and a red tachometer face into the equation. By the way, the seatbelts matched the stitching, so came in red or silver.

The Targa 4 GTS making its debut in Detroit.

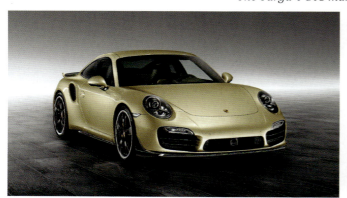

For the Aerokit Turbo, the front spoiler extended upwards ahead of the front wheels, and there was a new rear spoiler. The XAV option brought gloss black to the new front appendage, the standard sill trim and rear apron, the top part of the new rear spoiler (the base was in body colour), and the engine cover louvres. The XAF version had all these parts colour-keyed to the body. In both cases, the PAA aerodynamics system was left intact.

The 911 Carrera 'Style Edition' built solely for the Chinese market, being unveiled at the 2015 Shanghai Motor Show. Powered by the 3.4-litre engine but available in closed or open guise (with rear- or four-wheel drive), it featured, among other things, LED headlights, 'Turbo III' alloys, and the Sport Chrono package.

One of the limited edition cars built to celebrate 30 years since the founding of Porsche Italy.

fair share of home-grown exotica, but to celebrate 30 years since the founding of Porsche Italy, a special 30-off version of the Targa 4S was created. Finished in Gemini Metallic, with 'Sport Classic' wheels and a black leather interior featuring 'Pepita' cloth inserts on the seats, it was announced in May 2015 at a price of €167,911. Meanwhile, yet another model had joined the 911 ranks back in Stuttgart ...

The GT3 RS
While the strict GT3 was a road car that could be raced, the RS version was basically a racing car that could be used on the road. Knocking five seconds off the Nürburgring lap time posted by the GT3, the RS was the quickest of all the 911s on sale on that time when it came to covering the 13-mile (21km) Nordschleife circuit. Yes, there are some mad times being set nowadays, but to put things into perspective, it could lap the Nordschliefe over 30 seconds faster than the pole-setting Group A Jaguar XJ-S did in the 1983 ETCC.

Making its world debut at the 2015 Geneva Show, which opened on 5 March, the €181,690 GT3 RS was powered by the MA1/76 four-litre flat-six. This naturally-aspirated unit used the familiar 102mm bore combined with a longer 81.5mm stroke (achieved using forged titanium con-rods) to give a capacity of 3996cc. Red-lining at 8800rpm, with a 12.9:1 c/r, it developed 500bhp at 8250rpm, plus 338lbft of torque at 6250rpm.

Lifting the engine cover showed that the powerplant had a quite different appearance to its brethren, with a revised fan cover (there was no middle intake on the RS) and altered cut-outs in the carbonfibre dressing panel compared to the GT3. Titanium tailpipes added to the car's exotic aura.

While no manual gearbox was offered, the seven-speed PDK transmission had the same 'paddle neutral' feature as the GT3, plus a motorsport-derived 'Pit Speed' button on the centre console to limit speed. It came with the same internal gearing as the GT3, but combined with a 4.19:1 final-drive to give a CG1/95 designation.

Front and rear views of the GT3 RS.

The PTV limited-slip differential package was naturally included.

Power – and the ability to transmit it to the road – is one thing, but weight is the enemy of any high-performance machine. As such, magnesium alloy was adopted for the roof, the front wings and front and rear lids were made of carbonfibre, and the rear window was of a polycarbonate material. This not only saved about 10kg (22lb), it also lowered the car's centre of gravity, which is an important factor in improving handling dynamics.

Using the wider Turbo body as a starting point, the GT3 RS was certainly distinctive. While the front apron looked similar, the lip spoiler attached to it was heavier than that of the GT3, extending further up into the flared wheelarches.

Interior of the GT3 RS, this car having the standard full bucket seats combined with the optional black/orange trim. P03 and P07 seats were available free of charge.

In addition, the luggage compartment lid had a wide recess down its centre to remind folks of the 911s of yore – a feature that was carried through into the roof to create a 'double bubble' effect.

From the side, one could see vents cut into the top and trailing edge of the front wings, put there to increase downforce over the front axle. Moving back, apart from the beefier swage lines in the rocker panels, things looked similar to the GT3 until reaching the Turbo's intake on the leading edge of the rear fender. However, apart from the massive rear wing sitting above the engine, the bodywork aft of the wheelarch was closer to that of the GT3 than the turbocharged cars, with a re-profiled cut-out and a heavier dressing piece low down. The centre-lock wheels looked the same as those fitted to the GT3, but were actually a bigger diameter at the rear.

Around the back, naturally the three-position adjustable rear spoiler dominated the view, but the lid below it was different, too, aggressively styled and with the spoiler base having the exit grille rather than the bumper moulding. The black exhaust surround area was changed compared to the GT3 as well, now being full width, while the model badging became a simple 'GT3 RS' sticker to save weight.

Under the skin, there was a lowered and adjustable active suspension, rear axle steering, and the braking system off the GT3. The track was wider up front, making sense of the wheelarch extensions, which covered 265/35 ZR20s mounted on dark Platinum-painted 9.5J rims (silver optional). The Turbo body also provided a wider track at the back, with 21in wheels (12.5J) being employed, shod with 325/30 rubber – the widest tyres of any 911.

While the interior was based on that of the regular GT3, the 12-o'clock marker on the special steering wheel, titanium-colour tachometer face, various carbonfibre trim parts and fabric door releases gave a good idea of the

Close-up of the rear spoiler, engine cover and badging of the 911 GT3 RS model.

newcomer's purpose, further reinforced by the option of the Clubsport package, full bucket seats, a larger fuel tank and lightweight battery, the ability to delete numerous 'luxury' items to save weight, and the Sport Chrono package coming with the Track Precision app.

As for colouring, the RS was offered in White, GT Silver Metallic, Lava Orange and a purple shade called Ultraviolet. The interior was black with matching Alcantara in standard guise, as per the GT3, with extended leather trim available. There was also a pair of two-tone options for the RS, namely black with orange, and black with silver grey.

Weighing in at 1420kg (3124lb) and capable of dismissing the standing-quarter in 11.2 seconds, as *Car* magazine wrote at the time: "It's far from practical and may be too extreme for some, but it's still one hell of a driver's car."

The GT3 RS gradually began filtering through to export markets in the summer, further boosting the company's already booming sales. It was generally available from May in Europe, but early July in America, for instance, priced at $175,900,

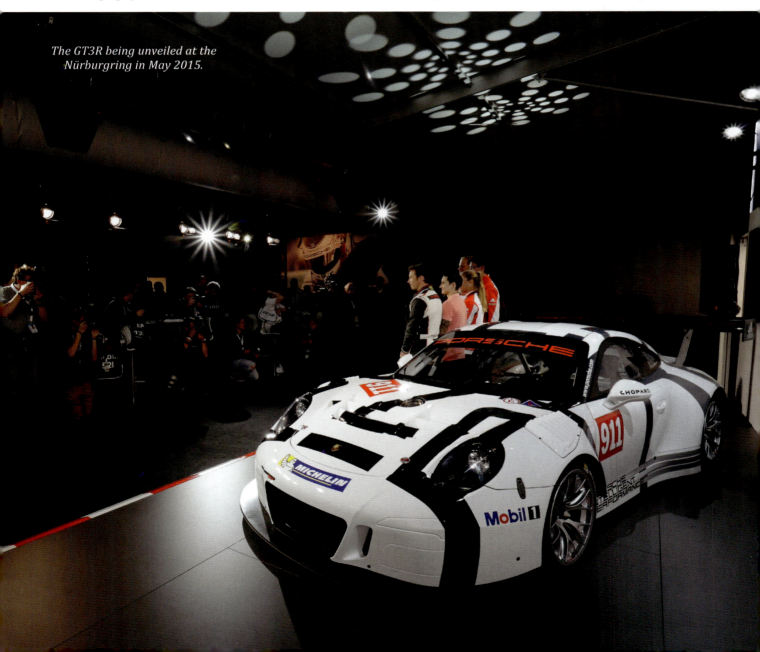

The GT3R being unveiled at the Nürburgring in May 2015.

and the likes of Australia from August, for those with a tidy $387,700 to spare.

By that time, Porsche had a new GT3 RS-based racer in its motorsport arsenal. Unveiled at an event to coincide with the 2015 Nürburgring 24-hour Race, the 911 GT3R was built to comply with FIA GT3 regulations, leaving owners with numerous motorsport options. The €429,000 car would also effectively take the place of the 911 GT America in the Stateside United SportsCar Championship, for that series would also adopt FIA GT3 regs for the 2016 season.

The 2015 racing season

The Porsche works continued to fight in the WEC and TUSC arenas, the former with an updated LMP1 car and a lightly revised RSR, while the American championship used the 470bhp RSR only. The 919 Hybrid duly won the LMP1 title for the Stuttgart maker, claiming the first of three consecutive wins at Le Mans along the way, while Richard Lietz sealed the GT crown in the final round of the season, both for himself and the factory, more than making up for the fairly mediocre Porsche showing in the GTE-Am category.

In the United SportsCar Championship, featuring more 911 interest, Porsche was keen to get a good result at the Daytona 24-hour Race (the first of 12 TUSC rounds, with four counting towards the North American Endurance Cup). It fielded two works cars in GTLM and loaned two works drivers to assist Bryan Sellers in the GTD category 911 RSR belonging to Team Falken Tire.

Having all led the GT field at various stages of the race, the three RSRs suffered numerous setbacks, including a coming together of the two works cars that cost them a huge amount of time, and the Falken machine had engine trouble. The Pilet/Lieb/Tandy RSR eventually finished fifth in Class, but at least the Alex Job Racing and Wright Motorsports 911 GT America models followed a Dodge Viper home in the GTD category to claim a couple of podium spots. Interestingly, the Wright Motorsports entry for the actor Patrick Dempsey was sponsored by Brumos – a legendary name and livery that would soon be consigned to the history books.

There were more niggling problems for the PCNA cars at a swelteringly hot Sebring, with the Falken RSR finishing ahead of them, and Long Beach wasn't kind to the team either. At least things started to look up at Laguna Seca, with a podium spot in GTLM and a GTD Class win for Patrick Lindsey and Spencer Pumpelly in a 911 GT America.

The GTLM cars didn't compete at Detroit (or Lime Rock, for that matter), so Watkins Glen was next, which counted towards the NAEC series within a series. Wolf Henzler and Bryan Sellers duly won the GTLM category for Team Falken Tire, followed home by works RSR. In Ontario, Porsche was able to celebrate again, as

The RSRs had a much better World Endurance Championship season in 2015, with Richard Lietz (standing closest to the right-hand car) declared number one driver after three Class wins, and Porsche crowned GTE-Pro champions.

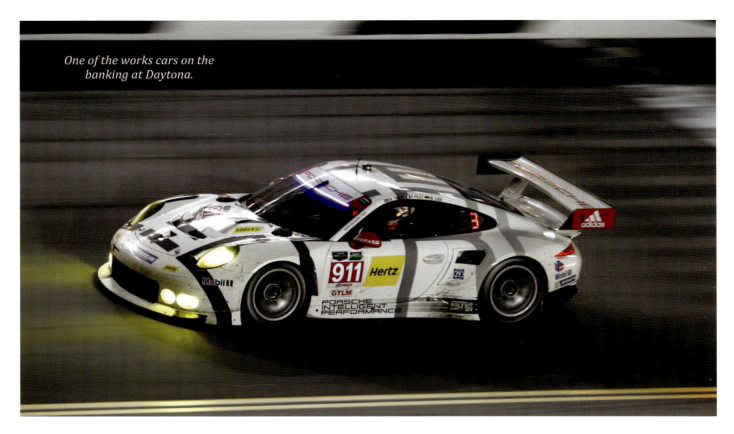

One of the works cars on the banking at Daytona.

Patrick Pilet and Nick Tandy won one for the factory team, staving off the threat from BMW and Chevrolet.

Soon after, the works cars finished one-two at Elkhart Lake, putting Porsche in the lead in the maker's title chase with only four rounds to go, and the success was duly repeated in Virginia, again via a one-two finish. Even though the momentum was broken in Texas, third, fourth and fifth for GTLM 911s kept Porsche in with a strong shout.

Patrick Lindsey and Spencer Pumpelly at Laguna Seca. The pair would also win the GTD Class at Road Atlanta later in the year, helped on that occasion by Madison Snow.

In the finale at Road Atlanta, Pilet, Tandy and Lietz teamed up to claim an overall win in the Petit Le Mans event – a first for a GT car since the start of the TUSC, and proof if ever it were needed that the 911 RSR had come of age. Although the winning margin was only a few seconds, it was enough to secure the GTLM title for Porsche and the drivers' crown for Patrick Pilet.

In the other big races, the 911 was featuring in all manner of top class Grand Touring car races as the GT3 era took hold – in large part due to the 'bang for your buck' element, and also probably because the regulations were fairly consistent compared to those in the LMP and headier GT categories, so it was easier to justify investing in a machine that could be used and readily updated

An appropriately-numbered works RSR on its way to victory in Ontario. This was the only TUSC round to be held outside the USA.

at reasonable cost. Of course, GT4 was popular for that very reason, but makers were less likely to gain publicity from it.

On saying that, somewhat ironically, there was hardly any Porsche interest in the Blancpain Endurance Series for 2015, with the only 911 runners competing in the amateur category, and the Blancpain Sprint Series also failed to attract serious Porsche entries – two teams attending just one meeting each in the end.

In the background, the European Le Mans Series was still running alongside the WEC, but it was perhaps telling that both championships shared the same weekend for their respective first rounds at Silverstone. All five ELMS races were over four hours, so shorter than WEC ones, but only Proton Competition and Gulf Racing UK fielded Porsche teams. Nonetheless, the latter equipe took the flag on home territory, but had to settle for just one more podium before the season ended; the Proton outfit was second once, but in the middle of the

Patrick Pilet pictured after clinching the TUSC GTLM title in Road Atlanta.

The Falken Motorsports team was third at the Nürburgring 24-hour Race, and surely had to be at short odds for a win in the following year.

pack in other rounds. As such, there was nothing for fans of the Stuttgart marque to get excited about, and only one team would be involved in the following season.

Audi was again victorious in the Nürburgring 24-hour Race, but at least the Falken Motorsports 911 gave them a run for their money, with Wolf Henzler, Peter Dumbreck, Martin Ragginger and Alexandre Imperatori finishing third, just one lap down on the Ingolstadt machine.

Moving farther afield, the SCCA World Challenge featured a lot of 911s. A remarkably consistent season gave Ryan Dalziel of EFFORT Racing third place in the top drawer GT standings (earning him the coveted Porsche Cup in the process); Porsche also secured the manufacturers' title, beating Ferrari by quite some margin.

In the Porsche Supercup, it was Philipp Eng who ultimately reigned

German VLN action, with a 991 coupé being chased by a pair of older 911 track warriors.

Austrian driver Philipp Eng fighting the Texan elements in the final round of the Porsche Mobil 1 Supercup.

supreme, although Sven Müller can count himself as unlucky, winning twice as many races as Eng, but failing to finish on two occasions, thus dropping the young German driver down the field. Müller would get his revenge, though, winning the 2016 Supercup title, albeit by a fairly narrow margin.

The 'Black Edition'

Fans of the Stuttgart marque would have known that the launch of a 'Black Edition' meant the imminent end of the model this stylish package was being applied to. In this case, it was the 911 Carrera and the Boxster, with the Cayman following a few months later.

The 3.4-litre 911, with a seven-speed manual transmission considered standard, was available in four versions – the 911 Carrera Black Edition, 911 Carrera 4 Black Edition, 911 Carrera Cabriolet Black Edition, and 911 Carrera 4 Cabriolet Black Edition, with prices ranging from €79,700 to €93,900, plus taxes.

It was a familiar formula: solid Black paintwork (with Jet Black Metallic as a €990 option), a black soft top (if fitted), a matching black interior, and a number of extras thrown in to create a strong value-for-money package. The 2015 car came with LED headlights with PDLS, 'Turbo III' wheels, the full park assistant package with camera, auto-dimming mirrors, heated seats with a Porsche crest on the headrests, a SportDesign steering wheel, the Bose sound system, and special treadplates.

Oddly, apart from the paint, the hood on the dropheads and the interior colour, so many of the regular options were offered, one wonders how many cars exist in the kind of specification outlined in the press material? Anyway, as usual, the Black Edition was sold worldwide. As an example, the first cars began arriving in Stateside dealerships at the end of July, with 911 prices starting at $88,800, plus a $995 delivery charge.

With 991.1s drifting into the traditional 2016 Model Year (and occasionally beyond, in the case of the GT3 variants, although not officially according to the way Model Year designations were allocated), we will pause here, and pick up the story again in the next chapter, which deals with the arrival of the 991.2 machines ...

The Carrera 4 coupé version of the 'Black Edition' model, introduced in May 2015 as a 2016 (G-Series) vehicle. In the end, 1084 C2 coupés were built, along with 572 drophead versions, 441 C4 coupés, and 275 C4 convertibles.

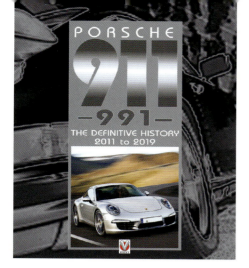

4

A major face-lift

The 911 had started life as a 2-litre machine. A decade later, with the base engine up to 2.7 litres, a turbocharged 3-litre model made it into the showrooms as Porsche's new flagship. Now, with the introduction of the 991.2 a further 40 years down the line, a twin-turbo 3-litre six was about to become the point of entry for the 911 range ...

The 991.1 was gradually phased out in stages as soon as the first of the 991.2 models were unveiled at 2015 Frankfurt Show. Even with the Mission E concept shown alongside them (the basis for the Taycan EV, eventually released as a production car at the 2019 edition of the IAA), there was still a great deal of interest in these new 911s the moment the doors opened at Frankfurt Messe on 17 September. The reason was not so much the styling (as had become the norm in recent mid-cycle face-lifts, the

Matthias Müller introducing the 991.2 to the press gathered in Frankfurt.

body was only mildly revised), but the all-new powertrain adopted for the new 911 range, which now used variations on a smaller 3-litre flat-six with twin-turbos to improve fuel economy and reduce emissions. Actually, the latest EURO 6 codes, due to kick in from September 2015, had left petrol cars unchanged, but there was certainly no harm in pushing 'green' appeal.

A new approach

Seeing as the turbocharged powerplant was the biggest change in the jump from 991.1 to 991.2 (or 911 II as it is sometimes designated), it is the flat-six engine we shall start off with in this section.

Looking through the parts books, comparing them side-by-side, one can see that much of the basic structure was the same in the move from the normally-aspirated MA1 (9A1) unit to the turbocharged MA2 (9A2) lump: the two-part crankcase, crankshaft, con-rods and pistons, ancillary drive system, cylinder heads, and 24v valvetrain were all refined rather than changed completely; even the basic cooling system was largely the same. With turbochargers installed, though, the intake manifolds and plenum chamber (what Porsche calls a 'distributor tube') above the engine were completely different, as was the air cleaner assembly. The new distributor tube was longer and narrower, and combined with shorter intake ports, this allowed the air-fuel mixture to cool before it entered the combustion chamber, enhancing ignition characteristics. Although less air made it into the cylinders, adjusting the boost pressure compensated for it.

Out of sight, a new alloy was used for the crankcase, cutting weight and improving rigidity, while a plasma beam was used to coat the cylinders with an iron-based material to reduce friction. The VarioCam Plus system was upgraded to control both IN and EX camshafts (previously intake only), and the high-pressure injectors were moved to an almost central position in the combustion chamber. With the plugs located in an adjacent off-centre spot,

The 3-litre bi-turbo MA2 engine, seen here in Carrera S guise, with turbochargers attached but minus the intercoolers.

this, combined with a revised piston crown shape, improved burn to such an extent that the secondary-air injection system previously used to heat the catalytic converters could be eliminated.

The addition of a turbocharger on each bank (both having their own aluminium alloy intercooler mounted above) obviously brought about other changes to the exhaust system, and required a fair bit of extra plumbing. It's also worth noting that the DME black

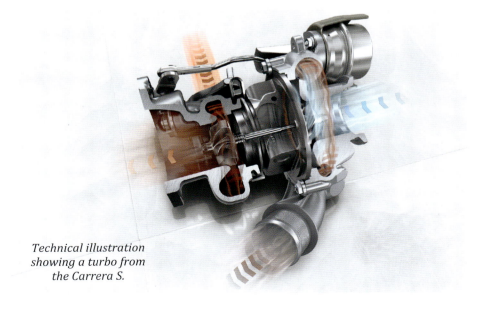

Technical illustration showing a turbo from the Carrera S.

box and the individual coils that sat atop the sparkplugs were changed at this time, too, while the lubrication system had some fairly heavy modifications applied to it at the bottom-end. Another interesting item was the ability to block the water pump and cut drive to the air-conditioning compressor, respectively improving warming-up times and reducing the load on the engine.

In detail, a new 91mm bore combined with a 76.4mm stroke resulted in a 2981cc displacement. As it happens, the same relationship was used in the face-lifted 981 models (the 718s) to give a 2-litre capacity, as they inherited a four-cylinder power-unit rather than retaining a six. This engine was duly employed on both the base and S grades, with beefier turbochargers, a revised exhaust and other tweaks like a new ECU providing the difference in output.

It all sounds fairly straightforward, but the changeover originally gave August Achleitner and his team of engineers a few concerns. One typically expects to lose high-end revs in a forced induction engine, and the lack of instant response is another factor that totally changed the 911's character for the vast majority of buyers.

Ultimately, a system was developed that reduced lag to previously unheard of levels, and other refinements enabled the Porsche to retain its heady red-line, which was considered another prime 911 attraction. Indeed, the old NA engine red-lined at 7600rpm on the tachometer, but official paperwork quotes 7800rpm as maximum revolutions. Likewise, with the 3-litre turbocharged units, the gauge in front of the driver (black on 370bhp machines, silver on the S, although black was a no-cost option) was marked 7400rpm, but the maximum revolutions was quoted as 7500rpm. As such, only 300rpm was lost in the transformation from 9A1 to 9A2, which is pretty remarkable.

Looking similar to its predecessor once installed (with fans either side of the central intake and suitable changes made to the identification plates), the new six was an excellent all-rounder in the end, endowed with lots of low-end torque spread over a wide rev-range, but still willing to spin freely over 7000rpm. A lot of work was done on the acoustics, too, to keep the Porsche soundtrack authentic.

For the record, with a 10.0:1 c/r, the MA2/01 base unit (or MDC/KA as it would be more commonly known) developed 370bhp at 6500rpm on 98-octane unleaded, along with 331lbft of torque at anywhere between 1700 and 5000rpm. With the same compression ratio but 1.1 bar of boost instead of 0.9, the MA2/02 Carrera S unit (aka the MDC/HA) gave 420bhp at the same revs, and a maximum of 368lbft of torque, also at the same revs. Despite the increases in power, the engines were said to be as much as 12 per cent more fuel-efficient than their equivalent MA1 predecessors.

The transmissions were familiar enough, albeit coming with different numbers due to revised gearing on third through sixth, improved shift feel and a slightly smaller double-plate clutch on the 7MT setup, and a new dual-mass flywheel borrowed from the manual gearbox for use on the PDK setup; the PDK's electronic control system was improved at the same time with a view to saving fuel.

The 370bhp RR car came with the G91/06 manual gearbox as standard or the CG1/15 PDK unit as an option, while the 420bhp variant was assigned the G91/05 and CG1/10; 4WD machines came with a choice of G91/35 and CG1/40 gearboxes.

Both the manual and PDK units now shared the same ratios across the board, with 3.91 on first, 2.29 on second, 1.58 on third, 1.18 on fourth, 0.94 on fifth, 0.79 on sixth, and 0.62 on seventh. Then things get confusing, not least because a technical paper released by the factory at the time would seem to contradict it. Anyway, the arrival of the Carrera T seems to confirm the real situation, so on 370bhp C2 and C4 models, the final-drive ratio was carried over (front and rear on the Carrera 4, of course). For the new S grade, the f/d was nudged from 3.44 to 3.59:1 on RR vehicles, which was duly combined with a front axle ratio of 3.46:1 on the four-wheel drive models.

Despite a weight gain of between 30 and 50kg (66 to 110lb), depending on the grade (the lightest 911 now tipped

The Carrera S engine viewed from the transmission end, this time with the intercoolers in place. Note the angle of the intercoolers – leaning the opposite way to those of the 911 Turbo.

The 911 Turbo S Exclusive GB Edition built for the British market has a number of special touches, such as black 'Sport Classic' wheels, the painted rear spoiler, intakes and mirrors, black door handles, and retro decals down the sides. The trim was much like that of the Club Coupé built for the US, although the Union Jack on the centre armrest lid was definitely unique. Priced at just over £150,000, a total of 40 cars were built: ten in red, 15 in white, and 15 in silver.

Finishing touches being applied to an Exclusive Edition Carrera S coupé for the Korean market.

Incidentally, the 'Experience Centre' in Atlanta finally opened in mid-2015 – some two-and-a-half years after the initial groundbreaking ceremony. The GTS Club Coupé officially went on sale at the same time.

Naturally, all of the new mainstream models filtered through to the other major export markets, one after another, with prices generally increasing by a very small amount compared to the 2014 Model Year. Pricing now started at £74,199 on the UK 911s, for instance – a jump of about £800, although no more changes were applied until the 991.1 run expired.

Italy had never been a really big market for Porsche, with more than its

Available in the four solid colours, and all the other contemporary 911 paint shades plus a model-specific Carmine Red Metallic, the first cars began arriving in domestic dealerships in November, with prices starting at €117,549 (including taxes).

Soon after, Porsche unveiled the 911 Targa 4 GTS at the 2015 Detroit Show, which opened to the public on 17 January. This was the first time a Targa body had been offered with GTS trim, and the only difference worthy of note compared to the other GTS models is the black 'Targa' badge on the roll-over hoop. Priced at €137,422 (the same as the Carrera 4 GTS Cabriolet), cars started arriving at German dealerships from mid-March.

As it happens, March 2015 saw the release of several new price lists in Germany, as, apart from a couple of increases, they also outlined the colour changes due to take effect in June that year. Anthracite Brown Metallic was dropped, and Lime Gold Metallic was replaced by a Lava Orange (M2A) hue; the GTS models still had Carmine Red (M3C) as an additional paint shade to choose from.

The increases we've just mentioned amounted to €800 on the Targa 4 and Targa 4S, although the price of the eight Carreras, the GT3 and the Turbos were kept the same as before. The latter models did have a new bodykit, however – the Aerokit Turbo, offered in gloss black (XAV) or body colour (XAF), and available for all four turbocharged variants through both the Exclusive and Tequipment catalogues, meaning retrofitting was possible. One could also now ask for a gloss black or body colour finish for the intake louvres either side of the Turbo's rear wheels, and painted rocker panel trim.

There were a few more common options, too, largely thanks to the introduction of the GTS grade, such as the darker LED headlights from that model (XEY), and the black SportDesign mirror arms (XCS) that were listed for it; painted sill trim (XAJ) was added for the GT3 as well. A satin black alloy wheel finish was also doubtless inspired by the GTS, as were the various Alcantara cubby lids, while other items included leather or Alcantara sunvisors, full bucket seats for the GT3 (P11), plus a new Exclusive leather interior package for most cars (DHA). Apart from that and a new Sport Chrono package for the GT3 (the 643 version with lap timer), there was little change, and the prices were, by and large, carried over once more.

Export market news

As new models trickled out of Stuttgart at a steady pace, US dealers were able to offer a huge range of 911s for the 2015 season, with prices starting at $84,300. Sales of the rear-engined icon had held up well thanks to this, for one would usually expect a heavy fall once the novelty of a new car had worn off. The policy of drip-feeding variants had obviously paid off, for 2014's US 911 sales were virtually identical to those of the 2013 CY, at around 10,500 units. The Macan robbed a few Cayenne sales, but helped boost PCNA's overall figure to 47,007 units – the number one share of 189,850 worldwide sales, and almost twice the number recorded for Germany.

Porsche Cars North America made good use of its new headquarters in Atlanta by unveiling the 60-off GTS Club Coupé there in January 2015, created to celebrate 60 years of the Porsche Club of America (PCA). Based on the 911 Carrera GTS, this $136,060 machine was finished in a special colour called Club Blau, and featured a full SportDesign bodykit, 'Sport Classic' wheels, and subtle black model badging on the doors. Inside, there was special red and blue stitching on the steering wheel (the wheel also had a red 12-o'clock marking), red contrast stitching elsewhere, carbonfibre trim parts, a '60' logo on the cubby lid, and commemorative model dash trim and treadplates. One could also order a key in the car colour, and floormats with the leather edges held together with red and blue thread.

The GTS Club Coupé for the American market.

The production process in Stuttgart

A series of pictures taken in March 2015 showing various stages of the production process, from mating the chassis components to the body, through to some of the final testing procedures (continues on next page).

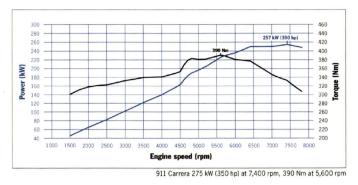
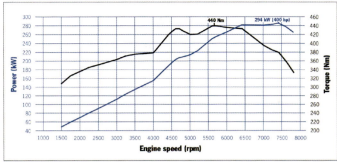
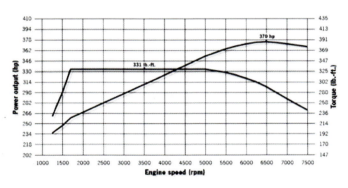
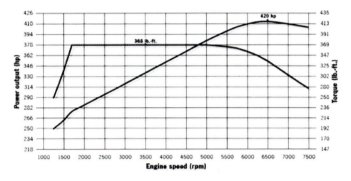

The power and torque curves for (top) the 3.4- and 3.8-litre NA Carreras, versus those for the new turbocharged models, with the 420bhp Carrera S model shown on the right. As one can see, the characteristics of the normally-aspirated units were quite different to those with forced induction.

the scales at 1430kg/3146lb), the added power and changes in gearing meant the new cars were even faster than before, at least on paper, with the top speed of the Carrera S coupé exceeding 190mph (304km/h); it had a 0-60 time of a fraction over four seconds, with 3.9 being possible with launch control activated on the PDK-equipped car with the Sport Chrono package.

As for the chassis components, a revised version of the PASM active suspension with new shock absorbers and revised springs and anti-roll bars was made standard, enhancing comfort and lowering the car by 10mm (0.4in); a slow-speed front axle lift system (474) was offered as an option to keep things practical, while rear axle steering (470) at last became an option on the S grades, combined with a new EPS ratio when fitted. Cars with the Sport Chrono package (with the single QR5 code replacing the old 639/640 ones) were given a new PSM mode, too, sitting somewhere in-between the existing on/off settings to allow a little more freedom of expression with a nanny still watching your back.

The brakes were uprated, with thicker front discs on the strict Carrera, and bigger 350mm (13.8in) diameter discs on the front of the Carrera S models. Those opting for the PCCB setup inherited bigger discs, too (up to 410mm/16.1in up front and 390mm/15.3in at the rear), while a new post-collision braking system was introduced as a standard item, tied-in with the airbag control unit, to try and limit further damage caused following a rear-end shunt.

The on-centre steering ratio was adjusted by a tiny amount, from 16.6 to 16.9:1, even though the steering wheel remained at a 375mm (14.8in) diameter. Additionally, whilst looking the same, the wheels were actually slightly different and now standardised at 8.5J up front and 11.5J at the rear, with the 19in code becoming 432, and the 20in rim morphing into the 433 in the process. Tyre sizes were also simplified, with the strict Carrera wearing 235/40 and 295/35 ZR-rated rubber with a reduction in rolling resistance, regardless of the body and C2 or C4 status, while the S grades came with 245/35 and 305/30 tyres.

There were no real surprises in the bodywork department, the update largely following contemporary fashion. The front bumper moulding was changed to resemble what can only be described as a 'Turbo-style' front-end – large outer intakes (now featuring three 'active' blades, which could either close for maximum aerodynamic efficiency, or open up in varying amounts to provide a specific amount of cooling in line with the driving situation), with the inner

Cutaway drawing of the strict Carrera Cabriolet with a manual gearbox. This illustration is ideal for showing the packaging of the new power-unit and its cooling system, as well as the chassis components.

part of the hefty moulded-in 'frame' angled inwards at the bottom to create an enclosure for the central intake, and the upper part providing a location point for the ultra-slim LED foglight-cum-indicator, or 'additional headlamp' as the folks in Stuttgart liked to call it.

Incidentally, the central mouth, situated below the number plate mounting area as usual, also had blades in it – two in this case. However, as before, the central intake was more for styling than anything else on most cars, as it was usually blanked off behind the pair of vanes. Below the mouth was a

A Carrera S coupé (left) pictured with a 370bhp Carrera Cabriolet – both shod with the standard issue wheels and tyres for the grade. Note the exhaust pipes on the convertible.

A useful catalogue illustration showing the latest front end styling revisions, with the 'active' intake blades closed in the left-hand side of the picture, and open on the right.

The new bi-xenon headlight design, with daytime running lights grouped around the main lens.

The grille over the engine cover evoked memories of earlier 911s, even though the louvre bars were facing in the opposite direction to the accepted Stuttgart norm.

heavy black lip spoiler (larger still on cars with the 030 PASM Sport Suspension, combined with greater extension on the rear spoiler), while above it, swage lines – like those of the contemporary Turbo – were moulded into the upper surface of the bumper cover, following the angle of the air intake frame. Aft of the ridges were new bi-xenon headlamps, with four DRLs grouped around the main headlight lens.

As mentioned earlier, the wheels looked much the same at first glance (both standard designs were surprisingly similar, in fact, although there were a few new options to make up for this), and the mirrors really were carried over. However, the eagle-eyed would have spotted the new door handles, which looked more upmarket for losing their grip shells.

Around the back, the rear deck lid now came with longitudinal gloss black louvres, designed to work in harmony with the intake requirements of the new engine. Aft of the grille, the variable position pop-up rear spoiler was made to double as a charge-air cooling aid, as well as an aerodynamic appendage, thus eliminating the need for side intakes like those seen on the 911 Turbo, although there were some vents cut into the rear apron corners, serving as outlets to channel hot air away from the intercoolers.

The rear combination lamps were

An action shot of the Carrera S coupé, this angle showing off the new rear-end styling rather nicely, as well as the standard exhaust system for the grade.

The latest PCM unit.

a touch sharper-looking than before, complete with four-point brake lights, while the high-mount brakelight was made wider, sitting in a black dressing piece above the engine cover grille; the Carrera 4s and their ilk continued to sport an additional red strip between the rear lights. Meanwhile, the exhaust pipe designs – and their surrounds – were similar, although the sports exhaust system (option 176) now had two round tailpipes sitting closer together, albeit not as tight as those found on the GT3.

Size-wise, the Gen II car was 8mm (0.3in) longer than the 991.1 version, and sat 10mm (0.4in) lower, thanks to the new suspension settings. There was also a tiny increase in the front track, but otherwise there were no other significant differences. The fuel tanks were also the same, still being fractionally bigger on the 4WD variants (albeit now officially classed as 67 litres, or 14.8 imperial gallons), although the front luggage capacity was upped seven per cent due to some careful re-arranging of the cargo space.

The biggest change to the interior was in making a newly-developed PCM unit with a navigation module and a ton of connectivity goodies a standard item. The author can well remember a review on the GT3, where the journalist noted how great the car was, but, in their opinion, it was badly let down in the Infotainment area. In an ultimate driving machine, does it really matter? An automobile is not a living room or office, and the amount of near misses on roads nowadays have doubtless increased in line with the proliferation of touchscreens and the wonderful world of 'do not use while driving' Infotainment.

Anyway, feeling the need to fall in line with other manufacturers, Porsche introduced a glass-screened version of the PCM unit to satisfy the whims of a new generation that seems unable to live for more than five minutes without something from an electronic device calling for their attention. At least the German maker kept the TV tuner an expensive option, thus making it less appealing, before dropping it completely, and a basic tracking system became a useful part of the package (readily upgraded via option 712), as did the voice command function.

Considering that most options remained unchanged in price since the debut of the 991 series, one wonders how much of the price hike applied to the 991.2 was to cover the PCM upgrade, as opposed to PASM – the other major gain on the spec sheet? With add-ons, there was a good €3500 in options on the older cars, suddenly made standard. Sadly, the handy electronic logbook element remained on the option list, despite the bold PCM move and the fact that it actually had something to do with motoring, and CDs were now considered a thing of the past – one listened to music via Bluetooth or a USB stick, or by specifying the digital radio option (priced at a hefty €400 plus tax). As such, the CD-changers were dropped from the options list, and old-school audiophiles like the author were left to ask their children how to download stuff to a USB. Once that was done, one could enjoy music through the standard 150W eight-speaker setup (previously 235W with nine speakers), or the Bose or Burmester 12-speaker upgrades, which were still available.

The other important change inside was the adoption of a fresh three-spoke steering wheel design, inspired by the 918 Spyder. Similar to the SportDesign wheel, it was chunkier, with chrome highlights on black, and a chrome ring on the airbag cover. A multi-function version was available, incidentally, and cars with the Sport Chrono package now came with a four-mode rotary switch (plus a 'Sport Response' button for overtaking manoeuvres once mass-production got under way) mounted below the right-hand spoke of the steering wheel. This move meant the console switches were eliminated, allowing the PASM and PSM ones to move forward, although the 'Sport' button remained on vehicles without the Sport Chrono option.

The ambience of the updated cockpit, with the new steering wheel making a big difference.

A manual car with the basic GT Sport steering wheel and Sport Chrono package, the latter bringing forth a new rotary mode switch (although expected, some of the early cars – like this one – lacked the 'Sport Response' button placed in the middle of this).

To go with the new steering wheel, a smaller-diameter GT Sport version (858) was released, looking much the same, but with screws locating chrome inserts on a darker three-spoke frame. The cruise control systems were also improved, and a new radar-controlled option called the Lane Change Assistant (or LCA, option

Preferred wheel options, with the standard 'Carrera' and 'Carrera S' rims, next to the (left to right) 'Carrera Classic,' 'RS Spyder Design' and 'Carrera Sport' wheels.

code 457) warned drivers of traffic approaching from behind that might be lurking in a blind spot zone.

Domestic sales

Classed as a 2017 model, the first domestic price list for the 991.2 range was issued on 7 September 2015. It included the new 911 Carrera coupé at €96,605 (including taxes), and the Carrera S version at €110,766. The only other cars at this stage were the Carrera Cabriolet at €109,695, and the Carrera S Cabriolet, which commanded €123,856.

Virtually all the options were carried over, including the pricing (it was mainly leather-related items that were subjected to increases, while features such as the 030 suspension upgrade were much cheaper due to the latest standard specifications, and restricted to the S

An arty series of pictures showing an early Carrera S with a number of options, including painted wheels and a sports exhaust, readily identified by the tailpipe design.

grade coupés only now), so there's no real point going over them again. We do need to look at some of the replacements and new items, though, and there were quite a few.

The new sports exhaust system we mentioned earlier came with chrome tailpipes. The sports tailpipes (XLT) were also chrome, but quoting the XLP code gave them a gloss black finish. Although the 176 system was illustrated in the first catalogue, it should be noted that both it and the two tailpipes variations were not officially available until the spring of 2016. It's also worth mentioning that no power kit was listed at this time.

As for wheels, the 'Carrera Classic' (427) design was rolled out for service again, albeit with a wider 11.5J rear rim. One could also opt for the 'RS Spyder Design' alloys (460), or the five-spoke XRD 'Carrera Sport' wheel – the former looked a lot like a centre-lock rim but with a traditional five-hole fixing, while the latter was rather like the 'Sport Classic' Fuchs-type wheel with reversed colouring. Wheel spacers were no longer listed, probably due to the wider standard rims, and the contrasting paint (CRX) option also seemed to disappear; body colour, gloss black, metallic black, satin black or a platinum shade were listed for wheel options instead.

While body kits, XEX and XXG lights, and the painted front spoiler, front air intake blades and rear apron options all fell by the wayside, the SportDesign mirror base could now be painted in gloss black (the same treatment could be applied to regular mirrors soon after via the DHD option code).

The Comfort Package went, and steering wheel heating was now restricted to the new multi-function wheel (489); the CLU contrast colour option was also dropped. The new 360mm (14.2in) diameter GT Sport wheel replaced the old 840 version, and the interior paint finishes were reduced, with new packages (EKA and EKB) taking their place instead. Painted gauges and seatbelt colour choices were much the same, with Bordeaux Red joining the fray, and completely replacing the blue option on the seatbelt front.

The leather packages were also revised (EKC and EKD), and a leather seats only option was no longer listed, along with a few of the other minor items. An Alcantara-trimmed GT Sport steering wheel now came as a set with a matching gearlever (EKL or EKM), and one could also specify Alcantara seat inserts (XWP) for just €300 plus tax. The aluminium, carbonfibre and wood packages were all assigned new

A 911 Carrera S Cabriolet with Platinum-painted wheels, darkened LED headlights, door decals, sports tailpipes, and an Exclusive wood interior (including a multi-function steering wheel, a Porsche crest on the centre box lid, and a number of additional leather trim items).

numbers, with the centre console trim now only available via one of these sets. New aluminium gearlevers augmented the latest carbonfibre and mahogany items, the carbonfibre steering wheel morphed from the XHL version to the heated XHW version (likewise the wood-rimmed wheel, from XHF to XHV), and lightweight carbonfibre floormats were offered for the first time, at €715 plus tax per set, in regular or personalised types.

The colour palette was almost completely revised, with only a handful of metallic paintwork options carried over. In addition, the Platinum Grey upholstery was replaced by a new Agate Grey shade, and the blue trim was dropped. Saddle Brown leather was added, and the more expensive hide trim options were also revised.

It should be noted that the Rhodium Silver and Sapphire Blue shades were not available until January 2016 on the 991.2, even though they were some of the few colours carried over from the earlier coachwork colour list; the same was true of the Racing Yellow hue, and the three new 'special' paint colours. Some of the leather trim was also delayed.

Mahogany Metallic was added in March 2016, along with the Sport-Tex

Standard colour & trim guide

These colour variations were available on mainstream Carreras from September 2015 until March 2017. Please see the text for variations applied to other model lines and specials.

Solid coachwork colours

Black (041), White (C9A), Guards Red (80K), and Racing Yellow (1S1).

Metallic coachwork colours

Jet Black Metallic (C9X), Agate Grey Metallic (M7S), Rhodium Silver Metallic (M7U), GT Silver Metallic (M7Z), Carrara White Metallic (S9R), Night Blue Metallic (M5F), Sapphire Blue Metallic (M5J), and Graphite Blue Metallic (M5G).

Special coachwork colours

Lava Orange (M2A), Carmine Red (M3C), and Miami Blue (M5C); Mahogany Metallic (M8Y) was added in March 2016. A 'colour to sample' option was also available.

Hood (convertible top) colours

Black, Red, Blue, and Brown. Hood always lined in black.

Leatherette (vinyl) trim

Black, Agate Grey, and Luxor Beige. Carpeting and floormats came in matching hues, as did the headlining.

Leather trim

Black, Agate Grey, Luxor Beige, and Saddle Brown. Carpeting and floormats came in matching hues; the headlining came in black on the black and brown options, or grey and beige to match the trim.

Regular two-tone leather trim

Graphite Blue with Chalk, Black with Bordeaux Red, and Black with Luxor Beige. Carpeting and floormats came in the lighter shade, with the roofliner in the darker one.

Sport-Tex leather and cloth trim

Black/Black with dark silver contrast stitching, and Chalk leather with Graphite Blue inserts. These two options were first listed in March 2016, but were not officially available until January 2017.

Special leather colours and natural leather trim

Graphite Blue, Bordeaux Red, Espresso, and two-tone Espresso with Cognac. Carpeting and floormats came in matching hues; the roofliner was black on the red option, or blue and brown to match the trim. A 'colour to sample' option was also available.

leather options, although the latter trim (basically leather outer seat facings combined with a heavyweight monotone fabric insert) would not be available until the start of 2017 in reality.

In the background, while Angela Merkel provided consistency in Germany as a whole (ultimately serving as Chancellor for four terms), there was a great deal of upheaval at VW as the 'Dieselgate' scandal came to a head. Things first started to unravel in mid-2014, with Martin Winterkorn duly resigning with a number of others in September 2015, only days after the face-lifted 911 was unveiled at the Frankfurt Show.

Replacing Winterkorn, Matthias Müller was appointed the new CEO of Volkswagen, this move allowing VW-Audi man Dr Oliver Blume to become Porsche's new boss at the same time, with the ex-finance supremo Lutz Meschke becoming his right-hand man. Interestingly, as part of the reshuffle, Detlev von Platen, who'd headed Porsche's US operations for several years with a good degree

Oliver Blume – Porsche's new President. Born in June 1968, he had been on the Porsche Executive Board since 2013, responsible for production and logistics at that time.

Michael Steiner – Porsche's new R&D supremo.

The Carrera 4S in coupé, convertible and Targa guises. All cars have been fitted with optional alloys and a sports exhaust.

Interior of the Carrera 4S coupé with a PDK gearbox and the Sport Chrono package.

Rolling chassis of the Carrera 4S.

of success, was appointed the Sales & Marketing Director at head office in Germany.

Another victim of the 'Dieselgate' episode, and one who actually served jail time for it, was Wolfgang Hatz. Although he was on hand for the 991.2 launch, he was suspended only days after introducing the new model alongside the Mission E concept at the IAA. His replacement, eventually made official in May 2016, was Dr Michael Steiner – an ex-Mercedes man, six years Hatz's junior, who had headed the Panamera project before moving further up the ladder.

Meanwhile, on 7 October 2015, the four-wheel drive versions of the new Carrera went on sale in Germany. All the options were the same, and there were only the obvious changes on the spec sheet, relating to engine sizes and/or body type. The newcomers included the 911 Carrera 4 coupé at €103,983 including taxes, the C4S coupé at €118,144, the Carrera 4 Cabriolet at €117,073, the Carrera 4S version at €131,234, the Targa 4 at the same price as the C4 drophead, and the 911 Targa 4S at €131,234 – the same as the top convertible.

Early thoughts

The press launch took place in Tenerife. Henry Catchpole was impressed with the Carrera S he drove, with plenty of torque available, delivered in a manner more associated with a normally-aspirated engine, a nice sound coming from the tail (a touch softer than before), and far better steering feel.

The challenge to provide more comfort without compromising handling is never an easy one, but virtually every report stated that Porsche had definitely succeeded in this area (only road noise was marked down). For some, the 911 had become almost too refined – the sharp bark from the exhaust was missing, the controls that told you everything (whether you needed to know or not), and the array of modern gizmos, from the Sport Chrono switch to the Infotainment upgrade, took the 991.2 into a different era. It should be said, though, that both of the latter items were appreciated by the majority of folks.

Writing for *Motor Trend*, Michael Febbo noted that the 370bhp 7MT Carrera he tried was "the best new car I've driven in years ... In reality, the base 911 is now a $100,000 car. The crazy thing – it's worth every penny."

One of the things that struck Febbo was the power delivery, which was far more linear than that of the 911 Turbo, and even the Carrera S, for that matter. He went on: 'I don't want to say the 991.2 feels like an older 911, it doesn't. A newer Porsche will never feel like an air-cooled car, and that isn't a bad thing. It does feel smaller, lighter, and more engaging than the 991.1 ever has to me. On twisting roads, it flows and shoots from corner to corner. It plays in the most serious way. This is the most rewarding 911 in quite some time, and that really is saying something."

One should remember, though, that quite a few regular 3.4- and 3.8-litre

The new 991.2 range was very well received in the press ...

991.1s were still coming off the line in the 2016 season. With Model Years now considered as starting on 1 June rather than September, as was the established and infinitely more sensible norm for decades, a handful of 3.4- and 3.8-litre engines were even classed as 2017 units, with these officially sporting an MAB code in place of MA1 in parts books. In reality, though, they were the same, and it's probably perfectly acceptable to use an MAB designation on these run-of-the-mill NA powerplants from day one. What is really odd, however, is that although engine numbers have been allocated, there are no VINs for 2017 cars with these engines, and the factory has stated none were built – a situation confirmed by VDA data, as the last 991.1 core line-up was built in the 2016 MY, and the last of the GT3 variants were considered 2016 vehicles even if they were produced after the factory-defined 2017 season kicked in. At least being aware of this grey zone may help someone in the future.

The Porsche stand at the 2015 Detroit Show, which opened to the public on 17 January, with a Turbo S Cabriolet in the foreground.

New 911 Turbos

With a new line of mainstream Carreras in place, the next model to be upgraded was the 911 Turbo, along with its Turbo S stablemate. Both would again be offered in coupé and drophead guise, with all four variants being listed in Germany from 1 December 2015, even though January's Detroit Show was marked down as the official debut. To confuse things further, they were classed as 2017 models!

Anyway, the key point was that both grades – the strict Turbo and the more powerful Turbo S – each gained another 20 horses in the tail and a 'dynamic boost function' that kept the engine on the boil when briefly releasing pressure on the throttle, thanks to some trickery with the DFI black box, the latest Sport Chrono package (previously standard on the S only), a number of chassis upgrades, some fresh styling features, and the latest Infotainment setup introduced on the Carreras.

Looking at the changes in detail, the MA1/71 became known as the MDA/BA (or MA1/72 in old terminology) thanks to modified inlet porting in the cylinder heads, and new fuel-injection nozzles that worked at a higher fuel pressure. All other leading features were carried

Power and torque curves for the new 911 Turbos, with the 540bhp car on the left, and the 580bhp on the right. Apart from the output levels, the delivery characteristics of the new power-units were very similar to those of their immediate predecessors.

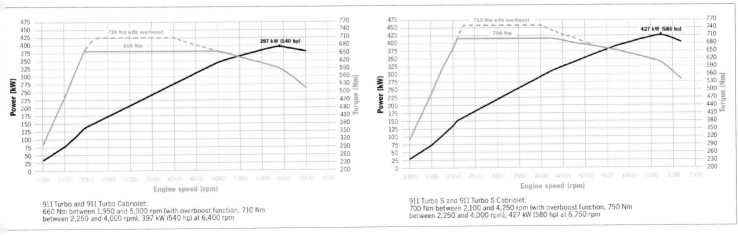

The preferred alloy wheel options for the new Turbo, with the 439 'Turbo' rim top left, the 449 'Turbo S' design on the right, and the optional 'Sport Classic' five-spoke rim in the bottom left corner.

over, with the only thing really changing being the power output, now listed at 540bhp at 6400rpm. Maximum torque was identical to before, kicking in at the same revs, and the exclusive use of a PDK transmission was kept, too.

Meanwhile, the MA1/71S morphed into the MDB/CA unit, with the power gain (580bhp at 6750rpm) achieved through the fitting of new turbos with larger compressor wheels; all other major technical details remained unchanged (to such an extent, that even the old catalogue picture of the engine was recycled with a fresh background grafted in to make it look new).

However, despite the additional power, which meant the Turbo S coupé could do the 0-60 sprint in under three seconds before going on to a top speed of 206mph (330km/h), fuel consumption was reduced by around six per cent on both engines courtesy of improvements in the electronic control systems for the 4WD drivetrain, especially those looking after the PDK's gearchange mapping (the gear ratios themselves were unchanged from the previous generation Turbos, although a new CG1/60 code was adopted to cover the upgrades).

As for the chassis tweaks, the new Turbos inherited the latest version of the PSM system from the 991.2 Carreras, giving more control to the driver whilst keeping a safety net in place. The active suspension and rear axle steering systems were carried over, and once

Front three-quarter shot of a 911 Turbo coupé, with this angle and lighting providing a nice view of the changes up front.

A Turbo S coupé on the move, with these pictures filling in the missing styling details. The inset shot shows the interior of the same car, with a multi-function version of the GT Sport steering wheel.

A plan view of a turbocharged convertible, showing off the shapely back wings and the latest engine cover design adopted on the four Turbo models.

more, the S was fitted with PDCC and ceramic brakes as standard.

Fresh alloys were introduced, with a similar situation to the Carreras. Indeed, the 439 'Turbo' wheel was much the same as its 429 predecessor, but at least the centre-lock 449 'Turbo S' rim was obviously new, with seven open spokes instead of ten. It should be noted that wheel sizes were increased on the strict Turbo model, upped to the 9J x 20 and 11.5J x 20 combination previously used on the Turbo S grades only; tyre sizes were carried over.

Styling-wise, the intake profiles were changed in the front bumper moulding, with the central one gaining a bit of a lip and a vane through the middle, while the outer pair were brought into line with those of the new Carreras – still angled the same way as the previous Turbos, and with two horizontal blades, but with very slim LED lights above the openings. In this case, the 'additional headlamp' was actually two narrow strips, and all cars now came with the so-called 'air blades' up front, supplementing the PAA active aerodynamics package.

In addition to the redesigned wheels and fresh paint colours (the same ones found on the Carreras from September 2015 onwards), the new Carrera's door handles were adopted, giving another distinguishing feature in profile. Around the back, 991.2 Carrera-type combination lamps were brought into the equation, while the rear bumper moulding was completely different, with more aggressive corner vents and the rear reflectors integrated into them. The engine cover grille also came in for attention, with the outer louvres replaced by gloss black longitudinal bars to match those of the new Carreras.

Inside, the biggest news was adopting the latest PCM unit as a standard item, again hooked up to the Bose sound system on the Turbos, but gaining parking sensors and a costly back-up camera was an unexpected bonus, as was getting cruise control for all cars. The GT Sport steering wheel (complete with a rotary mode switch for the Sport Chrono setup) was also new, but otherwise, the changes were restricted to the fresh colour palette – like the exterior shades, the same as the one introduced on the Carrera line from September 2015 onwards, with leather trim as standard in this case (two-tone trim was again considered the norm for the S grades, incidentally).

With the official domestic launch

A 911 Turbo Cabriolet taking a break on the challenging Kyalami circuit.

scheduled for the end of January 2016, the new 911 Turbo coupé was priced at €174,669 including taxes, while the S version commanded an additional €28,203; the Turbo Cabriolet was listed at €187,759, with the S again having a €28,203 premium over the 540bhp car.

Options were much the same as before, largely changed to suit new equipment levels and colours, or falling in line with the new Carreras. It's worth mentioning the lighting, though, as the codes were quite different. The LED PDLS Plus headlamps (standard on the Turbo S) went from the familiar 602 code to 632, and a dark version was made available via option XEY; dark-tinted rear lights could be ordered via the XXP code. Naturally, these items filtered through to the other 911s in due course.

A windscreen with a grey top band was now fitted to all Turbos as standard, and door mirrors could be upgraded via the latest Carrera options for those wanting to save weight or inherit a sportier appearance; the front axle lift facility (474) was another welcome addition. As with the Carreras, the trim packages and steering wheel options were revised (with Alcantara seat inserts being another variation to consider), although the bodykit was still available on the Turbo (in XAF or XAV guise), and the alloy wheel options were carried over, too.

The press was invited to try the new Turbos at the Kyalami track in South Africa, and judging by the rapturous reception the new cars got, the expense involved was well worth it. Virtually every report from the time gave a top marks rating (or damned close to it), dispelling fears that modern machines like the Audi R8 and McLaren 570S were starting to overshadow the evergreen 911.

Autocar summed things up nicely: "While a lot about the face-lifted 911 Turbo S remains the same, its intrinsic character has evolved, making it more memorable to drive than ever ... The crowning achievement is that the [ferociously quick] 911 Turbo S feels every bit at home on the road as it does on the track."

Corporate news
Things definitely seemed to be going Porsche's way. With 225,121 vehicles delivered in 2015, this beat the previous record set the previous year by a massive 19 per cent, largely thanks to strong sales in Europe (Germany in particular) and China. Indeed, China became Porsche's largest outlet at this time, taking just over 58,000 vehicles over the year.

Oliver Blume introducing the new 718 Boxster (this is an S model) at the 2016 Geneva Show. The white car is the one that interests 911 fans, though ...

Reflecting on 2015's performance, Oliver Blume said: "The figures reflect the pulling power of our brand, as well as the appeal of our products. Focusing completely on the development, production and sales of highly-emotional sports cars is paying off, but what is much more important for us is customer enthusiasm, a return on sales, and providing job security."

It looked like Blume's wishes would be achieved, too, as the relentless release of new models continued. Following hot on the heels of the 911 Turbo, it was the turn of the 982 series (labelled as the 718 in showrooms) to take a bow, with the four-cylinder turbocharged Boxster making its official debut at the 2016 Geneva Show; the tin-top Cayman version was first displayed at the Beijing Show a few weeks later. While Volkswagen's diesel exploits had a rather chequered history, the company's efforts in downsizing were highly-respected in engineering circles (with the excellent supercharged and turbocharged TSI unit being a case in point), and Porsche was doubtless able to benefit from this experience to augment its own extensive catalogue of data.

As well as the Boxster, visitors to the Geneva Show (which opened on 3 March), would have noticed there was another Porsche débutante in Switzerland – the 911R, which was given it's world première there ...

The 911R

As if the extensive 911 range wasn't baffling enough already, with 991.1s and 991.2s in the model mix, Porsche decided to introduce a 2016 MY car at the 2016 Geneva Show. As such, this was classed as a 991.1 machine, introduced almost six months after the 991.2s were launched as 2017 vehicles. And things used to be so logical!

Anyway, the 911R designation (with the R suffix standing for *Rennen*) means a lot to knowledgeable Porsche fans, as it was first given to a lightweight 911-based racer that went on to set a number of speed records back in 1967, and won the Tour de France Automobile outright in 1969.

Developed by Porsche's motorsport department in Flacht and limited to 991 units worldwide, the new 911R was not an out-and-out racer like its predecessor, but it was lighter than any of the newly-introduced 991.2 range (tipping the scales at 1370kg/3014lb), and was powered by the mighty 500bhp 4-litre engine from the GT3 RS, in this case, mated to a six-speed manual transmission.

Although the majority of engine specs were exactly the same as those for the RS (although a special model plate was made for the dressing piece around the fan shrouds), it should be noted that the compression ratio was listed at 13.2:1

The 911R was supposedly limited to just 991 units, although 1018 were built in the end, four as 2015 models. Despite so few being made available, the 911R had its own, beautifully-produced catalogue.

The view greeting 911R drivers, with a manual gearbox and a number of retro-style touches. The 911R was a full 50kg (110lb) lighter than the contemporary GT3 RS, with features such as the PCM unit and air-conditioning optional. Endowed with the same power as the RS and a 6MT gearbox, this meant that performance levels were truly exceptional.

Various publicity shots of the 911R, including the interior and engine bay.

for the R in factory-issued paperwork, as opposed to 12.9:1 for the RS. Considering the GT3 RS outlived the car it spawned, making it through to March 2017 in the end, this is very strange indeed.

One thing's for sure, the use of a G91/90 manual gearbox was a major deviation from the RS, with short throws and switchable automatic rev-matching, and gearing (3.75, 2.38, 1.72, 1.34, 1.08 and 0.88 combined with a 3.76:1 final-drive) that allowed a 0-60 time of 3.8 seconds along with a top speed in excess of 200mph (officially 323km/h).

Naturally, the chassis was uprated to handle the extra horses, with dynamic engine mounts, the latest PCCB ceramic brake setup, a 30mm (1.2in) lower PASM suspension (with an adjustment facility and ball-joints employed on some of the components), rear axle steering, PTV with a mechanical limited-slip differential, a recalibrated PSM system, and centre-lock forged alloys – basically a GT3 wheel and tyre combination, but with the rims painted in a matt Aluminium finish and black and silver Porsche crests on the locking nut; a satin Platinum or gloss black finish could be specified as a preferred option.

Interestingly, though, despite all this mechanical potency, in complete contrast to the Gundam-style GT3 RS, the bodywork changes were kept surprisingly low-key. This was doubtless the biggest charm point of the 911R, with racing technology shoehorned into a fairly standard-looking Carrera 4 coupé shell, which was slightly wider at the back, of course.

Notwithstanding, there were a few changes, such as the use of a GT3 front apron, a carbonfibre front lid beyond it (complete with a retro-style swage line down the middle), carbonfibre front wings that played host to regular bi-xenon lights, a magnesium alloy roof from the RS, GT3 side skirts (available painted on request), and a GT3 rear bumper moulding and diffuser surrounding the twin black pipes of the sports exhaust system; SportDesign mirrors and the use of a lightweight polycarbonate for the three back windows rounded things off. However, not having a huge rear wing made a massive difference to the car's appearance. Instead, the 911R came with a regular automatic pop-up rear spoiler, and a modified engine cover grille ahead of it – a tasteful frame with a 991.2-style high-mount brakelight assembly built into it, carrying a dark mesh insert (matching the other grilles scattered about the vehicle) with a distinctive '911R' badge on it.

As for the interior, black was the dominant theme, with silver contrast stitching, silver door pull loops, carbonfibre trim on the dashboard (with numbered plaque), centre console and model-specific treadplates, and an Alcantara headlining; extended leather trim was available, adding carbonfibre trim to the door cappings as well, although the latter was one of several carbon standalone options available. A nice touch was the green calibrations and white pointers on the black gauges, and the black spokes on the special leather-trimmed steering wheel.

Proof, if it were needed, that the 911R could indeed be ordered in just about any colour. This car was photographed in Werk I in the final days of 2016.

Full bucket seats with silver six-point belts were the norm, but P03 or P07 seats could be ordered for those who preferred a little more comfort, as well as standard black three-point seatbelts. The buckets and P03s were trimmed in black leather with Pepita cloth inserts (a natural dark brown and black two-tone scheme could also be specified, again combined with the classic houndstooth cloth), although, to save weight, the rear seats were removed, along with a lot of the noise insulation. Likewise, the PCM unit and air-conditioning were also ditched, becoming a no-cost option instead.

The catalogue listed White or GT Silver Metallic as the only body colours, which could then be left in a monotone state, or have green or red decorative stripes added on the bonnet, roof and engine cover. For the full effect, there was the option of the traditional-looking Tequipment or Exclusive 'Porsche' door stripes, which were available in black, green or red, and could be ordered on their own or combined with the upper body ones. However, the 'paint to sample' (or PTS) option meant virtually any body colour was possible, and the upper stripes could be ordered in other colours, too (such as white, black, blue, grey, orange or yellow), using this method.

Priced at €189,544 including taxes, interesting options included lighting upgrades, the Sport Chrono package with lap timer (643), a lightweight flywheel (187), lightweight battery (192), a larger fuel tank (082), carbonfibre mirror shells, and the front axle lift facility, which was probably a good idea on a car sitting as low as this one.

Britain's *Top Gear* summed up the 911R with the following prose: "For years, fast cars have been getting faster and faster. But they haven't necessarily been getting more exciting to drive. The 911R takes things back to basics. It reminds us that sports cars aren't all about the stopwatch, but the sensations, the experience, the moment ... They're about making us feel connected. Making us feel alive. And maybe – just maybe – the 911R is perfection."

The 2016 MY abroad

While Porsche had been messing around with its Model Year cut-off dates for some time (the colour charts tend to sum things up nicely), the majority of export markets still used traditional sales seasons, namely September or October for the introduction of a new Model Year. As such, with staggered releases and a string of early announcements (not to mention the R grade), confusion reigns supreme ...

Anyway, for 2016, the US range continued pretty much the same as it had for the 2015 season. There were no less than 21 variants of the 911 on sale, with prices starting at $84,300. In mid-October, it was announced that Klaus Zellmer (previously head of Overseas & Emerging Markets) would be the new PCNA President, and he could certainly count himself as lucky to be taking over the reins when he did – buoyant US sales

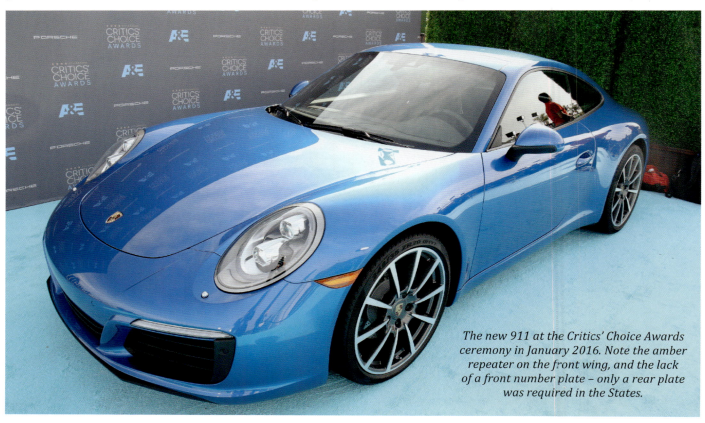

The new 911 at the Critics' Choice Awards ceremony in January 2016. Note the amber repeater on the front wing, and the lack of a front number plate – only a rear plate was required in the States.

A 911 Carrera coupé with sports exhaust blurring the US scenery.

(ultimately, another record year, with 51,756 Porsches finding new homes Stateside in 2015, largely thanks to the Macan and Boxster), the 991.2 had just been unveiled in Germany, and another US 'Experience Centre' set to open at the end of 2016, this time in Los Angeles, with the US motorsports arm (PMNA) using the same site.

In the meantime, the 991.2 range was launched in America in March 2016. The new 911 Carrera coupé was priced at $89,400, with the S version commanding $103,400. As for the open cars, the 911 Carrera Cabriolet was introduced at $101,700, with $115,700 being asked for the S; a delivery charge of around $1000 had to be applied to all vehicles, and, as before, a number of PCNA-unique packages were available, bundling popular options within an attractive price bracket.

The four-wheel drive models landed in showrooms in April, with the Carrera 4 coupé listed at $96,300, the C4S at $110,300, the C4 Cabriolet and Targa 4 at $108,600, and the Carrera 4S Cabriolet and Targa 4S at $122,600. The Turbos were also available from April (with prices ranging from $159,200), while the first 911R deliveries were expected at the tail-end of summer, with a base price of $184,900.

Perhaps not surprisingly with so many new models in the mix, 2016 went on to be another record-breaking year from a sales point of view, with 54,280 Porsches sold in the States. Rather oddly, though, only 8901 were 911s, compared with almost 10,000 in the 2015 CY, although, as noted earlier, the

A UK-registered coupé with the optional '911' badging and a sports exhaust.

Scene from the 2015 Tokyo Motor Show, the first major show to feature the Carrera 4 line-up. This is a C4S coupé with a Macan GTS, being introduced by Dr Erhard Mössle – the man in charge of engineering the 4WD models.

new lines were yet to have a full year on the market.

Meanwhile, times were certainly changing in Europe. In Britain, Theresa May replaced fellow Tory David Cameron as Britain's PM in May 2016, the latter having held the post for six years. It was an era of Brexit woes, and questions about the future of the European Union in general.

There were questions being raised regarding the role of automobiles in society, too, with electric vehicles seemingly being appointed as the way to save the planet, although it has to be said that without a 'green' source of renewable energy to charge them (as well as a cleaner way to produce and recycle batteries), the world simply isn't ready for such a big change, and certainly not within the timeframes being punted. It's ironic to be calling for a ban on IC engines just as they're delivering high levels of performance in a clean manner, but with Volkswagen about to overtake Toyota as the world's number one car manufacturer, this move towards EVs in the corridors of power would have a huge bearing on the company's engineering direction.

Anyway, back in the realm of 911s, Britain followed Germany's lead, issuing a price list for the new 3-litre turbocharged range on 7 October 2015. Including VAT at 20 per cent, the Carrera coupé was announced at £76,412, with 4WD adding £4986 to the invoice, and the more powerful S engine, another £4459 on top of that; the C4S coupé was priced at £90,843. Another £8841 brought the convertible and Targa bodies into play, with the latter available in four-wheel drive trim only, as elsewhere.

With a PDK transmission adding around £2400 to the bottom line, the GTS grades were still around at this time, ranging from £91,098 for the Carrera GTS coupé up to £104,385 for the Carrera 4 GTS Cabriolet and Targa 4 GTS models. The GT3 was still available, too, priced at just over 100K, while the older Turbos fetched between £121,523 and £151,782. The new 911 Turbo coupé would command £5402 more, with the S version gaining just £2728 in the transformation from 991.1 to 991.2, while the drophead Turbo pricing remained unchanged until the spring.

As March got under way, the 911 Turbo Cabriolet received a £5618 price hike, while the S version was hit with a £2832 one. At the same time, the 911R became available at £136,901 – over £5500 more than a GT3 RS or flagship Panamera, and almost three-and-a-half times the cost of one of the last base 2.7-litre Caymans. Things would then stay the same on the 911 front throughout the remainder of 2016.

Not surprisingly, the other major markets told much the same story in this 'world car' era. Porsche's distributor in Australia announced the new 991.2 range in September 2015, with prices starting at $239,300. Buyers wouldn't have expected to take delivery of a car that year, but at least it shows the pattern was there, and Japan followed Germany as well, with September and October looking after the 3-litre Carreras, and December the new Turbos. In Japan, prices of the 991.2 range started at 12,440,000 yen, and went all the way up to a hefty 28,650,000 yen – about 4,000,000 yen more than a Ferrari California T, although still a fair bit cheaper than a newer 488 Spyder model.

The 2016 racing season

There were no big surprises in the LMP1 programme, although VW Group "cost efficiency" dictated that both Porsche and Audi would run only two cars each all season (even at Le Mans), and Audi would duly quit the WEC arena at the end of 2016. Things were better for the Zuffenhausen brand, at least, with the manufacturers' and drivers' crowns in the bag thanks to the 919 Hybrid model.

The 470bhp RSR was subtly revised for the new season, mainly to comply with the latest regulations. Several aerodynamic changes were noted, including the use of a larger rear diffuser, and the rear wing being moved higher and further back; in addition, the 2016 cars received a modified front lip spoiler and heavier side sills to match. There was also a new seat and a bigger escape hatch in the roof to enhance safety, and a fresh colour scheme using white fading to black.

With the retirement of Olaf Manthey, Dempsey-Proton Racing would run the only RSR in the GTE-Pro Class in the full World Endurance Championship (officially classed as a customer team

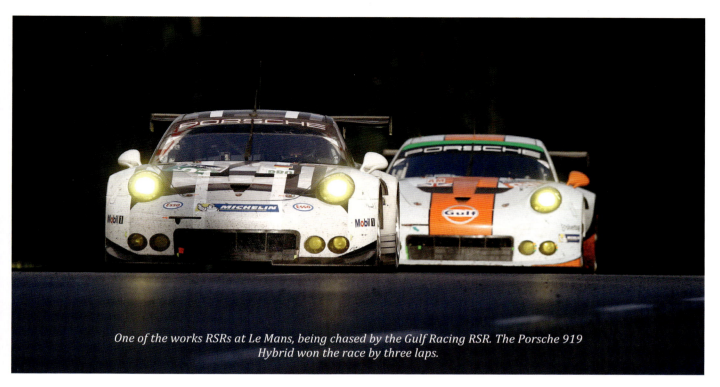

One of the works RSRs at Le Mans, being chased by the Gulf Racing RSR. The Porsche 919 Hybrid won the race by three laps.

The PCNA RSRs in the pitlane at Daytona.

despite the drivers, calling into question the "stepping up a gear" statement made on motorsport involvement at the end of 2015), with the KCMG and Abu Dhabi Proton Racing outfits getting varying levels of works assistance in the GTE-Am category. Gulf Racing also fielded a 911 RSR in the latter WEC Class, while Porsche Cars North America had the only two 911s in the GTLM section in IMSA's championship, with both factory cars running in the latest livery.

Meanwhile, the new 'customer' 911 GT3R was well-received, prompting Porsche to increase production up to around 40 vehicles. It would make its international debut at Daytona, with the factory also entering two GT3Rs in the Nürburgring 24-hour Race in a bid to promote it and hopefully bring the 24h trophy back to Zuffenhausen at the same time.

The GT driver line-up naturally included Lietz and Christensen, the defending WEC champions, along with Pilet, Makowiecki, Tandy, Bamber, Henzler, Long and Bergmeister. Between them, helped by Estre and Eng, they would cover the works and works-assisted campaigns in both the WEC and the IMSA series in the States.

Unfortunately, the 911 RSR failed to secure a solitary top three GTE-Pro finish all season in the WEC, and although the GTE-Am category bore better results, AF Corse won the team and drivers' title for Ferrari; Abu Dhabi Proton Racing finished the season in second.

Due to a change in sponsorship, the TUSC became known as the IMSA WeatherTech SportsCar Championship in 2016, adopting FIA GT3 regulations for the GTD Class along the way. Otherwise, it was business as usual, and Porsche Cars North America (PCNA) continued to support the 12-round series via a pair of works 911 RSRs entered in the GTLM category. As it happens, they were to be the only Porsches running in GTLM this particular season, although there were plenty of 911s in the GTD field.

Things got off to a reasonable start, with one works RSR delayed by driveshaft trouble at Daytona, but the other finished the 24-hour classic in third in GTLM, narrowly beaten by a pair of Corvettes; the GT3R scored second in Class (GTD) on its race debut courtesy of Black Swan Racing.

An accident cost the PCNA team dearly at Sebring, but the sister works car was third, keeping the RSRs in the hunt. Pilet and Tandy delivered the goods with a win at Long Beach, although the team struggled to come back from a poor qualifying session at Laguna Seca – at least Porsche stayed in touch with Chevrolet in the overall standings, and the GT3R scored its first GTD Class win thanks to Mario Farnbacher and Alex Riberas.

With Detroit for GTD only, the next GTLM round was at Watkins Glen, although the works cars were totally off the pace there. Starting on pole in Ontario, one would have expected better than sixth and eighth, but it was just one of those seasons; it was exactly the same story at Lime Rock, and Elkhart Lake wasn't much better.

A works car got on the podium at Virginia, but Chevrolet was now a long way ahead in the championship, and Ford opened the gap on Porsche, too. At least Texas was a reminder of last season, with PCNA RSRs first and second

The Park Place Motorsports GT3R in IMSA WeatherTech series action, seen here being hounded by an Audi.

One of the Manthey Racing GT3Rs at the Sepang 12-hour Race. Ultimately finishing in fifth, the sister car (number 911) came home in second overall.

in GTLM. However, Road Atlanta would prove to be the last outing for the old works cars – a new racing model was expected to be available in time for next year's season opener at Daytona. There was no fairytale ending, though, and Porsche finished 2016 in the middle of the maker's table in a dreary third place.

In other races, the Blancpain endurance and sprint events were really starting to strike a chord with enthusiasts, attracting entries from several prestigious names in the automotive world. For some reason, Porsche runners were few and far between, and limited to the Pro-Am ranks. Porsche stalwart IMSA Performance won one endurance round, but that alone wasn't enough to put the team in with a shout at the end of the year.

Proton Competition ran two 911 RSRs in the European Le Mans Series, with Wolf Henzler, Mike Hedlund and Robert Renauer winning the GTE Class in the second of six rounds (held at Imola). However, Aston Martin Racing and JMW Motorsport (a Ferrari team) were in a different league, and the Porsche outfit had to settle for fourth and sixth in the championship.

With the GTC Class dropped from the ELMS, the Le Mans Cup was born for LMP3 and GT3 runners, although primarily for amateur drivers. As if there weren't enough races already (including the Asian Le Mans Series, of course), the little-known VdeV Endurance Series for LMP and GT was at last taking off. The IMSA Performance 911 was the only Porsche contender of note, however, and it didn't really excel in this competition, made up of seven European events lasting either four or six hours.

Another newcomer was the Intercontinental GT Challenge – another SRO brainchild aimed at tempting manufacturers to back local teams, although, other than the Sepang 12-hour Race (handy after a Macau excursion for the Manthey team), Porsche did not get involved in this, its inaugural year.

Meanwhile, the more familiar SCCA-sanctioned Pirelli World Challenge had 11 rounds, with the GT Cup reserved for Porsche GT3 Cup drivers. No less than eight 911-based teams went for the big prizes, and there were a couple of Caymans in the lower categories, too, bringing some colour to the grids. Patrick Long and Michael Lewis had

A 911 in pole position in the German ADAC GT Masters series.

Sven Müller leading a line of Porsche Mobil 1 Supercup challengers at Silverstone.

> ### 991.1 production numbers
> Thanks to the sterling efforts of fellow Veloce scribe Adrian Streather, we can be fairly accurate on the 991.1 model mix. This is the overall picture of the mainstream line-up, including prototypes. Incidentally, according to the figures published in the VDA annuals, far less four-wheel drive variants were exported compared to their RR brethren in the regular Carrera lines – as little as half as many on average across the body and engine options.
>
> | Model | Total |
> |---|---|
> | Carrera (C2) coupé | 14,482 |
> | Carrera (C2) Cabriolet | 7292 |
> | Carrera 4 coupé | 2719 |
> | Carrera 4 Cabriolet | 1666 |
> | Targa 4 | 1407 |
> | Carrera S (C2S) coupé | 19,130 |
> | Carrera GTS (C2) coupé | 3638 |
> | Carrera S (C2S) Cabriolet | 11,321 |
> | Carrera GTS (C2) Cabriolet | 1656 |
> | Carrera 4S coupé | 10,664 |
> | Carrera 4 GTS coupé | 1872 |
> | Carrera 4S Cabriolet | 8070 |
> | Carrera 4 GTS Cabriolet | 1468 |
> | Targa 4S | 4286 |
> | Targa 4 GTS | 1526 |
> | GT3 coupé | 6063 |
> | GT3 RS coupé | 6128 |
> | Turbo coupé | 2984 |
> | Turbo Cabriolet | 1284 |
> | Turbo S coupé | 6902 |
> | Turbo S Cabriolet | 2727 |
>
> The remaining 991.1 production quota was made up of the 50th anniversary car (1968 units), GT3 Cup-based models (643 units), Black Edition cars (2372 units), and the 911R (1018 units).

a decent season in GT, while Michael Schein had an exceptional run of wins in the GTA Class. Unfortunately, both Long and Schein were pipped into second when the final points were calculated at the end of the year.

We were back to having two cars representing Porsche in the Super GT series in Japan, but apart from a single podium finish at Motegi for Naoya Yamano and Jorg Bergmeister, there was sadly nothing else to write home about.

Ending with something closer to home, one of the two works GT3Rs ran under the Manthey Racing banner crashed out of the Nürburgring 24-hour Race very early on, but the sister car was running well enough until it expired with five hours to go. In the end, it was a Mercedes-Benz one-two-three on the leaderboard.

Porsche started taking an interest in the ADAC GT Masters from this point onwards, with the KÜS car having

With a successful racing history dating back to the 996s, no less than 3031 specialised GT3 Cup cars had already been built by the time the 991.2 version was announced.

The 911 Targa 4S Exclusive Design Edition was announced in August 2016, limited to around 100 vehicles worldwide. Finished in Etna Blue combined with a Graphite Blue leather interior, darkened LED headlights, blue-painted badging and silver side stripes added character. There was also an added premium, of course – over $60K in the States.

works affiliations. The team ultimately came third after a strong second half to the season, launching David Jahn into the runner-up spot in the drivers' championship; Kevin Estre was fourth.

Finally, Sven Müller won both the Carrera Cup Deutschland and Supercup titles in 2016. In the latter, he won three of the ten rounds (in nine locations), narrowly beating Matteo Cairoli after the Italian was forced to retire in the first of the American double-header races.

Although it hadn't been an amazing GT season by Porsche standards, an exciting new RSR was on its way, and September 2016 had witnessed the launch of a new 911 GT3 Cup car. Now equipped with a 485bhp 4-litre NA six, revised aerodynamics and a new safety package, the 1200kg (2640lb) 991.2 version of the GT3 Cup car was reserved initially for the 2017 Supercup and certain Carrera Cup series,' but would be made available to a wider audience from 2018.

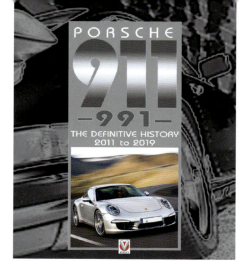

5

End of the line

While a new generation Panamera was released in time for the traditional 2017 season, 911 fans were more interested in the Porsche newcomers announced on 9 January 2017 – the eagerly-awaited 991.2 versions of the five existing GTS variants ...

Billed as being "faster and more capable than ever before," the GTS recipe was a familiar one, with a tuned power-unit (with output upped to 450bhp at 6500rpm), and sporty touches both inside and out to give the GTS models their unique character.

The engine changes were at the heart of the GTS transformation, of course. In this case, the Carrera S 3-litre bi-turbo MDC/HA six became the MDC/JA, pumping out an additional 30bhp thanks to the use of larger turbochargers, as well as providing an extra ten per cent of torque, which was available over a wide rev range.

All other drivetrain specifications were the same as the base MDC units, and the manual and PDK transmissions were carried over from the regular S lines, too, regardless of whether the owner went for an RR or 4WD layout, having the same type numbers and ratios. It should be mentioned, however, that a sports exhaust and the Sport Chrono package came as standard on the GTS line, allowing all five cars to top 188mph/300km/h.

The three four-wheel drive versions of the new GTS line.

A rear-wheel drive Carrera GTS coupé on the move, this angle and colour showing off most of the important styling features rather nicely, as well as the rear spoiler in its deployed position.

All cars were based on the wider C4 body, and came with a new SportDesign front apron (much like the old one, in reality, but with revised outer intakes to incorporate 991.2-style lights, complete with 'air blades' and a single horizontal vane in each), with swage lines ahead of the front lid to provide a 'family' look, and a black-painted spoiler lip. Bi-xenon lights with PDLS were the norm, incidentally, although many owners went for the darkened version of the LED headlights (option XEY) to give their car an established GTS look.

Around the side, one could see the SportDesign mirrors (swapped for regular items if folding mirrors were required), subtle black GTS decals on the doors (even on black cars, although a delete option was available), and the latest 20in 'Turbo S' centre-lock wheels in satin black shod with 245/35 and 305/30 rubber; 'Carrera S' rims were a no-cost option, by the way, finished in black, silver or body colour. On the Targas, the roll-over hoop was painted in satin black for the first time, with the bar's badging also becoming black, although a stock silver bar could be ordered if desired.

On the subject of badging, that on the tail remained in black, with either the full model name or optional '911' script under the 'Porsche' lettering. Above that, 4WD models kept the familiar red lighting strip that ran between the darkened rear combination lamps, while C2-based machines were given a grooved black dressing piece instead, as before.

The engine cover grille was now the same as the run-of-the-mill Carreras, fitting in with the car's image without the need for modification. Meanwhile, the pop-up rear spoiler looked standard enough, but was made to extend further than normal – the extra height balancing the new front end, thus reducing lift over both axles. A new option introduced at this time was the SportDesign package (XAT), bringing with it the same type of

Detail shots of the latest Targa 4 GTS.

Interior of the Carrera 4 GTS Cabriolet with the red-stitch version of the GTS package. Note the GT Sport steering wheel, which looked a little fussy if the multi-function buttons were added.

front spoiler already used on the GTS and a revised rear spoiler, which had a stronger trailing edge profile, albeit a long way from being a ducktail.

The only other difference was the sports exhaust system, finished in black and fitted to all cars, which brought the special diffuser insert that goes with those particular tailpipes into play. Otherwise, the rear bumper moulding was the same as that off any stock Carrera 4 model.

Under the skin, there was an active PASM suspension, as per the new Carreras, but the coupés were allowed to drop a further 10mm (0.4in), thus gaining what was previously an option. PDCC and rear axle steering could be specified as options, as could the front axle lift system and upgraded EPS. The braking system came from the Carrera S, with the latest PCCB ceramic disc setup available for those who push hard, but with even the heaviest car tipping the scales at just 1585kg DIN (3487lb), this was an unnecessary extravagance for most owners.

Inside, the established GTS ingredients were all there: Black partial leather-trimmed four-way power seats with Alcantara inserts and a 'GTS' logo in the headrest, Alcantara on the GT Sport steering wheel and gearlever, as well as the centre console lid, door furniture and headlining, black anodised brushed aluminium dash and gear surround trim, and the 'GTS' logo on the black tachometer face and treadplates. For techno freaks, the Sport Chrono package included an upgraded version of the Track Precision app, and the optional GTS package was rolled out for service once more, featuring carbonfibre trim pieces, a red tachometer dial, and red or silver contrast stitching, with seatbelts to match.

While sales began in January, cars were available from March 2017 in Germany, so used the revised colour and trim guide introduced at that time for the '2018' season, and yes, you've guessed it, the GTS was officially classed as a 2017 vehicle, with the first examples of the breed having an H-Serie chassis code! Confused? You should be ...

Anyway, the 911 Carrera GTS coupé was introduced at €124,451 (including taxes), with the 4WD version

Tail of the RR GTS convertible, with the black dressing piece clearly visible between the rear lights – a useful distinguishing feature to put some distance between the two- and four-wheel drive cars.

commanding €7378 more in basic 7MT guise. The rear-wheel drive GTS convertible was listed at €137,541, and €144,919 was the asking price for both the C4 GTS Cabriolet and the Targa 4 GTS. However, a new price list issued in March 2017 added around one per cent to the cost of GTS motoring.

Options were, in the main, carried over – pricing, too, although the 90-litre (20 imperial gallon) fuel tank was now a token €100 plus VAT instead of being free of charge, and the P01 and P03 seats were more expensive. The main changes came as a result of the 991.2 revamp, so the new PCM unit was supplied, cutting out many of the old extras, while trim packages were revised, and the 'Carrera S' wheels were naturally of the latest type (433s rather than 423s). Sport-Tex upholstery was offered, along with the new steering wheel options, and things like leather upholstery on the back of the shell seats, plus carbonfibre mirror housings and footmats.

Meanwhile, the XAA Cup bodykit was no longer available, of course, and the 602 and XXG lighting options were also dropped, leaving only darkened headlamps and rear light units to choose from. As for new items, there was the option of a painted HVAC control panel, or one could order the louvres on the engine cover in body colour (XAX), a rear screen only in privacy glass (XPR) and, from August 2017, have the triangular piece above the door mirrors made in carbonfibre (CSX). The newer things were naturally made available on other model lines at this time.

In the United States, Barack Obama (Dem) had moved into the President's office at the start of 2009, but in the second half of January 2017, handed over the keys to the White House to Republican Donald Trump.

Americans got to know of the 991.2-based GTS models at about the same time, of course (although strangely, Porsche decided to stay away from the Detroit Show), and a few months later – in April – the first of the five new GTS models started arriving in US dealerships, with prices ranging from $120,700 to $139,900 – actually $1700 more than first advertised.

As *Road & Track* noted at the time:

"It's hard to call a $120,000 Porsche a bargain, but the GTS package offers a better performance-to-dollar ratio than any other 911."

As expected, the GTS models found their way into the other export markets over the early part of spring. Great Britain got its GTS range in March, with prices starting from £94,316 and going up to £108,144. Australia wasn't far behind, with the price of entry for GTS motoring being a cool $300,500, while Japan's GTS line-up ranged from 17,500,000 yen up to 21,160,000 yen. Of course, with such a full range of options available, including the ability to delete badging, finding a model that looked just like one in the catalogue might prove difficult.

Another new GT3

Arriving far sooner than the majority of press members expected (assuming any new GT3 would be turbocharged), an evolution of the existing NA model was announced on 7 March 2017, just ahead of the Geneva Show opening to the public and a world première.

It was already a hard act to follow, so the easy way forward was to fit what was basically the 4-litre GT3 RS engine into the vehicle, instantly gaining 25bhp, and let the RS move further up the ladder. In some ways, it was a similar situation to the 1974 season, when the contemporary RS six became a 911 Carrera power-unit. They call it progress ...

Anyway, there were a number of important differences between the actual RS engine and the MA1/77 (MDG/GA) variant that powered the 2018 model GT3. There was a new, stiffer crankshaft with larger bearing areas, an iron-based cylinder lining, a fresh intake manifold design with a second flap added to boost torque and low-speed response, a modified valvetrain (the so-called 'rigid valve drive' doing away with automatic hydraulic adjustment) sitting atop modified heads, a higher c/r, larger radiators up front, and improvements in the lubrication system. All these revisions added up to a 500bhp/339lbft unit that would rev 200rpm faster, despite the adoption of a dual-mass flywheel.

With a sports exhaust as standard and a 9000rpm red-line, thus keeping the previous GT3 limit intact, it certainly had the kind of character enthusiasts admire. As *Car & Driver* noted: "If you're uncomfortable above 6000rpm, this isn't your Porsche. Because this is an engine that won't stop pulling until your cochleae burst into flame. This is an engine bred for Daytona, Sebring and Le Mans, and it makes you earn everything you get."

A seven-speed PDK transmission (CG1/92) was considered standard, although the G91/90 six-speed manual gearbox from the 911R was available

The new 2018 MY GT3 making its debut at the 2017 Geneva Motor Show. Oliver Blume can be seen holding the car's mirror, with recently retired Porsche racer Mark Webber standing next to him.

as a no-cost alternative for those who preferred a full array of pedals and were less bothered by academic 0-60 times simply by ticking the I486 box in the options list.

The gearbox and final-drive ratios were carried over from the regular GT3 (not the RS) and 911R, incidentally, meaning a top speed of just under 200mph (320km/h). Both transmission options came with dynamic engine mounts and a limited-slip differential via the PTV system, being electronically-controlled on the 1430kg (3146lb) PDK machines, and mechanical on the 1413kg (3109lb) 6MT vehicles.

As for the chassis components, the 2018 MY car inherited the latest PSM system, giving the driver more control over the amount of 'help' they wanted, and a retuned active suspension to improve responses, set approximately 25mm (1.0in) lower than a 911 Carrera and adjustable for track work. The rear axle steering progression was also recalibrated, although the brakes were familiar GT3 fare, as was the steering (the previous ratio was retained) and the wheels and tyre sizes; shod with freshly-developed Michelin rubber, the ten-spoke 'GT3' centre-lock alloys were finished in silver as standard, with satin Platinum, Black and Aluminium shades listed as costly options. For the record, previously Platinum had been the catalogue listing, with silver and gloss black offered as alternatives.

Regarding the styling changes, the redesigned front bumper moulding-cum-air dam was optimised for enhanced aerodynamic efficiency. The central intake edges were angled to resemble those of the new Turbos, but with additional smaller intakes outside in established GT3 fashion; the large outer intakes carried narrow 991.2-style lighting units, and a new interpretation of the 'air blade' concept. All five openings had mesh inside them, as before, and the rubber lip spoiler was still there, smoother in profile than before due to the pouting apron it was attached to, and continuing halfway up the wheelarch. The bi-xenon headlights were of the new design, with four-point DRLs, and while

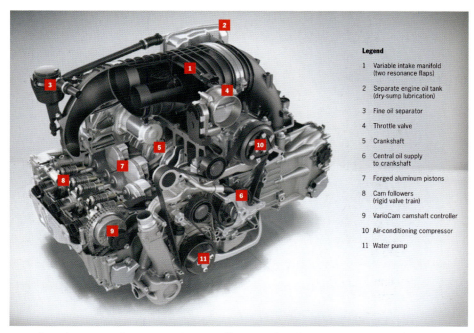

The 4-litre MDG/GA powerplant, as illustrated in the contemporary catalogue.

the regular LED headlamp upgrade was cheaper than before, the XEX option was no longer available.

The latest door handles were fitted, of course, and the eagle-eyed would have noticed the black side panels on the rear spoiler, as well as a '4.0' insert replacing the '3.8' one. Actually, the carbonfibre rear wing assembly sat 20mm (0.8in) higher than before, mounted on a new carbonfibre rear lid with completely new ram air scoops (also in black, but made of glassfibre) and an outlet, thus doing away with the one that was previously in the top of the bumper moulding.

The lightweight polyurethane rear apron played host to the latest tinted combination lamps (killing off the XXG option), and was less fussy than before – the outer vents being tighter, and the exhaust surround insert being wider. This minimalist approach was highlighted even more on US cars, which had a smaller area set aside for the registration plate, of course. Anyway, the wider mesh-filled dressing piece around the twin black exhaust pipes allowed hot air to escape that much easier, with a new underbody diffuser combined with the other aerodynamic tweaks to increase downforce by as much as 20 per cent compared to the outgoing GT3.

Available in all the '2018' exterior colours except Night Blue and Mahogany (with the four special shades costing far more than before), the interior was exclusively black. There wasn't much in the way of changes inside the cockpit, as it happens. Apart from the use of a GT Sport steering wheel (with a red 12-o'clock marker available via the 886 code), the adoption of the new PCM unit brought about the biggest changes, linked up to eight rather than four speakers, and coming with a Bose upgrade option as well. Of course, to save weight, the PCM unit could be removed (P98) free of charge, although this meant losing the Track Precision app, and there was no facility to delete the air-conditioning this time around.

The aluminium trim parts were still in place, with a body-coloured paint finish available as an option on most components. The regular Sports Seats Plus (P05) front seats were carried over, with the rear seats deleted once more to keep the car's weight down. However, the P01 bucket seat option now had a vertical red accent stripe with a 'GT3'

A GT3 on the move, with these angles showing off the latest styling revisions quite well.

logo on the Alcantara inlay, while the P03 chairs now came with a similar stripe in silver, pushing their price up at the same time. As before, to get the NCO Clubsport package (I003), one had to specify either the P01 or P03 seats.

As it happens, a few existing option prices changed, with the larger fuel tank no longer free of charge, and there was a hefty increase on the extended leather trim package. On saying that, the front axle lift facility was cheaper, so that helped balance things out. In addition, the anthracite grey P1A and P1B aluminium trim package became a NCO, along with a leather-clad steering wheel and gearlever option in place of the standard Alcantara covering.

New items for GT3 enthusiasts included the latest Sport Chrono package with lap trigger software, darkened LED headlights, gloss black mirror bases and/or carbonfibre shells, a carbonfibre window triangle piece, gloss black door handles, colour-keyed sill trim, painted 'Porsche' and/or model tail badges, a rear-only privacy glass option, a back-up camera, carbonfibre floormats, and leather trim to replace the aluminium parts on the dash and doors. Most of these things had filtered through from other lines, and likewise, the painted door handles (XJA) and black sports exhaust system (a 178 code) options were duly offered on the other 911 models, too.

Although a fair bit costlier than before, being listed at €152,416 (VAT included) in its native Germany, the latest GT3 knocked 12.3 seconds off its predecessor's Nordschleife lap time, which was seriously impressive. As Andreas Preuninger (the GT line boss) stated at the time: "A few years ago, lap times like this could only ever be achieved by thoroughbred race cars with slick tyres. The new GT3 achieves this with comparatively modest power, and is still fully suitable for everyday use."

This Nürburgring excursion was certainly a good way of whetting appetites, for while sales began as soon as the car was announced, the first domestic deliveries were not expected until mid-June, with export markets following later still.

Meanwhile, the press was busy

Interior of a GT3 with P03 seats and a PDK transmission. This car has carbonfibre trim inserts rather than the standard aluminium pieces (with a natural-coloured finish, although a darker version was listed as a no-cost option); the steering wheel is the stock item.

A different GT3 with P01 bucket seats and the regular brushed aluminium trim pieces.

singing its praises. Dan Prosser of *Auto Express* wrote: "As well as being the fastest and most powerful GT3 to date, this latest version is also the best. In just about every significant area it represents a step-change over the previous model, with better steering, a more sophisticated chassis and greater performance. It's just a pity GT3 ownership remains such an exclusive and selective club."

The GT3 proving its worth on the Nürburgring with test driver Lars Kern at the wheel.

As expected, the latest GT3 was a huge hit with the motoring press. This car pictured at the works has the 'correct' wheels and provides us with a clear view of the scoops in the engine cover, each having a mesh grille and feeding air into the power-unit. Incidentally, the new six had its two fans placed next to each other, inside the gap created by the scoops, with a small metal plaque on each, carrying 'GT3' and '4.0' logos, respectively. As such, the view was quite different for those who lifted the rear lid.

And the conclusion from the folks at *Top Gear*: "It feels small and light, narrow, hard and fast. You drive it on a British B-road, and wonder why almost everyone else gets it so wrong. You don't need more speed than this and I'm not sure there are many cars that deliver more sensation. Certainly none at this money. For the ability and engineering on offer here, £111,802 is a bargain."

The story so far …
With no reliable figures available for each model in the final years of the 991.2 run (thanks to Porsche having a policy of not releasing the data of late), here, at least, are the numbers – including pre-production vehicles built in the 2014 season – that take us up until the end of the 2017 Model Year. Due to their isolated nature, the GT3 Cup cars and limited edition Turbo S Exclusive coupés have not been included in this table.

Model	Total
Carrera (C2) coupé	8673
Carrera (C2) Cabriolet	3775
Carrera T coupé	77
Carrera 4 coupé	1695
Carrera 4 Cabriolet	1116
Targa 4	1655
Carrera S (C2S) coupé	6205
Carrera GTS (C2) coupé	3157
Carrera S (C2S) Cabriolet	3425
Carrera GTS (C2) Cabriolet	1368
Carrera 4S coupé	5445
Carrera 4 GTS coupé	2180
Carrera 4S Cabriolet	3963
Carrera 4 GTS Cabriolet	1548
Targa 4S	3910
Targa 4 GTS	2280
GT3 coupé	3917
GT3 RS coupé	24
GT2 RS coupé	105
Turbo coupé	1895
Turbo Cabriolet	1109
Turbo S coupé	4339
Turbo S Cabriolet	2340

Note: As a matter of interest, according to VDA figures, around three in every four cars were shipped abroad in the early 991.2 production phase.

More changes
A press release dated 21 March 2017 brought news of "comprehensive innovations for all Porsche lines" for the '2018' Model Year – the changing of the seasons seeming to come earlier and earlier. Anyway, much of it concerned enhanced connectivity, but more importantly, the colour charts were revised once more, with several changes outlined for the 911s.

The shortlived Mahogany Metallic hue was replaced by a Chalk shade (aka Crayon) from the start of June 2017 on the GTS, and as early as March on most lines (for the record, Chalk paintwork was actually listed from the start of the year, but ultimately came online in March 2017). Then, there was Saffron Yellow Metallic (a very special €8925 option restricted to the Turbos, and therefore not listed in the charts below), with four coats of paint giving a particularly deep finish. Meanwhile, Luxor Beige trim was almost wiped out, but otherwise things remained the same on the 911 front.

Still on a colouring theme, following on from the GTS introduction, buyers of the regular Targa 4 and Targa 4S models could also specify a roll-over hoop in satin black (591), albeit with a silver 'Targa' badge rather than a black one. One should also mention the SportDesign package (XAT) here, first listed in the January 2017 catalogue, and including new front and rear spoilers painted in body colour; the XAS code brought the front air dam moulding only, but in both cases, they were available for all of the Carreras.

The other important newbie to arrive via the GTS line was the 450bhp

---

Standard colour & trim guide
These colour variations were available on mainstream Carreras from March 2017, and stayed valid for just one year. Please see the text for variations applied to other model lines and specials.

Solid coachwork colours
Black (041), White (C9A), Guards Red (80K), and Racing Yellow (1S1).

Metallic coachwork colours
Jet Black Metallic (C9X), Agate Grey Metallic (M7S), Rhodium Silver Metallic (M7U), GT Silver Metallic (M7Z), Carrara White Metallic (S9R), Night Blue Metallic (M5F), Sapphire Blue Metallic (M5J), and Graphite Blue Metallic (M5G).

Special coachwork colours
Mahogany Metallic (M8Y) to June 2017, Chalk (M9A), Lava Orange (M2A), Carmine Red (M3C), and Miami Blue (M5C). A 'colour to sample' option was also available.

Hood (convertible top) colours
Black, Red, Blue, and Brown. Hood always lined in black.

Leatherette (vinyl) trim
Black, and Agate Grey. Carpeting and floormats came in matching hues, as did the headlining.

Leather trim
Black, Agate Grey, and Saddle Brown. Carpeting and floormats came in matching hues; the headlining came in black on the black and brown options, or grey to match the trim.

Regular two-tone leather trim
Graphite Blue with Chalk, Black with Bordeaux Red, and Black with Luxor Beige. Carpeting and floormats came in the lighter shade, with the roofliner in the darker one.

Sport-Tex leather and cloth trim
Black with dark silver contrast stitching, and Graphite Blue with Chalk.

Special leather colours and natural leather trim
Graphite Blue, Bordeaux Red, Espresso, and two-tone Espresso with Cognac. Carpeting and floormats came in matching hues; the roofliner was black on the red option, or blue and brown to match the trim. A 'colour to sample' option was also available.

The latest X51 power kit for Carrera S variants.

X51 power kit. Available for €10,139 for 7MT Carrera S models and €10,567 for those with a PDK transmission, it came with bigger turbos, a retuned ECU, the Sport Chrono package with dynamic engine mounts, a sports exhaust with silver tailpipes, carbonfibre dressing pieces (it actually looked a lot like the 991.1 unit when installed, apart from the '3.8' suffix changing to a '3.0S' one), and improvements to the brake cooling system.

The X51 upgrade was duly offered as a retrofit Tequipment option on cars equipped with the Sport Chrono package from June 2017. Although it seemed to disappear briefly, it duly returned to

A Targa 4S photographed at the works in the summer of 2017, fitted with a sports exhaust.

Nr 1,000,000

The one-millionth 911 – a Carrera S coupé finished in a special Irish Green shade with retro-style trim – was built on 11 May 2017, and following it down the line gives us an ideal opportunity to see contemporary production methods in action. The interior shot (on the next page) with Wolfgang Porsche at the wheel just about shows the commemorative plaque on the dash, above the glovebox. Fittingly, the car will be kept in the Porsche Museum.

(continues overleaf)

the fold, and given the inherent time delays involved between ordering and actually driving away 30bhp better off, one can almost ignore this blip, stating that the X51 option was available from March 2017 through to the end of 991.2 production.

The press release also mentioned a 0.9 to 2.0 per cent increase in pricing. In the case of the mainstream 911 Carreras, it was a fraction over one percentage point, taking a base Carrera coupé up to €82,281 plus tax (German VAT was still 19 per cent, by the way, having remained at that rate from 2007), and the C4S convertible and Targa 4S at the other end of the scale up to €111,381, or €132,543 with tax included.

However, apart from the Sport Chrono package as a notable exception (up €120 plus tax), the pricing on existing options remained largely unchanged. The 439 'Turbo' alloy wheel design was now listed, by the way, and the painted front spoiler option was back (along with a colour-keying package via the DAR code), while most of the other items had arrived with the GTS.

As for the Turbos, each grade received a blanket increase of €1900 plus tax. About the only significant change for the Turbo line-up was its new Saffron Yellow paint option that we mentioned earlier, and things like the painted tail badges introduced on the GT3. The equivalent to the DAR option on the Carreras was given the EPL code on the Turbos, incidentally, while ticking the CCM box brought forth painted air intakes up front combined with painted air outlet slats in the tail.

Yet more new 911s

As if the choice of 911s wasn't extensive enough already, with the multitude of options available blurring the defining lines between grades almost to the point of making them worthless, June 2017 saw the release of two more Turbo models. It must be said, though, that both of these variants really were rather special, and no amount of extras could have come up with an equivalent vehicle ...

The first car was the 911 Turbo S Exclusive coupé – an ideal promotional tool for the new Porsche Exclusive Manufaktur brand based in Zuffenhausen. Limited to just 500 units worldwide, it still had its own catalogue and price list, outlining the many unique features applied to these €259,992 hand-crafted machines.

The engine was modified via a power kit, transforming it into the MDB/CB unit – the additional 27 horses took the power output up to 607bhp, and combined it with 553lbft of torque. Typical carbonfibre plates confirmed it was an Exclusive version of the flat-six, while a special exhaust system (with four round tailpipes finished in black) provided a handy external distinguishing feature. The Sport Chrono package was fitted as standard, and PDK transmission was the only option.

As for the chassis components, there was an active suspension with the PDCC bits, an upgraded EPS system (usually an option, even on the Turbos) and rear axle steering. Unique 20in centre-lock wheels were provided in black with Golden Yellow highlights (black with silver highlights being a no-cost option), while the PCCB ceramic braking system rounded things off. Regarding the latter, the discs were of the normal type, but the calipers were painted black with Golden Yellow 'Porsche' lettering.

In reality, it was the bodywork and interior that made the coupé so special. In addition to having the Turbo Aerokit, the front lid, roof panel, side skirts, side intakes, central intake panel on the

Striking gold paintwork was considered standard for the 500-off Turbo S Exclusive model, with the grey and white liveries shown here available at no extra cost; the three other shades available were a €2654 option.

Classed as a 2018 model, according to official data, 156 Turbo S Exclusive 4WD coupés were built in the first year, and 354 in the second.

engine cover, upper rear wing, exhaust surround, and door mirror shells were all executed in carbonfibre. While the carbon weave was fully exposed in the smaller items, the luggage compartment panel and roof were painted in such a way that it looked like they had carbonfibre stripes running their length. Standard colour choices were Golden Yellow Metallic, Agate Grey Metallic and Carrara White Metallic, with Black, Guards Red and Graphite Blue Metallic classed as cost options.

Inside, the 18-way seats were upholstered in black leather, with perforated inserts and an underlay of Golden Yellow stripes – this way, the sporty effect was there without being too obvious; Golden Yellow contrast stitching was a no-cost option, which was carried over to the headrest logo. Black leather trim abounded elsewhere, set off by the carbonfibre package, GT Sport steering wheel with contrast stitching, and an alloy shift lever; a limited edition badge above the glovebox and carbonfibre treadplates added exclusivity. There wasn't much left to specify other than a few minor leather trim details, such as fuse box covers, and sunvisors in Alcantara to match the standard headlining. A four-piece leather luggage set was available, along with a matching titanium Porsche Design chronograph.

Regular options were few and far between: A front axle lift facility, rear wiper, privacy glass, the Porsche Active Safe and LCA systems, Porsche Entry & Drive, a garage door opener, the Burmester sound system, a speed limit warning gadget for the PCM unit, passenger-side map net, fire extinguisher, carbonfibre footmats, and an upgraded tracking system.

A couple of months after the launch, a special carbonfibre wheel was offered for the Turbo S Exclusive model only – a seven-spoke design that

Interior of a Turbo S Exclusive model pictured at the factory. This car has the contrast stitching, which was actually an option (albeit a no-cost one).

The handcrafted carbonfibre wheels that were offered as an option for the Turbo S Exclusive model; the carbon weave was left exposed, by the way. Note the 'Porsche Exclusive Manufaktur' front wing badges.

The exotic carbonfibre insert on the Turbo S Exclusive's engine cover, seen here with a matching Porsche Design watch. Another special mechanical timepiece was created for the GT2 RS as well, as it happens.

Design sketch by Woosung Chung for the GT2 RS.

shaved about 20 per cent off the weight of the regular alloys. The only problem is they were fairly nondescript, and cost a hefty €15,232 a set – enough to secure a contemporary Suzuki Celerio in Germany, and still have plenty left over to go on a nice touring holiday with it!

The second new 911 released in June 2017 was the GT2 RS. We'd been down this road a few times before, as it happens, with the GT2 model ultimately being the 911 Turbo equivalent to the GT3 and where it sits in relation to the Carrera line-up (the GT1 was a whole different ball game).

Unveiled at the Goodwood Festival of Speed on 30 June, at the heart of the GT2 RS was a modified version of the 3.8-litre Turbo S six, with significantly larger VTG turbochargers on each bank, and a special cooling system designed to spray water on the intercoolers in order to keep an optimum inlet temperature in peak load conditions (a special water tank was provided in the luggage compartment). In addition, the new air filter design and titanium exhaust system (with a single tailpipe in each corner) ensured free breathing, and also gave a weight saving of 7.5kg (16.5lb). Despite sporting a lower compression ratio (9.0:1), the various changes resulted in the MDH/NA engine pumping out no less than 700bhp, along with the same torque as the Turbo S Exclusive model.

Hooked up to a customised version of the seven-speed PDK transmission (the Type CG1/80, with ratios of 3.91, 2.29, 1.58, 1.18, 0.94, 0.79 and 0.67, combined with a 3.96:1 final-drive), the 1470kg (3234lb) rear-wheel drive GT2 RS could dismiss the 0-60 yardstick in 2.7 seconds before going on to a top speed of 212mph (340km/h). More impressive was the fact that the GT2 RS would go on to break the Nürburgring-Nordschleife production car lap record with a time of six minutes and 47.3 seconds, taking almost five seconds off the previous record, and on stock UHP tyres, too.

Naturally, keeping such performance in check calls for a well-sorted chassis. The PSM stability management and PTV systems were fine-tuned, and the ball-jointed and adjustable active suspension with rear axle steering made the most of the Michelin ZR-rated rubber – 265/35s on 20in aluminium alloy rims up front, and 325/30s on larger diameter 21in wheels at the back. The huge footprint helped the standard PCCB braking system do its job properly as well, of course.

The body styling was a case of form following function in its purest sense. The front air dam and bumper moulding was plain and simple, with huge openings finished with titanium-coloured mesh grilles to maximise the flow of cooling air. The lip spoiler extended into the leading edge of the front wheelarch, but in a more dramatic fashion than with the GT3 RS released a couple of years beforehand.

Between the bi-xenon headlights, there was a slit cut into the front apron, as per the GT3 RS (albeit with a carbonfibre dressing piece), and the latter model also provided the carbonfibre front wings and front lid, although the aforementioned panel, left unpainted, now had NACA ducts on either side of its central groove to improve brake cooling. More GT3 RS parts were found in the magnesium alloy roof and rocker panels, with additional carbonfibre parts used for the intake dressing pieces on the rear wings, just aft of the door handles, and the shells of the SportDesign mirrors. The side and rear windows were made of lightweight glass to save a few more grammes, and the stick-on decals on the doors were repeated on the tail with the same gallant aim in mind.

Incidentally, the ten-spoke centre-lock wheels were painted in White Gold

The 700bhp engine of the GT2 RS, seen in partial cutaway guise and when placed in situ.

reserved for the tail-end. The huge adjustable carbonfibre rear wing looked similar to the GT3 RS one, with the same vent in the carbonfibre 'ducktail' element, but it was actually slightly different, with restyled end pieces on the upper spoiler (left with exposed weave) and modified forged aluminium mounts. The carbonfibre air scoop insert in the engine cover was also new, largely following the lead of the contemporary GT3, but far more intricate.

Moving down, naturally the rear combination lamps were of the 991.2 variety, coming with a dark lens effect, while the hefty black rear apron served as both a trailing edge of the rear wheelarch and an exhaust surround. As mentioned earlier, there was a single large bore gloss as standard, but a silver, stain black or Platinum finish could be specified; the same options were available for the lightweight magnesium alloy rims supplied in the Weissach Package, too, as it happens, while the PCCB calipers were back to their usual yellow hue.

The biggest styling changes were

Front and rear views of the GT2 RS in regular guise (without the Weissach Package detailing, in other words). Priced at €285,220 including taxes, the GT2 RS was the most powerful street-legal 911 ever built, and the only rear-wheel drive Turbo variant available during the 991 run.

The alloy wheels released with the 700bhp machine, seen here in White Gold – the standard finish.

tailpipe in each corner, while titanium mesh grilles covered the hot air outlets each side of them. It should be mentioned that the central outlet was placed quite high up compared to the GT3 variants, due to the modified underbody panelling and diffuser.

Inside, black leather formed the starting point for the trim, with red Alcantara used for the seat inserts (full buckets were standard, made from carbonfibre), door furniture, the centre cubby lid, the steering wheel rim, and the headlining. While black Alcantara was used on the gearshift and to cover the area left bare by the absence of the rear seats, red seatbelts and door release pulls set off the carbonfibre trim used on the centre console, dash and door cappings, as well as the model-specific treadplates. An interesting touch was the red or black stripes painted on the PDK selector baseplate, and the titanium-coloured tachometer face. The PCM communications unit was standard, along with air-conditioning, although the former could be deleted via the P98 option code, and the latter the 574 one.

Incidentally, the GT2 RS could be painted in one of the four solid colours, or the GT Silver, Chalk, Miami Blue and Lava Orange shades according to the catalogue, although the Exclusive option was always there for those wanting a unique hue.

Another way of securing a unique look was to order the €25,000 plus tax P70 Weissach Package. This replaced the magnesium alloy roof panel with a fractionally lighter carbonfibre one and, to add interest, a central bar was painted on the front lid, with exposed carbon weave surrounding it, while the new roof was painted in the centre and edges only to match. Also included were forged magnesium alloy wheels that looked a little like the 'Turbo S' rims from the time, saving 11.4kg (25lb), carbonfibre anti-roll bar assemblies, 'Porsche' lettering on the upper face of the rear wing, a titanium rear roll cage (12kg/26lb lighter than the Clubsport version, but deleted via the 808 option code if not required), red six-point seatbelts (full buckets or the P03 seats were required), special 'Weissach Package' logos repeated throughout the interior, and exposed carbonfibre detailing on the steering wheel spokes and shift paddles.

Other options included the Sport Chrono setup, cruise control, a bigger fuel tank, the front axle lift system, LED headlights, automatic dimming mirrors, black door handles and/or mirrors, badge deletion, carbonfibre window triangle pieces, extended leather trim parts, contrast stitching on the regular RS trim, a black and red leather trim package, black leather with black Alcantara upholstery (with or without red contrast stitching), black leather on the steering wheel rim and gear selector, black leather door capping inserts, an alloy pedal set, P03 or P07 seats, seat heating, coloured seatbelts, coloured gauge dials, painted interior components, Alcantara sunvisors and embossed centre console lids, the Bose sound system, a passenger-side net, fire extinguisher, illuminated door guards, carbonfibre floormats, and the familiar Clubsport Package, which was available as a no-cost option on the GT2 RS (six-point seatbelts to go with it were an extra, however).

Writing this book, it's fair to say there has been one headache after another on the research front. According to the parts catalogue, the GT2 RS didn't

The rather busy standard interior of the GT2 RS. More subtle colouring was available for those wanting it.

A GT2 RS with the Weissach Package, readily identified by its striking paintwork and magnesium alloy wheels.

Interior of a car with the Weissach Package – the plaque above the glovebox confirming this to be the case in the dashboard picture, while the second image leaves us in little doubt with regard to what we're looking at.

have a distinct set of chassis numbers, although they did in reality – 'AD' in the North American code becoming 'AE,' for instance, to cover the engine specification changes. It's something worth bearing in mind anyway.

Most magazine testers were in awe of this latest Stuttgart creation, many struggling to put into words the sheer brute force of the beast. *Top Gear* stated at the time of the launch that "it feels like technology has caught up with the concept … Tyres, throttle and stability control plus turbo management have honed (but not tamed) the GT2's historic wildness. The result is a sensationally fast car, one that's also far sharper, more drivable and controllable than it has any right to be. It doesn't feel electronically managed either, not for a second, but wonderfully mechanical."

Interestingly, *Autocar* noted: "The GT2 RS is a spectacular driver's car, but it isn't quite the ultimate GT derivative – a GT3 has more absorbing handling and an engine you'd treasure for longer. This is the proof, however glorious, that the 911 strays narrowly out of its depth when it tries to beat hardcore supercars at their own game."

The saying that you can have too much of a good thing springs to mind. Notwithstanding, looking down the production numbers, it's remarkable that of the 35,000 or so 911s built in the 2018 Model Year, over one-third of them were exotica – 6098 GT3s, along with 3397 RS versions, plus a further 3336 GT2 RS models (three of them being Clubsport spec). In addition, no less than 452 GT3 Cup machines were built – 164 more than the 2016 and 2017 totals put together.

One had to wonder how much longer petrolheads would be able to get their fix, though. While Porsche was quick to mention its GT racing campaign would continue, the company also announced it was ending its LMP1 involvement in the World Endurance Championship and preparing to enter the Formula E arena instead come the 2019 season. Add in the Mission E project and governments listening to the battle cry of the 'Green' brigade, and the future looked a little bleak to say the least …

The 2017 Frankfurt Show

Running from 14-24 September (with two press days beforehand), the 67th IAA provided the recently-unveiled third generation Cayenne with its public debut, as well as the 911 GT2 RS, as it happens, as there had been no major shows since its surprise announcement on 30 June. However, the marketing folks saw the Frankfurt Show as an opportunity to introduce yet another 991.2 variant – the 911 GT3 with Touring Package.

Available only on the six-speed manual version of the GT3 (specifications and pricing remained unchanged on the base vehicle, with only the emissions and fuel consumption ratings adjusted slightly), the biggest change when specifying the NCO Touring Package was the removal of the fixed rear spoiler, replacing it with an adaptive one instead.

In more detail, the 032 version of the Touring Package included a new engine cover insert with a mesh grille and 'GT3 Touring' badge, a Carrera-style rear spoiler with a small colour-keyed Gurney flap on its trailing edge, chrome exhausts, the deletion of the 'GT3' badge on the tail, bright side window trim instead of black, regular Carrera lighting units, chrome headlight washer nozzles, and a two-tone Porsche crest on the wheel centres. Inside, the seats were given a black fabric insert and Porsche crest on the headrests, while the Alcantara usually found on the steering wheel rim, gearlever, door furniture and centre console box lid was replaced with leather; stitching came in black rather than silver-grey. In addition, the dashboard trim, door cappings and gear surround were executed in black anodised brushed aluminium (along with the treadplate insert), and the rear centre tunnel gained some carpeting. Leather door cappings, leather sunvisors, and an embossed Porsche crest on the cubby lid were available as stand-alone options for the Touring Package.

Meanwhile, the 039 Touring Package (also free of charge) was basically the same, except dark-tinted light units were fitted at both ends, and the tailpipes went back to being black, as did the window trim, washer nozzles, and 'Porsche' lettering at the back.

Apart from a handful of Alcantara parts being dropped, the option list remained the same for vehicles equipped with the Touring Package. As it happens, a few new items had crept onto the list since the GT3's debut six months earlier, including an XGT wheel option (satin black paint with a red coachline on the outboard flange), leather trim on the steering column, leather upholstery for the backs of the sports seats, leather on the rear centre tunnel, and (from January 2018) blue seatbelts.

Export round-up

With so many model variations coming at staggered intervals, it's time to catch up with the export market situation before another batch of vehicles makes it into the showrooms, for – almost unbelievably – there were still more to come before the 991-series finally ran its course.

In the States, 2018 Model Year 911 prices started at $91,100, which was a figure doubtless chosen by someone sporting a wry smile. What it did mean, though, was that the cost of Porsche motoring had not increased to any significant extent, although the chances of driving a car away for that kind of money was remote, given the reams of paper used to describe the tempting array of options.

As mentioned earlier, people seemed to be plumping for models higher up the range anyway – easy credit and low interest rates presumably having a bearing on the model mix. For 2018, there was certainly plenty of choice, including the newcomers to the GT line.

Despite being displayed at the 2017 New York Show (held in April), the 2018 version of the GT3 was not available in America until the autumn of 2017, thereby justifying its MY classification. With GT3 prices starting at $143,600, it was actually pretty good value, and made all the more attractive when the first of the Touring Package models arrived Stateside in early 2018 with no additional cost over the standard car, as per Germany.

For those that really wanted to impress the neighbours, there was always the $257,500 Turbo S Exclusive, or for those that were willing to wait until the start of 2018 to take delivery, the GT2 RS, which commanded a whopping $293,200. Being more sensible for everyday use, there was always the Carrera T, but we'll come to that in a moment ...

In Britain, everything was ticking along gently, with a slight price increase for 2018 – no-one could moan, in reality, as they'd remained the same since the spring of 2016. With prices starting at £77,891, forking out a little more could have secured a special limited run model for the UK market known as the 'British Legends Edition' (available from early October 2017).

Based on the Carrera 4 GTS coupé and priced at just over £120,000 apiece, these cars were finished in Guards Red, Carrara White or Sapphire Blue, and came with a host of options fitted as standard, including chassis upgrades and the SportDesign exterior goodies. The main point was to celebrate the achievements of a British racing driver, so each car came with a signed B-post badge – that of Richard Attwood on red cars, Nick Tandy on white ones, and

The catalogue pages added to the American GT3 brochure to cover the new Touring Package. The model helped US 911 sales to hold steady, and allow another new PCNA record year – up to 55,420 units for 2017.

The blue version of the 'British Legends Edition' pictured with the car that inspired its colour scheme.

Derek Bell on blue machines, each having a connection with that particular shade.

At the top end of the scale, those with £207,506 to spare could have gone for the flagship GT2 RS model, or alternatively bought five basic 718 Caymans in a selection of colours!

There were no surprises in Australia and Japan, with model releases keeping in time with the events unfolding in Stuttgart – unfolding at quite a pace, too, with the Carrera T being announced on 22 October 2017 as another 2018 model ...

The Carrera T
Based on the strict Carrera coupé, the T grade (with the 'T' standing for Touring) was an interesting model, with a similar concept to the GT3's Touring Package – sporting, but less showy – and in this case, added performance through a reduction in weight.

The 370bhp six was left untouched, hooked up to a 7MT gearbox as standard, but with a PDK transmission still offered as an option. The manual gearbox was pushed as the way to go, however, coming with a stubbier gearlever with an embossed shift pattern in red, a shorter final-drive ratio (the S grade's 3.59:1), and a mechanical lsd via the PTV setup to enhance the driving experience; the PDK version had the regular shifter and retained the 3.44:1 final-drive found on the other C2 models.

Chassis upgrades included the lowered 030 PASM Sport suspension not usually available on the 991.2 version of the strict Carrera, which also brought with it a heavier front lip spoiler. Rear axle steering, something else restricted to the S as a rule, was available on the T as an option, while 20in 'Carrera S' wheels were made part of the standard package, finished in a Titanium colour.

As well as the different front spoiler profile, Agate Grey-painted SportDesign mirrors added another feature, with the same colour used on the engine cover slats and tail badges; the model-specific door stripes were a take it or leave it thing. A sports exhaust system with black tailpipes rounded off the exterior differences, although it should be noted that lightweight glass was used for the rear and side windows (unless you ticked the 540 option box to bring back normal glazing).

Black leather was chosen for the interior, with the four-way P05 seats coming with Sport-Tex fabric inserts; gloss black trim was used in place of Galvanosilver parts, and a leather-wrapped GT Sport steering wheel was made a standard fitment. In keeping with the lightweight theme, black fabric loops replaced the inner door releases, while sparser sound-deadening material allowed the engine note to filter through to the cockpit in a less restricted fashion.

Surprise, surprise, as well as the majority of regular items, there were specific options available for the T model: Specifying full bucket seats was combined with the deletion of the rear

A 911 GT3 pictured at the 2017 Tokyo Motor Show, priced at 21,150,000 yen in 6MT or PDK guise, but with lhd only. For the record, the contemporary manual Carrera coupé (the entry-level 911) was listed at 12,440,000 yen (with left- or right-hand drive), while the flagship GT2 RS (also lhd or rhd) was a whopping 36,560,000 yen.

The Carrera T making its show debut at the LA Show at the end of 2017. Only a few were built in the 2017 Model Year, but the number soon leapt to 2669 units in the 2018 MY.

A useful catalogue page showing a manual Carrera T with the yellow version of the Carrera T Interior Package.

seats (secured via the P11 code) in America, although the rear seats could be deleted on their own in most other countries (the first time this option had been offered on a modern Carrera), while the Carrera T Interior Package (090) brought with it contrast colouring – the seatbelts, stitching, the '911' logo on the headrests, pinstripes on the seat inserts and door opening loops could be ordered in yellow, red or silver rather than the stock black hue. Hardcore enthusiasts looking to ditch weight and complication could also choose whether to have the PCM unit or not as well.

Tail of the Carrera T. Much was made of the links with the 911T of the past in promotional material, but the new car was of a far higher calibre than its namesake – the original car had been little more than an entry-level model, in reality. Using the 'Touring' moniker in full would have probably been a better idea.

Available in the four standard 911 solid colours, plus Jet Black Metallic, Carrara White, GT Silver, Miami Blue and Lava Orange, the 1425kg (3135lb) Carrera T was priced at €107,553 including taxes.

Car & Driver called the Carrera T "purist perfection," while the folks at *Top Gear* wondered if the other 20-odd 911s were really necessary such was the all-round ability of this newcomer. Having remarked on the £7500 premium over the regular Carrera coupé in a dubious manner at the offset, by the end of the magazine's test, it's value for money was no longer questioned: "It's terrific," they said. Being totally frank, it would be the author's 911 of choice, too ...

In the export markets, the first batch of Carrera Ts was expected to arrive in the USA in March 2018 (two months behind Germany), with the model priced at $102,100. Many of the major outlets had received the T by that time, with most of the right-hand drive countries being furnished with Carrera Ts by the end of the year.

The 2017 racing season

While the LMP1 field was dwindling fast in the World Endurance Championship, with Audi gone and no-one stepping up to take its place, Porsche built some cars to fend off Toyota's challenge, and made a real effort on the GT front.

New LM-GTE regulations were exploited to the limit on a new version of the 911 RSR, with every aspect of the vehicle overhauled. First, the 3996cc NA flat-six was tuned to deliver a few more horses (around 510bhp was quoted), and then turned around so that the layout went from an RR one to an MR one, with the six-speed transmission now sticking out the back rather than the engine, just like a Cayman.

Indeed, the styling would have reminded onlookers of a Cayman GT4 on steroids. The aggressive aerodynamic package (with bulging wheelarches joined at the bottom via an extension of the flat underbody) was crowned by a huge rear wing and diffuser unit. Even the mirrors were shaped with the ultimate in efficiency in mind, such was

A 911, but not as we know it ... The mid-engined RSR developed for the 2017 racing season. Inside, in line with contemporary motorsport practice, the cockpit looked more like the control room of a spaceship than a traditional 911.

the care and attention to detail after a rather poor GT showing in 2016.

Steel brake discs were retained, hidden by 18in forged alloys shod with Michelin racing rubber. Tipping the scales at 1243kg (2735lb), initially seven cars were built, including three for testing, two for the IMSA campaign, and two for the WEC.

With regard to the latter, thanks to a new contract with Manthey Racing, it was back to a two-car factory-run equipe known as the Porsche GT Team (the same name as used in the States, as it happens), which would stay in place over the next few seasons; Dempsey-Proton Racing returned to the GTE-Am category.

Unfortunately, while Porsche won the LMP1 championship (conquering Le Mans along the way), as well as the drivers' title to go with it, the new RSR's career got off to a painfully slow start, failing to pick up any wins and leaving the Stuttgart maker in third place in the manufacturers' league table (Ferrari took the GTE honours, with Ford in second place).

Across the Atlantic, CORE Autosport would run the IMSA WeatherTech Sports car Championship programme on behalf of PCNA, using the Porsche GT Team moniker (the same as that used for the World Endurance Championship equipe) for the GTLM campaign. The regular drivers were Patrick Pilet and Dirk Werner in number 911, and Kevin Estre and Laurens Vanthoor in 912.

As always, the season kicked off with the Daytona 24-hour Race. Suspension trouble delayed one car, but the Pilet/Werner/Makowiecki machine was second in Class, giving the new RSR a fine debut; the GT3R of Alegra Motorsports won the GTD category, adding a little icing to the cake. However, the celebrations didn't last long, for, although they were fast, the works RSRs finished seventh and eighth at Sebring after a run of bad luck.

Estre and Vanthoor put their car on the podium at Long Beach, but had to settle for eighth in Texas; Pilet and Werner were fourth in Class. With Detroit for GTD models only, the works machines weren't out again until Watkins Glen, by which time Daniel Armbruster had taken Jens Walther's place as the head of the PMNA operation that sold and serviced racing cars in the States.

Gianmaria Bruni stepped into Estre's shoes at the Glen, finishing sixth in GTLM with Vanthoor, one place ahead of the works sister car, but BMW's win knocked Porsche down to fourth in the standings, and any thoughts of fighting for the Endurance Cup were best forgotten if one was to be realistic. Despite starting on pole and clocking a

Patrick Pilet and Dirk Werner giving the new RSR its first ever victory at Lime Rock.

A 911 leading the field in the Spa 24-hour Race.

fastest lap, the RSR's finishing positions were the same in Canada.

At last, everything came good at Lime Rock, with the 510bhp works cars first and second in GTLM, and the 500bhp GT3R of Park Place Motorsports winning the GTD Class into the bargain. An accident at Elkhart Lake dropped the number 911 car down the field, but number 912 was second. A poor result at Virginia, where Porsche just couldn't seem to get on the pace, was followed by a third at Laguna Seca.

Despite only taking fifth and sixth in GTLM at Road Atlanta, somehow Patrick Pilet and Dirk Werner scored just enough to secure the North American Endurance Cup title, with Porsche second in the maker's division. It went quite a long way towards making up for Porsche trailing Chevrolet, BMW and Ford in the regular IMSA season.

In the other big events, the Nürburgring 24-hour Race didn't go to plan, with the top Porsche (a 911 GT3R) finishing in sixth overall. Meanwhile, the European Blancpain GT Series attracted just one Porsche team to the Pro Cup (which duly entered just one race), and another to the Pro-Am version in the endurance championship. It was a disappointing season, full stop. On the sprint side of the equation, Klaus Bachler and Kevin Estre entered one round as professionals, but only succeeded in making up the numbers.

The European Le Mans Series was still going – the ACO's desire to be seen as independent as strong as ever, despite its involvement with the FIA WEC. A handful of LMGTE cars supported the LMP2 and LMP3 machines that were the series' main attraction, but with only one 911 amongst them, run by Proton Competition. This duly won its Class in the final round of the ELMS season, but the Ferraris were hard to beat this year.

Further afield, the Pirelli World Challenge (sanctioned by the USAC rather than the SCCA from 2017) provided Porsche with the perfect arena in which to shine. Patrick Long was crowned GT champion driving a GT3R for Wright Motorsports, while the GTA category was dominated by 911 pilots – James Sofronas of GMG Racing came out ahead in the end.

Having largely given the inaugural year a miss, Porsche duly joined the Intercontinental GT Challenge for 2017, backing the Walkinshaw GT3 team with technical assistance and drivers (Bamber, Estre and Vanthoor), along with the Competition Motorsports GT3R (Long and Lieb). The Walkinshaw machine was involved in an accident, but

High-speed VLN action in Germany. Fred Makowiecki and Lars Kern won this late-October round of the series with their GT3R.

the other was second overall, and winner of the Class A Pro-Am Class.

Fourth in the Pro category was the best the GT3R drivers could do in the Spa 24-hour Race. Porsche made a big effort for the Laguna Seca round, even fielding the PMNA cars, but the Audis ruled supreme. With the Sepang 12-hour Race cancelled due to a lack of entries, that brought the IGTC series to a premature end, and Audi was able to take the GT3 title with ease. At least the GT4 crown went Stuttgart's way thanks to the Cayman contingent.

There were only two 911s in the

Michael Ammermüller pictured during a quiet moment.

Japanese Super GT series for 2017, scoring three third places between them over the year. In fact, it was the same teams representing the Stuttgart brand for 2018 as well, but that year there was only one podium finish to their credit. Things got worse again in 2019, with one car and a string of bad results. Different team, same story in 2020 and 2021, until they moved over to the Toyota Supra for 2022, with no more Porsche outfits to take their place.

The battle for this year's Porsche Supercup (2017 being the first season to employ the Type 991.2 GT3 Cup model) went right down to the wire, with Matt Campbell making an impressive late charge, but Michael Ammermüller doing just enough to beat Dennis Olsen in the end – the German driver finished the season on 193 points, seven clear of Olsen. Ammermüller, who had a single-seater career behind him, would ultimately go on to win the Supercup title again in 2018 and 2019.

The GT3 RS

The various triumphs of the LMP1 cars had done a good job of masking the distinct lack of silverware garnered by the new RSRs in the WEC and IMSA arenas. As such, Porsche's hard-earned reputation for motorsport superiority remained intact, and provided the perfect sales pitch for the latest 911 production car – the rear-wheel drive GT3 RS ...

Announced on 20 February 2018, just ahead of its public debut at the Geneva Show, the new GT3 RS was the third road-legal Porsche GT model to be unveiled within a year, and had the honour of becoming the most powerful series-production normally-aspirated 911 to date.

Closely based on the 4-litre engine in the 2018 GT3, with all the same leading specifications, the MDG/GB unit used in the RS version released an additional 20bhp, and a little more torque to boot. Developed under Thomas Mader, the biggest changes came via a new titanium exhaust system, and a ram air arrangement like that of the GT2 RS. As such, the new GT3 RS had intakes cut into the leading edge of the rear wings like its immediate predecessor, and a new engine cover insert to suit, with the view under the latter lid being quite different to the regular GT3 one, and that of the GT2 RS for that matter.

Oliver Blume presenting the new GT3 RS to press members at the 2018 Geneva Show, which also witnessed the debut of the Mission E Cross Turismo model. The striking Lizard Green hue was used as a signature colour for this latest GT car.

The view greeting folks who lifted the lid above the GT3 RS's engine – very different to that of the strict GT3 model, which had the two fans in the centre, and huge, featureless pieces of square trunking each side of them. The RS unit developed 520bhp, along with 347lbft of torque. For the record, although the output remained unchanged, from May 2019, maximum power was developed at 8400rpm rather than 8250, and torque peaked at 6250rpm instead of 6000.

Front and rear shots of the new GT3 RS finished with Chalk paintwork. With its large rear wing, the GT3 RS produced significantly more downforce than the strict GT3 once speeds increased to a certain level.

The GT3 RS came with a PDK transmission only, sporting familiar internal ratios of 3.75, 2.38, 1.72, 1.34, 1.11, 0.96 and 0.84, but in this case combined with a shorter 4.19:1 final-drive. The PDK's dual clutches were still 202mm (7.9in) and 153mm (6.0in) in diameter, incidentally, as they had been on the original 991 GT3 of 2013 vintage, and, as per the strict GT3, came with PTV Plus as standard; the Chrono Package, however, remained on the option list.

The chassis was largely GT3 fare, with the regular GT3 brakes and the PCCB system as an option. However, there were new helper springs at the front-end, a recalibrated rear axle steering system, and the larger wheel and tyre combination found on the GT2 RS was employed: forged 9.5J x 20 alloys with 265/35 rubber up front, and 12.5J x 21 rims shod with 325/30s at the back were borrowed from the 700bhp model, but in this case finished in a satin Aurum colour as standard with an 'RS' logo in the black wheel centre. For those wanting the ultimate in unsprung weight, the GT2 RS-type mag-alloys were available as an option.

With styling work overseen by Peter Varga, the GT3 RS was largely a mix and match job. It had the polyurethane apron off the strict 2018 GT3, the carbonfibre front lid and wings from the GT2 RS, the 'double bubble' magnesium alloy roof off the GT2 RS, the rear wings via the GT2 RS (with black plastic intakes rather than carbonfibre ones, as per the front wing vanes in order to keep costs in check), the rear apron off the current GT3, and the engine cover and rear wing from the GT2 RS, albeit with a different, rather plain grille insert and re-profiled matt black titanium endplates on the upper spoiler.

The SportDesign mirrors were colour-keyed, like the regular GT3, but the rear and side windows were produced in lightweight glass (a privacy version was available via the XPS option code). Hefty model-specific decals adorned the lower part of the doors, although their deletion was possible, along with the one on the tail if desired. In keeping with the motorsport image, niceties like painted rocker panels, headlight washer nozzle colouring and black door handles were gone, as well as some of the older and less efficient lighting options.

The GT3 RS had its own colour schemes, incidentally. The four solid paint options found on most other 911s were there, plus Lizard Green (the new car's signature colour), Lava Orange, GT Silver, Chalk and Miami Blue.

Inside, the two-seater layout was typical Porsche GT, as was the black leather trim with silver-grey detailing, and Alcantara on the door furniture, centre box lid and headlining. Full bucket seats were standard (black leather with matching Alcantara inserts), although P03 and P07 seats could be specified free of charge, and seat heating was okay on these; the standard seatbelts were supplied in silver-grey.

The GT Sport steering wheel came with shift paddles, Alcantara on the rim and a yellow 12-o'clock marker, while silver-grey fabric door pulls and carbonfibre interior trim parts like those found on the GT2 RS continued the sporting theme. The PCM and eight-speaker sound system was fitted as standard, but it could be deleted, as per the regular GT3; the air-conditioning could also be ditched via the 574 option code. Reduced sound-deadening material also helped shave a few more grammes off the kerb weight.

Ultimately, everything combined to create a 1430kg/3146lb car that could dismiss the 0-60 dash in three seconds dead (fractionally faster than its predecessor) according to the press release, and could boast a catalogued top speed of 195mph (312km/h).

Priced at €195,137 including German taxes, options were largely the same as those for the regular GT3, except the Touring Package wasn't listed. A big

Interior options for the new GT3 RS, with the Weissach Package (or WP) adding new logos on seat headrests and a plaque on the dashboard.

change, though, was the availability of the GT2 RS model's Weissach Package, which then allowed the buyer to upgrade to magnesium alloy wheels (452) if they wished. Unlike the GT2 RS version of the WP, which carried the same option code, the wheels were separated on this model, with the no roll cage option (808) being dealt the same situation. It all added up to the same in the end, with the P70 bundle at €17,850 including VAT and the mag-alloys at €11,900. It should be noted also, that the front lid, roof, rear wing and mirrors were left unpainted on the GT3 RS with Weissach Package, at least according to official paperwork. However, with Porsche's mad level of Exclusive options (including the PTS one), this may help to explain why the author has seen quite a few GT3 RSs for sale with the lined GT2 RS WP-style paintwork.

Of the other changes, an alloy fuel cap was supplied as standard, although the front axle lift system was significantly more expensive than it was on the strict GT3. The Clubsport Package came with black seats and belts plus a regular roll cage, or one painted in Lizard Green. Wheel paint options were still there, but the Aluminium finish was gone, with Aurum taking its place (strangely, Aurum gold was listed as standard in German literature, but still noted down as a cost item), and the red coachline on the black wheel option (XGT) was replaced by a bright green on black one (XGS).

Most of the existing interior trim packages were not available on the RS. Instead, various new extended leather packages were listed in black, with 11 choices of contrast stitching, or, for the really adventurous, there was a Black/Lizard Green upholstery option, which came with green seat inlays and detailing. The option of green seatbelts was a new thing, and the red interior parts colouring offered on the GT3 became green on the RS. Otherwise, even cruise control was still available!

Works driver Kevin Estre teamed up with Lars Kern to set a Nürburgring-Nordschleife lap time some 24 seconds faster than that posted by the previous GT3 RS model, which is truly remarkable. Borrowing so much of its technology from the motorsport programme, one

Another good day at the Nürburgring ...

shouldn't be surprised, but 24 seconds is an eternity in racing ...

The fast lap was made possible by the ease with which one could use all the power, and this was noted on numerous occasions in the various road tests that followed. As *Motor Trend* stated: "The focus of the RS is readily apparent and freakishly accessible. Never did it feel threatening or edgy." Having it for the odd track days would be a must, though, according to the writer, who used the comparison of buying a powerboat as something to go fishing with. On the other hand, several magazines said it was "livable around town" as long as one bought the front axle lift option to make it more practical in everyday situations. Exceptional sales would point to it being an acceptable compromise, at least, which is exactly where the PASM suspension comes into its own.

Springtime in Stuttgart

With the coming of spring 2018, the main 911 colour chart was simplified a little. The Rhodium Silver, Sapphire Blue, and Graphite Blue paint shades were dropped; the Saddle Brown trim option also fell by the wayside, but otherwise things remained the same.

A new GT3 RS photographed at the works, this car having the optional Weissach Package. As one can see, the 'correct' colouring, as seen in the catalogues, is quite different to that of the equivalent GT2 RS.

Standard colour & trim guide

These colour variations were available on mainstream Carreras from April 2018 to the end of 991 production. Please see the text for variations applied to other model lines and specials.

Solid coachwork colours
Black (041), White (C9A), Guards Red (80K), and Racing Yellow (1S1).

Metallic coachwork colours
Jet Black Metallic (C9X), Agate Grey Metallic (M7S), GT Silver Metallic (M7Z), Carrara White Metallic (S9R), and Night Blue Metallic (M5F).

Special coachwork colours
Chalk (M9A), Lava Orange (M2A), Carmine Red (M3C), and Miami Blue (M5C). A 'colour to sample' option was also available.

Hood (convertible top) colours
Black, Red, Blue, and Brown. Hood always lined in black.

Leatherette (vinyl) trim
Black, and Agate Grey. Carpeting and floormats came in matching hues, as did the headlining.

Leather trim
Black, and Agate Grey. Carpeting and floormats came in matching hues, as did the headlining.

Regular two-tone leather trim
Graphite Blue with Chalk, Black with Bordeaux Red, and Black with Luxor Beige. Carpeting and floormats came in the lighter shade, with the roofliner in the darker one.

Sport-Tex leather and cloth trim
Black/Black with dark silver contrast stitching, and Chalk leather with Graphite Blue inserts.

Special leather colours and natural leather trim
Graphite Blue, Bordeaux Red, Espresso, and two-tone Espresso with Cognac. Carpeting and floormats came in matching hues; the roofliner was black on the red option, or blue and brown to match the trim. A 'colour to sample' option was also available.

The Touring Package for the GT3 had brought leather on the rear centre tunnel (XZM) onto the regular 911 option list, along with Miami Blue seatbelts. The other new option released at around this time was an exterior package that brought with it window frame trim in gloss black.

Meanwhile, on the corporate front, Matthias Müller stepped down as Volkswagen's CEO in the spring of 2018, with Dr Herbert Diess (a brand manager quoted as being "a man of action" in *The Guardian*) taking his place in early April; Oliver Blume continued to head the Porsche camp, though.

A few weeks later, on 11 May, Porsche announced its latest GT motorsport challenger – the 2019 model GT3R. Making more effort in the GT arena certainly made sense, for the LMP1 programme was officially dead, and the Stuttgart maker had started building mid-engined RSRs for customer use. At a cool €991,000 apiece, the 510bhp machines needed to start earning their keep, and concentrating on one discipline until the Formula E excursion kicked off seemed to be a good way forward. Sending four works RSRs to Le Mans was a positive sign that would ultimately be handsomely rewarded …

An Evolution package had been created for GT3R runners in 2018, as it happens. However, the announcement of a new model – arriving in plenty of time to prepare for the 2019 season – must have been welcomed by the various teams around the world that remained loyal to the brand.

Based on the latest RS model, the GT3R's 4-litre DFI engine delivered up to 550bhp through a six-speed sequential gearbox and mechanical lsd (with a traditional 911 RR layout). Sporting a wild aerodynamic package, the body panels were almost exclusively carbonfibre, with polycarbonate windows to further reduce weight, while 18in BBS alloys covered meaty 390mm/15.3in and 370mm/14.6in diameter steel brake discs, serviced by an updated ABS system for enhanced precision. With a full, ultra-modern race-spec interior and air jacks, as well as the latest safety features and kits available

Cover of the German catalogue for the GT3 R racer. Other language editions exist, all with the same content.

to suit FIA endurance or IMSA races, the new GT3R came in white only, and was listed at €459,000 plus taxes.

Then, on 8 June, as part of the company's '70 Years of Porsche Sports Cars' anniversary celebrations, the 911 Speedster Concept model was unveiled at an event in Stuttgart-Zuffenhausen. Evoking memories of its namesake from the past, especially the 993 version, the C4 Cabriolet-based machine came with a 4-litre GT3 engine hooked up to a six-speed manual gearbox, and 21in centre-lock Fuchs-style alloys. Four months later, when a second Speedster Concept model was displayed at the Paris Salon (this time finished in Guards Red, or Indischrot, with new wheels and a different interior), it was announced that the two-seater would go into production in the first half of 2019, limited to 1948 units.

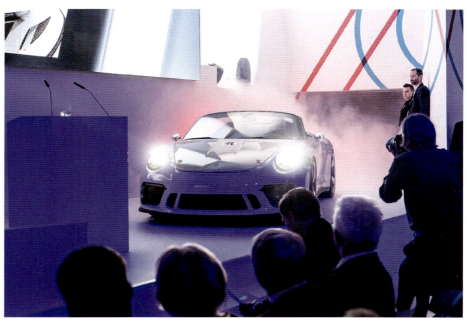

The 911 Speedster Concept being unveiled at the factory, and an overhead view of this rather special machine.

The Speedster Concept II displayed at the Paris Salon in the early part of October 2018.

A 911 GT2 RS-based special was unveiled at the Rennsport Reunion in California in September 2018. Marketed as a tribute to 'Moby Dick' (the famous 935 racer), only 77 of these 700bhp 1380kg/3036lb machines were made available, priced at just over €700,000 apiece. With an 18in racing wheel and tyre combination, they could only be used on the track or private roads, with paintwork according to customer choice.

The 911 Targa 4 GTS Exclusive Manufaktur Edition of October 2018 vintage, with sales restricted to Germany only, sadly.

Only a week later, Porsche released the 911 Targa 4 GTS Exclusive Manufaktur Edition for the home market. Finished in Agate Grey, a lot of the GTS model's black detailing was changed to silver (including the Targa bar and mirror shells) and set off by 'RS Spyder' wheels painted in satin White Gold. Tastefully trimmed in brown leather, with a matching roof panel, the asking price of €187,961 somehow seemed well justified.

Export review

As had become the norm, new models filtered through to export markets as and when, rather than a Model Year range being announced at the start of a specific season, and then largely untouched. Life was certainly a lot easier for historians back in the days of yore, that's for sure.

About the only model we haven't touched on for America so far is the new GT3 RS, which landed in the States in the autumn of 2018, priced at $187,500. On top of this, if the owner wanted to go the whole hog, there was the Weissach Package at $18,000, mag-alloys at $13,000, the PCCB braking system at $9210, the front axle lift facility at $3490, and a bigger fuel tank at $140; deleting the air-conditioning and/or communication setup came FOC.

Incidentally, with regard to the new strict GT3, officially, there was no 2019 model ... Well, there was, with plenty of cars for sale in the States with a 2019 VIN code, some even coming with their original window stickers to add further weight to the statement. After all, if PCNA called it a 2019 MY on paperwork they've issued with the vehicle and the chassis numbers tie-up, then that's exactly what it is.

Anyway, this constant flow of new models and product lines helped PCNA set yet another new sales record at the end of 2018, marking almost a decade of steady growth. With 57,202 units delivered through 190 dealers, the 911 accounted for 9647 sales, with the Macan selling in roughly the same numbers as the 718s, Panamera and Cayenne combined.

Detlev von Platen noted: "The capacity of the 911 to fascinate is stronger than ever." This was not simply marketing hype, for the sales figures backed him up, with only the fashionable SUVs outselling the evergreen icon. Strong growth in China and the Asia-Pacific region saw to it that Porsche as a whole set another record, too, with more than 256,000 global deliveries.

The right-hand drive markets continued to play 'follow the leader' and fell into line with Germany's product releases. Pricing was carried over in Great Britain for the 2019 season proper, but the cost of Porsche motoring was soon set to increase in a big way. In Australia, 911 starting prices stayed at $220,500, and there was no change in Japan either.

Star-struck in LA

Porsche chose the 2018 Los Angeles Show to provide the world première of the 992 series – the latest generation in a long line of 911s. Launched in Carrera S and Carrera 4S coupé guise only at

The 992-series 911 making its debut at the 2018 LA Show. The 2020 Model Year S coupés were released first, followed by S Cabriolets, and then 385bhp models started joining the ranks before a wave of newcomers began flooding the dealerships.

this stage, the styling was very similar to that of the 991, but somehow sharper and more athletic, and the interior was given a thorough makeover. The 450bhp engine was familiar enough, but now hooked up to an eight-speed PDK transmission.

Rather than dwell on the 992, given the amount of space needed for 991 topics, we will leave it at that for now, suffice to say that orders could be placed straight after the car's California debut, with prices starting at €120,125, representing a jump of about €8000 on the equivalent 991.2 Carrera S coupé.

On the following day, it was the turn of the 911 GT2 RS Clubsport to

The 911 GT2 RS Clubsport, expected to reach its first batch of happy owners by May 2019.

take a bow. Limited to 200 units, the 700bhp coupé was given the Clubsport treatment inside (with only one Recaro seat fitted), complete with a number of features borrowed from the new GT3R model, and tipped the scales at 1390kg (3058lb). Although the car wasn't road legal, with racing rubber and the required FIA-approved safety features already in place in its revised catalogue guise, there were hopes the €405,000 machine could be used in SRO-organised events, like the Blancpain GT Series and Intercontinental GT Challenge.

Interestingly, the GT2 RS set a lap record at Road Atlanta, and then captured the one at Road America, too. Not surprisingly, *Which Car?* named it the 'Performance Car of the Year,' but the supercar was making news for other reasons, too, once it was realised that four had gone down with the *Grande America* in the Bay of Biscay, en route to Morocco, in March 2019. Luckily for the owners, Porsche agreed to build replacements for them.

Race digest

If the timing of Model Years in the modern era has you as confused as the author, then the calendar for the World Endurance Championship will have you questioning your sanity. Although F1 and the WRC retained its traditional annual format, for some reason the 2018 WEC season became 2018-19, with certain events held twice. This could have been why Porsche withdrew its LMP1 racer earlier than expected, of course, as the company was eager to prepare for the Formula E campaign, which finally kicked off in November 2019 as far as the Stuttgart maker was concerned. Anyway, to keep things tight, let's start with the 2018 series' that actually happened in that year, then take a look at the 2018-19 WEC season after that.

In IMSA racing, Patrick Pilet, Nick Tandy and Fred 'Mako' Makowiecki were leading the GTLM field at Daytona at one point, but accident repair lost them a lot of time, and eventually they finished eighth in Class, two spots behind their teammates. The GTD category was best forgotten, with the top finisher amongst the 911 GT3Rs coming home 76 laps down on the GTD winner.

Thankfully, things went much better at Sebring, with the number 911 car winning and its stablemate coming third, sandwiching a BMW M8. The celebrations didn't last long, though, for the suspension broke on Bamber while he was leading at Long Beach, and the other works machine had to settle for sixth in Class; the GTD gladiators were still a long way off the pace at this point in the proceedings.

A win for the Bamber/Vanthoor pairing at Mid-Ohio put Porsche at the top of the maker's league table, but the Stuttgart firm dropped to second after

The pair of factory RSRs pictured at Daytona. The team's fortunes would improve once the IMSA circus moved to Sebring.

On the way to victory at the Mid-Ohio circuit ...

recording a third and fourth in the GTLM category at Watkins Glen; bad luck in Ontario dropped the German team down to third. Nothing changed after a third and fifth in Class at Lime Rock, and the GT3Rs were still struggling to make any sort of impact in GTD.

There was a slight change in fortunes at Elkhart Lake, for while the works cars were fourth and fifth, at least Patrick Long and Christina Nielsen claimed GTD honours for the Wright Motorsports outfit. Long and Nielsen got on the podium again in Virginia, but a fifth and DNF were pencilled in against the RSRs. At Laguna Seca, the 911 car went out after a tangle at the start, but number 912 was just 2.5 seconds off a win; Jorg Bergmeister and Patrick Lindsay (Park Place Motorsports) were second in GTD as well, with the GT3R sadly coming good far too late in the season to make a difference.

At the Petit Le Mans, where the works cars sported some retro paintwork, the combination of Pilet/Tandy/Makowiecki proved to be a winning one (in GTLM at least), while a puncture and drive-through penalty cost their teammates dearly, dropping them to sixth in Class, although they finished on the same lap as the other RSR. Notwithstanding, Porsche had had better seasons in the States, with third in GTLM and sixth in GTD being the end result for 2018; Pilet and Tandy missed out on the Endurance Cup by just a single point.

In the other big American series, the Pirelli World Challenge, Scott Hargrove had a great season to come second in the top GT category, while fellow 911 GT3R exponent (and works pilot) Michael Christensen was close behind in third. For the record, a pesky Ferrari 488 GT3 driver was declared the champion.

In the European Le Mans series, Proton Competition ran two 911 RSRs, and EbiMotors and Gulf Racing one

One of the works cars at the Petit Le Mans event, where the opportunity was taken to revive some old Porsche racing livery.

apiece. Although the latter was never really in with a shout, EbiMotors won a round, and both Proton machines took the flag, meaning Porsche claimed the silverware at three of the six rounds that made up the ELMS for 2018. Proton Competition rightfully came out on top of the LMGTE pile at the end of the year.

As usual, the Blancpain GT Series was split 50/50 between endurance and sprint races, with the two disciplines treated as separate championships under a single umbrella. While the Sprint Cup had no Porsche runners, the Endurance Cup had plenty of them, with works interest stronger than ever before – Manthey Racing entered all five rounds with Romain Dumas, Fred Makowiecki and Dirk Werner piloting its 911 GT3R in the Pro Class, while Timo Bernhard, Earl Bamber and Laurens Vanthoor had a similar car for Spa in KÜS livery; Black Swan Racing also ran a GT3R in the famous Belgian 24-hour epic, but in the Pro-Am category. However, despite the star-studded line-up, the results were frankly dreadful all year.

The Intercontinental GT Challenge series was also supported by the works, made up of the Bathurst 12-hour Race, the Spa 24-hour Race (shared with the Blancpain series), the Suzuka 10-hour Race, and the eight-hour event at Laguna Seca. In the Pro category, Manthey Racing would handle the first three rounds, with Wright Motorsports looking after things in California; Black Swan Racing and Craft-Bamboo Racing also had a strong entry. However, Mercedes-Benz and Audi dominated, with Porsche a distant third in the final standings.

After a disappointing 2017 season, the ADAC GT Masters campaign wasn't much kinder to the KÜS outfit this year either, despite the driver roster – Timo Bernhard, Marc Lieb and Kevin Estre assisting Klaus Bachler and Adrien de Leener. However, Mathieu Jaminet and

The Manthey 911 GT3R Evolution pictured at Spa during the Blancpain GT Series. Note that while the front lid was changed via the Evolution package (along with the corner appendages up front), the engine cover was not revised. This is a point worth clarifying, as one particular press release obviously missed something in the translation from German.

Robert Renauer of Precote Herberth Motorsport did just enough to take the drivers' championship by a single point, which was a magnificent achievement ...

The 2018-19 WEC

The first trip of the season to Spa (in May 2018) saw Christensen and Estre guide car 92 into second in the GTE-Pro category, just behind a Ford GT, while Lietz and Bruni (91) were fourth in Class. The 911 RSRs were up with the leaders in the GTE-Am battle, too, so the season started off promisingly enough.

Four works cars were entered at Le Mans, two of them in retro colours aping the Rothmans Group C era livery and the 'Pink Pig' paintwork that was used on 'Big Bertha' in the 1971 race at the Sarthe. While car 94 dropped out with suspension trouble, and 93 had its share of problems, too, the other factory RSRs finished first and second in the GTE-Pro Class; Christian Ried, Matt Campbell and Julien Andlauer won the GTE-Am silverware for the Dempsey-Proton outfit.

The latter combi won their Class again at Silverstone, although the number 91 car was disqualified over its ride height (as were both of the LMP1 Toyotas, as it happens). At least the sister works machine finished on the podium, keeping Porsche at the top of the GTE table. It was off to the Far East for the last two races of 2018, first to Fuji Speedway, then Shanghai. Christensen and Estre duly won their Class in Japan, and the two works cars got on the GTE-Pro podium in China (the GTE-Am runners did well in both events, too).

With the New Year celebrations over, the WEC championship continued with a round at Sebring, held just a day before the IMSA 12-hour classic, which only raises further questions regarding

Robert Renauer (left) and Mathieu Jaminet – winners of the ADAC GT Masters title for 2018.

the FIA's scheduling. Anyway, Lietz and Bruni duly won the GTE-Pro category (the sister car finished a lap behind, fifth in Class), and the Dempsey-Proton team was victorious once more in GTE-Am.

Back to Europe, and a return visit to Spa, this time in May 2019. In crazy weather, including snow at one point, Lietz was unlucky to be handed a drive-through penalty, dropping him down the field to 22nd overall, but the Christensen/Estre car moved into third in Class as a result, sealing the championship title for Porsche. The weekend was made all the sweeter by the Dempsey-Proton team holding off a Ferrari and Aston Martin challenge to score a third straight win in the GTE-Am category.

Starting on 15 June and ending on the following day, Le Mans was included for the second time in the so-called 'Super Season.' Of course, winning the famous 24-hour race was almost as good as winning the world title – it had stood alone for many years before being brought back into the rejuvenated WEC fold. There was also the drivers' crown to think of, so all the stops were pulled out, with another four-car assault. This time, cars 91 and 92 gained some gold striping to replace the regular red one, while 93 and 94 paid tribute to the legendary Brumos equipe ...

The 'Pink Pig' 911 RSR of Christensen/ Estre/Vanthoor taking the flag at Le Mans in June 2018, in the second round of the 2018-19 WEC.

While Christensen and Estre were ninth in Class (with Vanthoor helping), and were thus the last of the four works machines (the others finished second, third and seventh in GTE-Pro), they had done enough to secure the drivers' championship. In addition, Jorg Bergmeister, Patrick Lindsay and Egidio Perfetti won the GTE-Am Class, making them champions of their category, and their Team Project 1 outfit the top team as this strange season finally drew to a close.

A Dempsey-Proton 911 RSR at Fuji Speedway in October 2018.

Michael Christensen (left) and Kevin Estre – world champions for 2018-19.

The Team Project 1 RSR with its drivers (l-r): Jorg Bergmeister, Patrick Lindsay and Egidio Perfetti.

The production Speedster

Developed by Porsche's motorsport department, with two concept display models to whet the appetite and most of the hardware already well-known to fans of the marque, there were few surprises in the production version of the 911 Speedster, which was made available from 7 May 2019.

The engine was borrowed from the GT3, but tuned to give a fraction more power and torque – a 10bhp increase, giving a total of 510bhp DIN at 8400rpm, and 8lbft of additional torque to give 347lbft at 6250rpm. Apart from the adoption of individual throttle bodies to sharpen response, all other leading specifications were carried, although with the loss of the ram air scoops (air was pulled in from a long slit halfway down the rear fairing), the view under the Speedster's engine cover looked a lot like that of the 911R rather than the GT3, coming with new logos on the two metal plates dressing the central intake area.

The Speedster was equipped with a six-speed manual gearbox only, sending drive to the rear wheels through a limited-slip differential included in the PTV system. As well as being able to handle the torque easier, it was also lighter than the 7MT unit, and that was an important point for this model, which incorporated a number of weight-saving ideas, just like the original Speedsters of the fifties.

The chassis components were basically from the GT3 parts bin, although a PCCB braking system was fitted as standard, with traditional yellow calipers being the norm. A front axle lift facility was still an option, however, as was a bigger fuel tank.

Not surprisingly, the front end was borrowed from the GT3, with regular bi-xenon headlights as standard, framing the front lid off the older GT3 RS, with its strong feature line running down the centre; this led back to a lowered windscreen, which was unique to the Speedster.

Around the side, the height of the front screen became even more evident, with a black frame and colour-keyed SportDesign mirrors below. The 20in centre-lock alloy wheels were clearly borrowed from the GT3, being the same size (and shod with the same rubber), but had a coloured Porsche crest in the centre. The standard wheel spec was satin black paint, by the way, although a silver, Aluminium or Platinum finish was available, as well as black with a red coachline.

Continuing back, the twin 'streamliner' fairings positioned behind the seats sat high at their leading edge, butting up to what amounted to a miniature Targa bar (actually a stylised housing for the high-mount brakelight, painted satin black and carrying black 'Speedster' badges) and then tapered back to meld into the tail profile. These distinctive fairings sat above the wider C4-type rear wings, the 1852mm/72.9in overall width they provided being highlighted by a matt black section ahead of the rear wheelarch that doubtless reminded older enthusiasts of the first 911 Turbo.

The carbonfibre fairing panel dominated the view at the back, too, stopping short of the pop-up rear spoiler, the latter being trimmed at its leading edge to provide a place for an elongated black 'Porsche' insert. The dark rear combination lamps and black 'Speedster' badge sat on (and in) a contemporary GT3 rear bumper moulding, with the

The production Speedster, seen here in regular guise (the red car), and with the optional Heritage Design Package. Although the Talbot mirrors and unique alloy wheels from the concept vehicles did not make it through to this stage, most of the features found on the show cars were adopted.

August Achleitner retired as head of 911 development in April 2019, handing the reins to Dr Frank-Steffen Walliser, who'd been heavily involved with Porsche's motorsport programme for a while. Walliser is pictured here raising a trophy at Le Mans.

number plate cut-out shaped to suit local sizing, with dual black exhaust pipes poking out of the centre of the lower insert, as per the GT3.

In keeping with its illustrious Speedster predecessors, the hood was a lightweight affair. To put up the top, the fairing moved up rather like a regular trunk after using a centre console switch to release it; this allowed the hood to be manually pulled forward onto the screen header. Next, the fairing was lowered again, so the 'tails' on the hood could be locked into locating pieces on the side of the fairings, and the switch then locked everything in place. Dropping the hood was basically a reverse of the sequence using a different switch. Incidentally, the hatches on the top of the fairings were there to allow the Cabriolet's roll-over safety mechanism to work unhindered.

Paintwork options were virtually the same as the contemporary Carreras – only Night Blue was not available, with Lizard Green taking its place on the colour palette instead. The fabric hood came in black only.

The black interior featured full bucket seats with a special numbered plaque on the firewall behind them, although the 18-way P07 chairs were available at no extra cost. Full leather trim (along with extended leather components) was an option, as was red contrast stitching (including a red door pull loop to replace the black one, and red logos on the seat headrests), and a red marker on the GT Sport steering wheel rim. The carbonfibre dash, console and door capping pieces were augmented by carbonfibre treadplates, although one could specify a painted interior package if preferred. Air-conditioning and the PCM unit were deleted, but could be put back as NCOs; power windows remained standard.

Coming with a numbered Porsche Design chronograph created specifically to go with each vehicle, €270,000 was the asking price for the basic 1465kg (3223lb) car, with an additional €21,634 needed to secure the Heritage Design Package.

The latter, available on silver cars only, featured a white front mask and wing 'arrow' decoration, older-style Porsche crests, race number roundels, white 'Porsche' decals above the sills, Platinum- or silver-painted wheels hiding black brake calipers, and gold badging. Inside, the black trim was swapped for a two-tone black and cognac one, with silver-painted trim parts and blackened aluminium treadplates. The wild paintwork could be deleted, by the way, or you could go in at the deep end and specify a race number for the roundels!

Other major options not already mentioned included darkened LED headlights, gloss black mirror arms and/or carbonfibre shells, gloss black door handles, painted rocker panels, clear stone chip protection panels on the rear wings rather than black ones, the Sport Chrono package, cruise control, an alloy pedal set, the Bose sound system, a back-up camera, seat heating, coloured seatbelts, a fire extinguisher, and footmats.

The Speedster made its US debut at the 2019 New York Show, which was actually classed as the official launch of the production model, but the first Stateside deliveries were not expected to reach dealers much before the end of the year. Priced at $275,750, as *Car & Driver* stated at the time, the "Speedster makes a case for less is more."

In the UK, the £211,599 price-tag (including VAT) didn't stop *Evo* magazine giving it a five-star rating, or stop it selling out within a few days of orders being taken. Down Under, the asking price was

Interior of a Speedster with the red contrast stitching option. Note the numbered plaque between the seats.

$604,800, while in Japan (where less than 100 were allocated), it was about double the 16,660,000 yen needed to buy a new 992 Carrera S coupé.

The 2019 race scene
In the IMSA series, the Porsche factory cars had dominated the early part of the Daytona 24-hour classic, but various outside influences combined to drop the 510bhp RSRs down to third and fifth in the GTLM Class when the flag dropped. As for the new GT3R, the Park Place Motorsports car was eighth in the GTD category, although only one lap adrift of the winning Lamborghini.

It was back to winning ways at a wet Sebring, though, with the number 911 vehicle first in GTLM, closely followed by its stablemate in fifth, which finished on the same lap. Things were tight in GTD also, so sixth for Patrick Long, Patrick Lindsay and Nicholas Boulle was not as bad as it sounds ...

Interestingly, positions were reversed in Long Beach, with Earl Bamber and Laurens Vanthoor winning the GTLM Class, while Patrick Pilet and Nick Tandy were fifth, securing the top spot for Porsche in the maker's classification. Bamber and Vanthoor won again at Mid-Ohio, with teammates Pilet and Tandy third.

The cars were then shipped to augment the other works machines at Le Mans before returning to the States for the Watkins Glen six-hour classic. Despite a poor qualifying session, Pilet and Tandy lifted the GTLM trophy, with Bamber and Vanthoor a lap down in sixth. This duly extended Porsche's lead, and the gap only widened after a first and third for the works cars at Ontario, followed by a second and fourth at Lime Rock. The GT3R came good at Lime Rock, incidentally, with Zach Robichon and Dennis Olsen giving it a maiden GTD victory there – a feat Robichon repeated at the next round with Matt Campbell backing him up; the works cars were third and seventh in Class, with Ford showing the way on this occasion.

Porsche fans were treated to a GTLM one-two in Virginia, but the team struggled in Laguna Seca, meaning that the Petit Le Mans at Road Atlanta would

For Daytona and Sebring, Porsche ran the works IMSA cars in Brumos colours. This picture was taken at the Sebring race weekend (during a dry spell), but the famous livery would be called out for service again at Watkins Glen and Ontario.

decide the manufacturers' title. Sporting Coca-Cola livery in the finale, the works cars took fifth and sixth – enough to secure GTLM honours, and give Earl Bamber and Laurens Vanthoor the drivers' crown; Patrick Pilet and Nick Tandy finished the season in second place, while Zacharie Robichon was third in the GTD title chase.

Ford won the GTLM category in the North American Endurance Cup (sponsored by Michelin, and still consisting of the same four rounds borrowed from the main IMSA season), and Mercedes took GTD honours, but it was a very good year for Porsche, nonetheless.

As for the other disciplines, in the European Le Mans Series, with LMP2 and LMP3 cars dominating the grid, Dempsey-Proton Racing was the only Porsche team to enter all six rounds, and

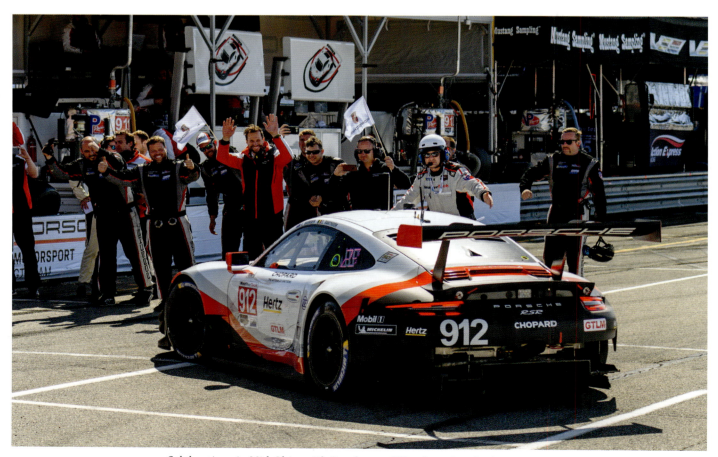

Celebrations in Mid-Ohio, with Bamber and Vanthoor in winning ways.

was duly rewarded with second place in the LMGTE championship – the only bright spot in a Porsche versus Ferrari battle that the Italian maker can claim to have won convincingly. Despite the odd win, the ADAC GT Masters series was also best forgotten.

In the Intercontinental GT Challenge, however, Bathurst provided an excellent swansong for the older 2018-spec GT3R, as Dirk Werner, Matt Campbell and Dennis Olsen guided an Evolution model to victory. Laguna Seca saw the latest car taking up grid positions, but the Wright Motorsports car retired whilst leading, and the Park Place Motorsports machine had to settle for a close third after eight hours of racing.

The Porsche camp was much happier in Spa, though, with works drivers helping GPX Racing and ROWE Racing 911 GT3Rs to a one-two victory in the Ardennes. A third for Dirk Werner, Matt Campbell and Dennis Olsen at Suzuka put Porsche second in the championship as it entered the final phase with a trip to Kyalami. However, a brilliant drive from Nick Tandy (aided and abetted by Dennis Olsen and Mathieu Jaminet) and other good finishes from 911 drivers gave Porsche the IGTC title for the first time.

There was plenty of Pro-level Porsche team interest in the Blancpain GT Series Endurance Cup, and although there were race wins for Dinamic Motorsport and GPX Racing, it was Lamborghini that garnered all the good publicity at the end of the season. Only the Italian Dinamic outfit bothered with the sprint side of the equation, entering a car for Sven Müller and Giorgio Roda in the final round, and, being frank, they probably wish they hadn't.

The Pirelli World Challenge was rebranded the Blancpain GT World Challenge America at this point, melding with other SRO promotions. Four teams were running new GT3Rs, while a fifth one fielded an older model. On saying that, only Alegra Motorsports and Wright Motorsports had Pro Class entries, and these are the ones that ultimately interest us. It was the latter team, with Patrick Long and Scott Hargrove driving,

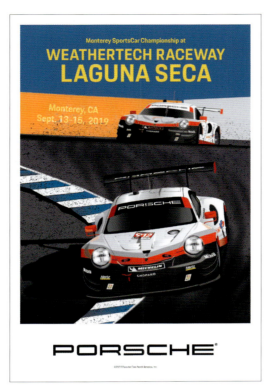

Poster for the Laguna Seca round of the IMSA series.

that did the best, ending the season in fifth after five podium finishes (including a win).

One Manthey 911 GT3R was placed second on the track at the Nürburgring 24-hour Race (desperately unlucky not to win, in reality), but a technical inspection after the event deemed that the engine's output was too high, and the car was subsequently disqualified. With another fancied Manthey 911 going out early, the fact that the older GT3R of Dennis Olsen, Matteo Cairoli, Lars Kern and Otto Klohs was promoted to fourth as a result was of little consolation to the team.

The 4.2-litre 911 RSR-19
The latest weapon in Porsche's GT armoury was unveiled at the Goodwood Festival of Speed in the early part of July 2019, just ahead of the 2019-20 WEC season in which it would compete; the updated 4.2-litre car would join the IMSA series in 2020 proper, with

En route to victory in the Bathurst 12-hour Race – proof, if any were needed, that the old GT3R still had the potential to shine.

A big change was in the exhaust system, with the pipes now exiting in front of the rear wheels to help reduce weight and allow the diffuser to be redesigned as part of an aerodynamic package upgrade that enhanced downforce and stability.

In the planning stages since 2017, it was eventually homologated on 1 July 2019, with Christensen/Estre and Lietz/Bruni listed as the drivers in the 2019-20 WEC campaign. Initially, the RSR-19 would be available for factory use only, but it was hoped that it would be available to private customers by the second half of 2020.

In the end, though, Aston Martin was able to claim the GTE-Pro crown (the British marque accumulated 332 points, versus 289 for Porsche, and 250 for Ferrari – the only makers involved). Christensen and Estre had to settle for third in the drivers' championship, while Ferrari dominated the GTE-Am arena.

The end of an era

The final 991-series 911 rolled off the line on 20 December 2019. "The last car to enter and pass down the serial production line," implying that there may have been a handful of vehicles still being finished in the Exclusive workshop. Whatever the case, a Speedster with the Heritage Design Package bound for America was officially the last of 233,540 991s built.

As it happens, the last car was built just as the world went into a state of flux due to the COVID-19 outbreak. Unlike the Lehman Shock, which had warning signs that were duly ignored, COVID came right out of the blue. The end result was much the same, though, with many firms brought to their knees as global lockdowns were enforced, and supply chains failed to deliver. However, no-one could oppose the loss of trade, as the death toll was quite horrific in the early days of the outbreak. Indeed, the last 991 built – the Speedster in the pictures – was ultimately auctioned by PCNA for a COVID charity. It fetched a final bid of $500,000, which PCNA then matched, meaning that a cool million dollars was donated in the end ...

The new 911 RSR making its debut at the 2019 Goodwood Festival of Speed.

2019 being completed with the existing 4-litre version.

Although it looked similar to the MR vehicle that spawned it at first glance, and was much the same in its overall concept, the 911 RSR-19 was developed almost from the ground up.

Retaining the mid-engined layout of the 2018-19 machine, the NA boxer engine was enlarged to 4194cc. While the output didn't change much, with around 515bhp available, the extra capacity gave a better spread of power, delivered to the rear wheels via a fast-acting six-speed sequential gearbox that was lighter than before, yet more rigid.

The last 991 model coming down the line and receiving some final checks.

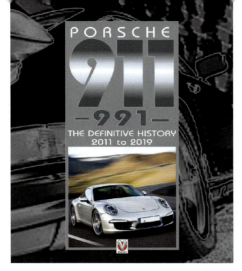

Appendix I

Year-by-year range details

Here are the brief specifications of all the 991-type Porsches, arranged in chronological and engine size order. Column one shows the model, the second column carries engine details (to be used in conjunction with Appendix II), while the third contains any useful notes. The introduction date refers to the start of domestic market sales (not the first deliveries), and only production road cars are listed for each Model Year (now considered as starting on 1 June rather than September, as was the established norm for decades). Therefore, prototypes, pure racing variants, and market-specific and/or minor limited editions are not shown:

2012
Model	Engine	Notes
Carrera coupé	MA1/04 (3.4)	Introduced September 2011. Both 7MT and PDK versions available.
Carrera Cabr	MA1/04 (3.4)	Introduced December 2011. Both 7MT and PDK versions available.
Carrera S coupé	MA1/03 (3.8)	Introduced September 2011. Both 7MT and PDK versions available.
Carrera S Cabr	MA1/03 (3.8)	Introduced December 2011. Both 7MT and PDK versions available.

2013
Model	Engine	Notes
Carrera coupé	MA1/04 (3.4)	
Carrera Cabr	MA1/04 (3.4)	
Carrera 4 coupé	MA1/04 (3.4)	Introduced September 2012. Both 7MT and PDK versions available.
Carrera 4 Cabr	MA1/04 (3.4)	Introduced September 2012. Both 7MT and PDK versions available.
Carrera S coupé	MA1/03 (3.8)	
Carrera S Cabr	MA1/03 (3.8)	
Carrera 4S coupé	MA1/03 (3.8)	Introduced September 2012. Both 7MT and PDK versions available.
Carrera 4S Cabr	MA1/03 (3.8)	Introduced September 2012. Both 7MT and PDK versions available.

2014
Model	Engine	Notes
Carrera coupé	MA1/04 (3.4)	
Carrera Cabr	MA1/04 (3.4)	
Carrera 4 coupé	MA1/04 (3.4)	
Carrera 4 Cabr	MA1/04 (3.4)	
Carrera S coupé	MA1/03 (3.8)	
Carrera S Cabr	MA1/03 (3.8)	
Carrera 4S coupé	MA1/03 (3.8)	
Carrera 4S Cabr	MA1/03 (3.8)	
GT3 coupé	MA1/75 (3.8)	Introduced March 2013, but officially classed as an early 2014 model. PDK only.
Turbo coupé	MA1/71 (3.8)	Introduced May 2013, but officially classed as an early 2014 model. PDK only.
Turbo S coupé	MA1/71S (3.8)	Introduced May 2013, but officially classed as an early 2014 model. PDK only.

2015

Model	Engine	Notes
Carrera coupé	MA1/04 (3.4)	
Carrera Cabr	MA1/04 (3.4)	
Carrera 4 coupé	MA1/04 (3.4)	
Carrera 4 Cabr	MA1/04 (3.4)	
Targa 4	MA1/04 (3.4)	Introduced January 2014, but officially classed as an early 2015 model. Both 7MT and PDK versions available.
Carrera S coupé	MA1/03 (3.8)	
Carrera GTS coupé	MA1/03S (3.8)	Introduced October 2014. Both 7MT and PDK versions available.
Carrera S Cabr	MA1/03 (3.8)	
Carrera GTS Cabr	MA1/03S (3.8)	Introduced October 2014. Both 7MT and PDK versions available.
Carrera 4S coupé	MA1/03 (3.8)	
C4 GTS coupé	MA1/03S (3.8)	Introduced October 2014. Both 7MT and PDK versions available.
Carrera 4S Cabr	MA1/03 (3.8)	
C4 GTS Cabr	MA1/03S (3.8)	Introduced October 2014. Both 7MT and PDK versions available.
Targa 4S	MA1/03 (3.8)	Introduced January 2014, but officially classed as an early 2015 model. Both 7MT and PDK versions available.
Targa 4 GTS	MA1/03S (3.8)	Introduced January 2015. Both 7MT and PDK versions available.
GT3 coupé	MA1/75 (3.8)	
GT3 RS coupé	MA1/76 (4.0)	Introduced March 2015. PDK only.
Turbo coupé	MA1/71 (3.8)	
Turbo S coupé	MA1/71S (3.8)	
Turbo Cabr	MA1/71 (3.8)	Introduced September 2013, but officially classed as an early 2015 model. PDK only.
Turbo S Cabr	MA1/71S (3.8)	Introduced September 2013, but officially classed as an early 2015 model. PDK only.

2016

Model	Engine	Notes
Carrera coupé	MA1/04 (3.4)	To May 2016.
C2 'Blk Ed' coupé	MA1/04 (3.4)	Introduced May 2015. Both 7MT and PDK versions available. To May 2016.
Carrera Cabr	MA1/04 (3.4)	To May 2016.
C2 'Blk Ed' Cabr	MA1/04 (3.4)	Introduced May 2015. Both 7MT and PDK versions available. To May 2016.
Carrera 4 coupé	MA1/04 (3.4)	To May 2016.
C4 'Blk Ed' coupé	MA1/04 (3.4)	Introduced May 2015. Both 7MT and PDK versions available. To May 2016.
Carrera 4 Cabr	MA1/04 (3.4)	To May 2016.
C4 'Blk Ed' coupé	MA1/04 (3.4)	Introduced May 2015. Both 7MT and PDK versions available. To May 2016.
Targa 4	MA1/04 (3.4)	To May 2016.
Carrera S coupé	MA1/03 (3.8)	To May 2016.
Carrera GTS coupé	MA1/03S (3.8)	To May 2016.
Carrera S Cabr	MA1/03 (3.8)	To May 2016.
Carrera GTS Cabr	MA1/03S (3.8)	To May 2016.
Carrera 4S coupé	MA1/03 (3.8)	To May 2016.
C4 GTS coupé	MA1/03S (3.8)	To May 2016.
Carrera 4S Cabr	MA1/03 (3.8)	To May 2016.
C4 GTS Cabr	MA1/03S (3.8)	To May 2016.
Targa 4S	MA1/03 (3.8)	To May 2016.
Targa 4 GTS	MA1/03S (3.8)	To May 2016.
GT3 coupé	MA1/75 (3.8)	
GT3 RS coupé	MA1/76 (4.0)	
911R coupé	MA1/76 (4.0)	Introduced March 2016. All production classed as 2016 MY programme, although most built later. 6MT only.
Turbo coupé	MA1/71 (3.8)	To November 2015.
Turbo S coupé	MA1/71S (3.8)	To November 2015.
Turbo Cabr	MA1/71 (3.8)	To November 2015.
Turbo S Cabr	MA1/71S (3.8)	To November 2015.

2017

Model	Code	Notes
Carrera coupé	MDC/KA (3.0)	Introduced September 2015, but officially classed as an early 2017 model. Both 7MT and PDK versions available.
Carrera Cabr	MDC/KA (3.0)	Introduced September 2015, but officially classed as an early 2017 model. Both 7MT and PDK versions available.
Carrera S coupé	MDC/HA (3.0)	Introduced September 2015, but officially classed as an early 2017 model. Both 7MT and PDK versions available.
Carrera GTS coupé	MDC/JA (3.0)	Introduced January 2017, as late 2017 model. Both 7MT and PDK versions available.
Carrera S Cabr	MDC/HA (3.0)	Introduced September 2015, but officially classed as an early 2017 model. Both 7MT and PDK versions available.
Carrera GTS Cabr	MDC/JA (3.0)	Introduced January 2017, as late 2017 model. Both 7MT and PDK versions available.
Carrera 4 coupé	MDC/KA (3.0)	Introduced October 2015, but officially classed as an early 2017 model. Both 7MT and PDK versions available.
Carrera 4 Cabr	MDC/KA (3.0)	Introduced October 2015, but officially classed as an early 2017 model. Both 7MT and PDK versions available.
Targa 4	MDC/KA (3.0)	Introduced October 2015, but officially classed as an early 2017 model. Both 7MT and PDK versions available.
Carrera 4S coupé	MDC/HA (3.0)	Introduced October 2015, but officially classed as an early 2017 model. Both 7MT and PDK versions available.
C4 GTS coupé	MDC/JA (3.0)	Introduced January 2017, as late 2017 model. Both 7MT and PDK versions available.
Carrera 4S Cabr	MDC/HA (3.0)	Introduced October 2015, but officially classed as an early 2017 model. Both 7MT and PDK versions available.
C4 GTS Cabr	MDC/JA (3.0)	Introduced January 2017, as late 2017 model. Both 7MT and PDK versions available.
Targa 4S	MDC/HA (3.0)	Introduced October 2015, but officially classed as an early 2017 model. Both 7MT and PDK versions available.
Targa 4 GTS	MDC/JA (3.0)	Introduced January 2017, as late 2017 model. Both 7MT and PDK versions available.
GT3 coupé	MA1/75 (3.8)	To May 2017.
GT3 RS coupé	MA1/76 (4.0)	To May 2017.
Turbo coupé	MDA/BA (3.8)	Introduced December 2015, but officially classed as an early 2017 model. PDK only.
Turbo S coupé	MDB/CA (3.8)	Introduced December 2015, but officially classed as an early 2017 model. PDK only.
Turbo Cabr	MDA/BA (3.8)	Introduced December 2015, but officially classed as an early 2017 model. PDK only.
Turbo S Cabr	MDB/CA (3.8)	Introduced December 2015, but officially classed as an early 2017 model. PDK only.

2018

Model	Code	Notes
Carrera coupé	MDC/KA (3.0)	
Carrera T coupé	MDC/KA (3.0)	Introduced October 2017 as a 2018 model. Both 7MT and PDK versions available.
Carrera Cabr	MDC/KA (3.0)	
Carrera S coupé	MDC/HA (3.0)	
Carrera GTS coupé	MDC/JA (3.0)	
Carrera S Cabr	MDC/HA (3.0)	
Carrera GTS Cabr	MDC/JA (3.0)	
Carrera 4 coupé	MDC/KA (3.0)	
Carrera 4 Cabr	MDC/KA (3.0)	

Targa 4	MDC/KA (3.0)	
Carrera 4S coupé	MDC/HA (3.0)	
C4 GTS coupé	MDC/JA (3.0)	
Carrera 4S Cabr	MDC/HA (3.0)	
C4 GTS Cabr	MDC/JA (3.0)	
Targa 4S	MDC/HA (3.0)	
Targa 4 GTS	MDC/JA (3.0)	
GT3 coupé	MDG/GA (4.0)	Introduced March 2017 as an early 2018 model, and last cars officially sold as 2018 models in most countries, including Germany. However, North America had a proper 2019 car. Both 6MT and PDK versions available.
GT2 RS coupé	MDH/NA (3.8)	Introduced June 2017 as an early 2018 model. PDK only.
Turbo coupé	MDA/BA (3.8)	
Turbo S coupé	MDB/CA (3.8)	
Turbo S Exc. coupé	MDB/CB (3.8)	Introduced June 2017 as an early 2018 model. PDK only.
Turbo Cabr	MDA/BA (3.8)	
Turbo S Cabr	MDB/CA (3.8)	

2019

Carrera coupé	MDC/KA (3.0)	Replacement released July 2019.
Carrera T coupé	MDC/KA (3.0)	To December 2019.
Carrera Cabr	MDC/KA (3.0)	Replacement released July 2019.
Carrera S coupé	MDC/HA (3.0)	Replacement released November 2018.
Carrera GTS coupé	MDC/JA (3.0)	To December 2019.
Carrera S Cabr	MDC/HA (3.0)	Replacement released January 2019.
Carrera GTS Cabr	MDC/JA (3.0)	To December 2019.
Carrera 4 coupé	MDC/KA (3.0)	Replacement released September 2019.
Carrera 4 Cabr	MDC/KA (3.0)	Replacement released September 2019.
Targa 4	MDC/KA (3.0)	To December 2019.
Carrera 4S coupé	MDC/HA (3.0)	Replacement released November 2018.
C4 GTS coupé	MDC/JA (3.0)	To December 2019.
Carrera 4S Cabr	MDC/HA (3.0)	Replacement released January 2019.
C4 GTS Cabr	MDC/JA (3.0)	To December 2019.
Targa 4S	MDC/HA (3.0)	To December 2019.
Targa 4 GTS	MDC/JA (3.0)	To December 2019.
GT3 coupé	MDG/GA (4.0)	To December 2019.
GT3 RS coupé	MDG/GB (4.0)	Introduced February 2018, but officially classed as an early 2019 model. PDK only. To December 2019.
GT Speedster	MDG/GA (4.0)	Introduced May 2019. 6MT only. To December 2019. Final 991-series car built.
GT2 RS coupé	MDH.NA (3.8)	To December 2019.
Turbo coupé	MDA/BA (3.8)	To December 2019.
Turbo S coupé	MDB/CA (3.8)	To December 2019.
Turbo S Exc. coupé	MDB/CB (3.8)	To December 2019.
Turbo Cabr	MDA/BA (3.8)	To December 2019.
Turbo S Cabr	MDB/CA (3.8)	To December 2019.

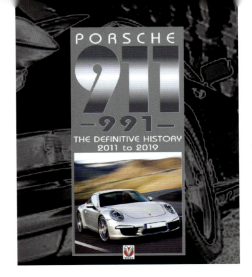

Appendix II

Engine specifications

The following is a survey of all the engines employed in the 991 series, complete with the leading specifications, and any other notes of interest. Only power-units employed in series production road cars are covered by this appendix, with production dates referring to official Model Year (MY) allocations, clearly laid out in the notes in Appendix I to avoid confusion:

Type MA1/03
Production (MY)   2012-2017
Cylinders   Six, water-cooled
Main bearings   Seven, in alloy block
Valve operation   Dohc per bank, 24v, in alloy heads
Bore & stroke   102.0 x 77.5mm
Cubic capacity   3800cc
Compression ratio   12.5:1
Fuel delivery   Direct fuel-injection (DFI)
Hp @ rpm   400bhp (294kW) DIN @ 7400
Torque @ rpm   324lbft (440Nm) @ 5600
Serial numbers   C*C 00501-, D*D 00501-, E*E 00501-, F*F 00501-, G*G 00501-, & H*C 00501-

Notes: Used in the Carrera S/4S and Targa 4S models (MT or PDK). Also known as the MAB/03 unit for 2017.

Type MA1/03S
As per MA1/03, except:
Hp @ rpm   430bhp (316kW) DIN @ 7500
Torque @ rpm   324lbft (440Nm) @ 5750

Notes: Optional X51 power kit version of Carrera S unit, fitted as standard on all 2015 MY onwards GTS models. Also known as the MAB/03S for 2017, at least unofficially, but the use of a suffix offers a useful distinction for our purposes.

Type MA1/04
Production (MY)   2012-2017
Cylinders   Six, water-cooled
Main bearings   Seven, in alloy block
Valve operation   Dohc per bank, 24v, in alloy heads
Bore & stroke   97.0 x 77.5mm
Cubic capacity   3436cc
Compression ratio   12.5:1
Fuel delivery   Direct fuel-injection (DFI)
Hp @ rpm   350bhp (257kW) DIN @ 7400
Torque @ rpm   288lbft (390Nm) @ 5600
Serial numbers   C*C 00501-, D*D 00501-, E*E 00501-, F*F 00501-, G*G 00501-, & H*C 00501-

Notes: Used in the strict Carrera, Carrera 4 and Targa 4 models (MT or PDK). Also known as the MAB/04 unit for 2017.

Type MA1/71

Production (MY)	2014-2016
Cylinders	Six, water-cooled
Main bearings	Seven, in alloy block
Valve operation	Dohc per bank, 24v, in alloy heads
Bore & stroke	102.0 x 77.5mm
Cubic capacity	3800cc
Compression ratio	9.8:1
Fuel delivery	Direct fuel-injection (DFI), with twin turbos
Hp @ rpm	520bhp (383kW) DIN @ 6000
Torque @ rpm	487lbft (660Nm) @ 1950-5000
Serial numbers	E*E 00501-, F*F 00501-, & G*G 00501-

Notes: Used in the strict Turbo models (PDK only).

Type MA1/71S

As per MA1/71, except:
Hp @ rpm	560bhp (412kW) DIN @ 6500
Torque @ rpm	516lbft (700Nm) @ 2100-4250

Notes: Used in the Turbo S models (PDK only).

Type MA1/75

Production (MY)	2014-2017
Cylinders	Six, water-cooled
Main bearings	Seven, in alloy block
Valve operation	Dohc per bank, 24v, in alloy heads
Bore & stroke	102.0 x 77.5mm
Cubic capacity	3799cc
Compression ratio	12.9:1
Fuel delivery	Direct fuel-injection (DFI)
Hp @ rpm	475bhp (350kW) DIN @ 8250
Torque @ rpm	325lbft (440Nm) @ 6250
Serial numbers	E*E 00501-, F*F 00501-, G*G 00501-, & H*H 00501-

Notes: Used in the GT3 model (PDK only).

Type MA1/76

Production (MY)	2015-2017
Cylinders	Six, water-cooled
Main bearings	Seven, in alloy block
Valve operation	Dohc per bank, 24v, in alloy heads
Bore & stroke	102.0 x 81.5mm
Cubic capacity	3996cc
Compression ratio	12.9:1
Fuel delivery	Direct fuel-injection (DFI)
Hp @ rpm	500bhp (368kW) DIN @ 8250
Torque @ rpm	338lbft (460Nm) @ 6250
Serial numbers	F*F 00501-, G*G 00501-, & H*H 00501-

Notes: Used in the GT3 RS model (PDK only), and 911R (6MT only). Factory data suggests a 13.2:1 c/r on the 911R application.

Type MDA/BA
As per MA1/71, except:
Production (MY)   2017-2019
Hp @ rpm   540bhp (397kW) DIN @ 6400
Serial numbers   H*H 00501-, J*J 00501-, & K*K 00501-

Notes: Also known as the MA1/72 unit.

Type MDB/CA
As per MA1/71S, except:
Production (MY)   2017-2019
Hp @ rpm   580bhp (426kW) DIN @ 6750
Serial numbers   H*H 00501-, J*J 00501-, & K*K 00501-

Notes: Also known as the MA1/72S unit.

Type MDB/CB
As per MA1/71S, except:
Production (MY)   2018-2019
Hp @ rpm   607bhp (446kW) DIN @ 6750
Torque @ rpm   553lbft (750Nm) @ 2250-4000
Serial numbers   J*J 00501-, & K*K 00501-

Notes: Used in the Turbo S Exclusive model (PDK only).

Type MDC/HA
Production (MY)   2017-2019
Cylinders   Six, water-cooled
Main bearings   Seven, in alloy block
Valve operation   Dohc per bank, 24v, in alloy heads
Bore & stroke   91.0 x 76.4mm
Cubic capacity   2981cc
Compression ratio 10.0:1
Fuel delivery   Direct fuel-injection (DFI), with twin turbos
Hp @ rpm   420bhp (309kW) DIN @ 6500
Torque @ rpm   368lbft (500Nm) @ 1700-5000
Serial numbers   H*C 00501-, J*C 00501-, & K*C 00501-

Notes: Also known as the MA2/02 unit. Used in the Carrera S variants (MT or PDK).

Type MDC/JA
As per MDC/HA, except:
Hp @ rpm   450bhp (331kW) DIN @ 6500
Torque @ rpm   405lbft (550Nm) @ 2150-5000

Notes: Used in the Carrera GTS variants (MT or PDK). Also available as the X51 option for regular Carrera S models.

Type MDC/KA
As per MDC/HA, except:
Hp @ rpm   370bhp (272kW) DIN @ 6500
Torque @ rpm   331lbft (450Nm) @ 1700-5000

Notes: Also known as the MA2/01 unit. Used in the strict Carrera and Carrera T variants (MT or PDK).

Type MDG/GA

Production (MY)	2018-2019
Cylinders	Six, water-cooled
Main bearings	Seven, in alloy block
Valve operation	Dohc per bank, 24v, in alloy heads
Bore & stroke	102.0 x 81.5mm
Cubic capacity	3996cc
Compression ratio	13.3:1
Fuel delivery	Direct fuel-injection (DFI)
Hp @ rpm	500bhp (368kW) DIN @ 8250
Torque @ rpm	339lbft (460Nm) @ 6000rpm
Serial numbers	J*J 00501-, & K*K 00501-

Notes: Also known as the MA1/77 unit. Used in the GT3 model (MT or PDK). Tuned to give 510bhp (375kW) and 347lbft (470Nm) in the 2019 GT Speedster (MT only).

Type MDG/GB

As per MDG/GA, except:

Production (MY)	2019
Hp @ rpm	520bhp (383kW) DIN @ 8250
Torque @ rpm	347lbft (470Nm) @ 6000
Serial numbers	K*K 00501-

Notes: Variation on the MA1/77 unit. Used in the GT3 RS model (PDK only). Advertised as the most powerful normally-aspirated 911 production engine to date. From May 2019, maximum power developed at 8400rpm, and maximum torque peak adjusted to 6250rpm.

Type MDH/NA

As per MA1/71S, except:

Production (MY)	2018-2019
Compression ratio	9.0:1
Hp @ rpm	700bhp (515kW) DIN @ 7000
Torque @ rpm	553lbft (750Nm) @ 2500-4500
Serial numbers	J*J 00501-, & K*K 00501-

Notes: Used in the GT2 RS model (PDK only). Most powerful 911 production engine to date, period.

---

www.veloce.co.uk
All current books and ebooks • New book news • Special offers

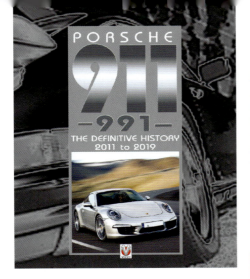

Appendix III

Chassis numbers & production figures

Please note that the following are start of run sanction numbers, with the factory-assigned Model Year (MY) being more important than the Calendar Year (CY). GTS models were batched in with the regular Carrera S run, incidentally, so they are not shown separately, while the 'Black Edition' was included in the strict Carrera numbers. Likewise, the Turbo S (including the special 2018-2019 Exclusive edition) is batched with the regular Turbo, the 911R with the later G-Serie GT3 RS codes, and there was no distinction between RR or 4WD vehicles.

The 'US' entry includes Canada, while the 'CH' entry includes China, Korea, Mexico and Brazil; the * in the code is a check digit, either replaced by a number from 0 to 9, or the letter X. Having an 'S' as the 11th digit in the chassis code indicates that the car was built in Stuttgart.

C-Serie models

2012 MY	Carrera coupé	WP0ZZZ 99ZCS1 00061-
	Carrera coupé (US)	WP0AA2 A9*CS1 06061-
	Carrera coupé (CH)	WP0AA2 99*CS1 06061-
	Carrera Cabr	WP0ZZZ 99ZCS1 35061-
	Carrera Cabr (US)	WP0CA2 A9*CS1 40061-
	Carrera Cabr (CH)	WP0CA2 99*CS1 40061-
	Carrera S coupé	WP0ZZZ 99ZCS1 10061-
	Carrera S coupé (US)	WP0AB2 A9*CS1 20061-
	Carrera S coupé (CH)	WP0AB2 99*CS1 20061-
	Carrera S Cabr	WP0ZZZ 99ZCS1 45061-
	Carrera S Cabr (US)	WP0CB2 A9*CS1 54061-
	Carrera S Cabr (CH)	WP0CB2 99*CS1 54061-

D-Serie models

2013 MY	Carrera coupé	WP0ZZZ 99ZDS1 00061-
	Carrera coupé (US)	WP0AA2 A9*DS1 06061-
	Carrera coupé (CH)	WP0AA2 99*DS1 06061-
	Carrera Cabr	WP0ZZZ 99ZDS1 35061-
	Carrera Cabr (US)	WP0CA2 A9*DS1 40061-
	Carrera Cabr (CH)	WP0CA2 99*DS1 40061-
	Carrera S coupé	WP0ZZZ 99ZDS1 10061-
	Carrera S coupé (US)	WP0AB2 A9*DS1 20061-
	Carrera S coupé (CH)	WP0AB2 99*DS1 20061-
	Carrera S Cabr	WP0ZZZ 99ZDS1 45061-
	Carrera S Cabr (US)	WP0CB2 A9*DS1 54061-
	Carrera S Cabr (CH)	WP0CB2 99*DS1 54061-

E-Serie models

2014 MY	Carrera coupé	WP0ZZZ 99ZES1 00061-
	Carrera coupé (US)	WP0AA2 A9*ES1 06061-
	Carrera coupé (CH)	WP0AA2 99*ES1 06061-
	Carrera Cabr	WP0ZZZ 99ZES1 35061-
	Carrera Cabr (US)	WP0CA2 A9*ES1 40061-
	Carrera Cabr (CH)	WP0CA2 99*ES1 40061-
	Carrera S coupé	WP0ZZZ 99ZES1 10061-
	Carrera S coupé (US)	WP0AB2 A9*ES1 20061-
	Carrera S coupé (CH)	WP0AB2 99*ES1 20061-
	Carrera S Cabr	WP0ZZZ 99ZES1 45061-
	Carrera S Cabr (US)	WP0CB2 A9*ES1 54061-
	Carrera S Cabr (CH)	WP0CB2 99*ES1 54061-

	GT3 coupé	WP0ZZZ 99ZES1 80061-
	GT3 coupé (US)	WP0AC2 A9*ES1 83061-
	GT3 coupé (CH)	WP0AC2 99*ES1 83061-
	Turbo coupés	WP0ZZZ 99ZES1 60061-
	Turbo coupés (US)	WP0AD2 A9*ES1 66061-
	Turbo coupés (CH)	WP0AD2 99*ES1 66061-

F-Serie models

2015 MY	Carrera coupé	WP0ZZZ 99ZFS1 00061-
	Carrera coupé (US)	WP0AA2 A9*FS1 00061-
	Carrera coupé (CH)	WP0AA2 99*FS1 00061-
	Carrera Cabr	WP0ZZZ 99ZFS1 37061-
	Carrera Cabr (US)	WP0CA2 A9*FS1 37061-
	Carrera Cabr (CH)	WP0CA2 99*FS1 37061-
	Targa 4	WP0ZZZ 99ZFS1 30061-
	Targa 4 (US)	WP0BA2 A9*FS1 30061-
	Targa 4 (CH)	WP0BA2 99*FS1 30061-
	Carrera S coupé	WP0ZZZ 99ZFS1 10061-
	Carrera S coupé (US)	WP0AB2 A9*FS1 10061-
	Carrera S coupé (CH)	WP0AB2 99*FS1 10061-
	Carrera S Cabr	WP0ZZZ 99ZFS1 43061-
	Carrera S Cabr (US)	WP0CB2 A9*FS1 43061-
	Carrera S Cabr (CH)	WP0CB2 99*FS1 43061-
	Targa 4S	WP0ZZZ 99ZFS1 33061-
	Targa 4S (US)	WP0BB2 A9*FS1 33061-
	Targa 4S (CH)	WP0BB2 99*FS1 33061-
	GT3 coupé	WP0ZZZ 99ZFS1 82061-
	GT3 coupé (US)	WP0AC2 A9*FS1 82061-
	GT3 coupé (CH)	WP0AC2 99*FS1 82061-
	GT3 RS coupé	WP0ZZZ 99ZFS1 85061-
	GT3 RS coupé (US)	WP0AF2 A9*FS1 85061-
	GT3 RS coupé (CH)	WP0AF2 99*FS1 85061-
	Turbo coupés	WP0ZZZ 99ZFS1 60061-
	Turbo coupés (US)	WP0AD2 A9*FS1 60061-
	Turbo coupés (CH)	WP0AD2 99*FS1 60061-
	Turbo Cabr	WP0ZZZ 99ZFS1 72061-
	Turbo Cabr (US)	WP0CD2 A9*FS1 72061-
	Turbo Cabr (CH)	WP0CD2 99*FS1 72061-

G-Serie models

2016 MY	Carrera coupé	WP0ZZZ 99ZGS1 00061-
	Carrera coupé (US)	WP0AA2 A9*GS1 06061-
	Carrera coupé (CH)	WP0AA2 99*GS1 06061-
	Carrera Cabr	WP0ZZZ 99ZGS1 38061-
	Carrera Cabr (US)	WP0CA2 A9*GS1 41061-
	Carrera Cabr (CH)	WP0CA2 99*GS1 41061-
	Targa 4	WP0ZZZ 99ZGS1 30061-
	Targa 4 (US)	WP0BA2 A9*GS1 32061-
	Targa 4 (CH)	WP0BA2 99*GS1 32061-
	Carrera S coupé	WP0ZZZ 99ZGS1 10061-
	Carrera S coupé (US)	WP0AB2 A9*GS1 22061-
	Carrera S coupé (CH)	WP0AB2 99*GS1 22061-
	Carrera S Cabr	WP0ZZZ 99ZGS1 43061-
	Carrera S Cabr (US)	WP0CB2 A9*GS1 54061-
	Carrera S Cabr (CH)	WP0CB2 99*GS1 54061-

	Targa 4S	WP0ZZZ 99ZGS1 33061-
	Targa 4S (US)	WP0BB2 A9*GS1 36061-
	Targa 4S (CH)	WP0BB2 99*GS1 36061-
	GT3 coupé	WP0ZZZ 99ZGS1 83061-
	GT3 coupé (US)	WP0AC2 A9*GS1 84061-
	GT3 coupé (CH)	WP0AC2 99*GS1 84061-
	GT3 RS coupé	WP0ZZZ 99ZGS1 85061-
		WP0ZZZ 99ZGS1 88061-
	GT3 RS coupé (US)	WP0AF2 A9*GS1 87061-
		WP0AF2 A9*GS1 92061-
	GT3 RS coupé (CH)	WP0AF2 99*GS1 87061-
		WP0AF2 99*GS1 92061-
	911R coupé	WP0ZZZ 99ZGS1 94001-
	911R coupé (US)	WP0AF2 A9*GS1 95001-
	911R coupé (CH)	WP0AF2 99*GS1 95001-
	Turbo coupés	WP0ZZZ 99ZGS1 60061-
	Turbo coupés (US)	WP0AD2 A9*GS1 66061-
	Turbo coupés (CH)	WP0AD2 99*GS1 66061-
	Turbo Cabr	WP0ZZZ 99ZGS1 72061-
	Turbo Cabr (US)	WP0CD2 A9*GS1 78061-
	Turbo Cabr (CH)	WP0CD2 99*GS1 78061-

H-Serie models

2017 MY	Carrera coupé	WP0ZZZ 99ZHS1 00061-
	Carrera coupé (US)	WP0AA2 A9*HS1 06061-
	Carrera coupé (CH)	WP0AA2 99*HS1 06061-
	Carrera Cabr	WP0ZZZ 99ZHS1 38061-
	Carrera Cabr (US)	WP0CA2 A9*HS1 41061-
	Carrera Cabr (CH)	WP0CA2 99*HS1 41061-
	Targa 4	WP0ZZZ 99ZHS1 30061-
	Targa 4 (US)	WP0BA2 A9*HS1 32061-
	Targa 4 (CH)	WP0BA2 99*HS1 32061-
	Carrera S coupé	WP0ZZZ 99ZHS1 10061-
	Carrera S coupé (US)	WP0AB2 A9*HS1 22061-
	Carrera S coupé (CH)	WP0AB2 99*HS1 22061-
	Carrera S Cabr	WP0ZZZ 99ZHS1 43061-
	Carrera S Cabr (US)	WP0CB2 A9*HS1 54061-
	Carrera S Cabr (CH)	WP0CB2 99*HS1 54061-
	Targa 4S	WP0ZZZ 99ZHS1 33061-
	Targa 4S (US)	WP0BB2 A9*HS1 36061-
	Targa 4S (CH)	WP0BB2 99*HS1 36061-
	GT3 coupé	WP0ZZZ 99ZHS1 83061-
	GT3 coupé (US)	WP0AC2 A9*HS1 84061-
	GT3 coupé (CH)	WP0AC2 99*HS1 84061-
	GT3 RS coupé	WP0ZZZ 99ZHS1 85061-
	GT3 RS coupé (US)	WP0AF2 A9*HS1 87061-
	GT3 RS coupé (CH)	WP0AF2 99*HS1 87061-
	Turbo coupés	WP0ZZZ 99ZHS1 60061-
	Turbo coupés (US)	WP0AD2 A9*HS1 66061-
	Turbo coupés (CH)	WP0AD2 99*HS1 66061-
	Turbo Cabr	WP0ZZZ 99ZHS1 72061-
	Turbo Cabr (US)	WP0CD2 A9*HS1 78061-
	Turbo Cabr (CH)	WP0CD2 99*HS1 78061-

J-Serie models

2018 MY	Carrera coupé	WP0ZZZ 99ZJS1 00061-
	Carrera coupé (US)	WP0AA2 A9*JS1 05061-
	Carrera coupé (CH)	WP0AA2 99*JS1 05061-
	Carrera Cabr	WP0ZZZ 99ZJS1 36061-
	Carrera Cabr (US)	WP0CA2 A9*JS1 38061-
	Carrera Cabr (CH)	WP0CA2 99*JS1 38061-
	Targa 4	WP0ZZZ 99ZJS1 28061-
	Targa 4 (US)	WP0BA2 A9*JS1 29061-
	Targa 4 (CH)	WP0BA2 99*JS1 29061-
	Carrera S coupé	WP0ZZZ 99ZJS1 10061-
	Carrera S coupé (US)	WP0AB2 A9*JS1 22061-
	Carrera S coupé (CH)	WP0AB2 99*JS1 22061-
	Carrera S Cabr	WP0ZZZ 99ZJS1 40061-
	Carrera S Cabr (US)	WP0CB2 A9*JS1 47061-
	Carrera S Cabr (CH)	WP0CB2 99*JS1 47061-
	Targa 4S	WP0ZZZ 99ZJS1 30061-
	Targa 4S (US)	WP0BB2 A9*JS1 34061-
	Targa 4S (CH)	WP0BB2 99*JS1 34061-
	GT3 coupé	WP0ZZZ 99ZJS1 64061-
	GT3 coupé (US)	WP0AC2 A9*JS1 74061-
	GT3 coupé (CH)	WP0AC2 99*JS1 74061-
	GT2 RS coupé	WP0ZZZ 99ZJS1 80061-
	GT2 RS coupé (US)	WP0AE2 A9*JS1 85061-
	GT2 RS coupé (CH)	WP0AE2 99*JS1 85061-
	Turbo coupés	WP0ZZZ 99ZJS1 51061-
	Turbo coupés (US)	WP0AD2 A9*JS1 56061-
	Turbo coupés (CH)	WP0AD2 99*JS1 56061-
	Turbo Cabr	WP0ZZZ 99ZJS1 59061-
	Turbo Cabr (US)	WP0CD2 A9*JS1 62061-
	Turbo Cabr (CH)	WP0CD2 99*JS1 62061-

K-Serie models

2019 MY	Carrera coupé	WP0ZZZ 99ZKS1 00001-
	Carrera coupé (US)	WP0AA2 A9*KS1 03001-
	Carrera coupé (CH)	WP0AA2 99*KS1 03001-
	Carrera Cabr	WP0ZZZ 99ZKS1 27001-
	Carrera Cabr (US)	WP0CA2 A9*KS1 29001-
	Carrera Cabr (CH)	WP0CA2 99*KS1 29001-
	Targa 4	WP0ZZZ 99ZKS1 18001-
	Targa 4 (US)	WP0BA2 A9*KS1 20001-
	Targa 4 (CH)	WP0BA2 99*KS1 20001-
	Carrera S coupé	WP0ZZZ 99ZKS1 09001-
	Carrera S coupé (US)	WP0AB2 A9*KS1 14001-
	Carrera S coupé (CH)	WP0AB2 99*KS1 14001-
	Carrera S Cabr	WP0ZZZ 99ZKS1 31001-
	Carrera S Cabr (US)	WP0CB2 A9*KS1 36001-
	Carrera S Cabr (CH)	WP0CB2 99*KS1 36001-
	Targa 4S	WP0ZZZ 99ZKS1 22001-
	Targa 4S (US)	WP0BB2 A9*KS1 25001-
	Targa 4S (CH)	WP0BB2 99*KS1 25001-
	GT3 coupé (US)	WP0AC2 A9*KS1 49061-
	GT3 RS coupé	WP0ZZZ 99ZKS1 58061-
	GT3 RS coupé (US)	WP0AF2 A9*KS1 64061-
	GT3 RS coupé (CH)	WP0AF2 99*KS1 64061-

GT Speedster	WP0ZZZ 99ZKS1 70061-
GT Speedster (US)	WP0CF2 A9*KS1 72061-
GT Speedster (CH)	WP0CF2 99*KS1 72061-
GT2 RS coupé	WP0ZZZ 99ZKS1 95061-
GT2 RS coupé (US)	WP0AE2 A9*KS1 55061-
GT2 RS coupé (CH)	WP0AE2 99*KS1 55061-
Turbo coupés	WP0ZZZ 99ZKS1 38061-
Turbo coupés (US)	WP0AD2 A9*KS1 40061-
Turbo coupés (CH)	WP0AD2 99*KS1 40061-
Turbo Cabr	WP0ZZZ 99ZKS1 42061-
Turbo Cabr (US)	WP0CD2 A9*KS1 44061-
Turbo Cabr (CH)	WP0CD2 99*KS1 44061-

Production figures

The numbers provided here, obtained with the help of Adrian Streather, are for Model Years (MY) rather than calendar years (CY), as per the modern method of calculating production in Zuffenhausen. One can see from the text that some MY designations are difficult to understand, but the chassis number allocations are created in this way, so we will stick with the format to avoid further confusion. Including the 100 prototype and pre-production coupés (mostly S grade), annual 991-series output was as follows:

	991.1	991.2	Total
2010 MY	100	-	100
2011 MY	4058	-	4058
2012 MY	25,708	-	25,708
2013 MY	29,710	-	29,710
2014 MY	31,501	79	31,580
2015 MY	27,663	3697	31,360
2016 MY	4546	27,065	31,611
2017 MY	-	33,788	33,788
2018 MY	-	35,336	35,336
2019 MY	-	10,289	10,289
Total number 991.1 models			123,286
Total number 991.2 models			110,254
Grand total (including prototypes)			233,540

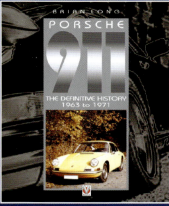

ISBN: 978-1-845844-54-7

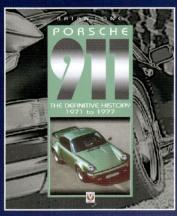

ISBN: 978-1-845844-55-4

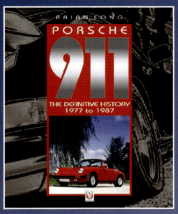

ISBN: 978-1-845844-58-5

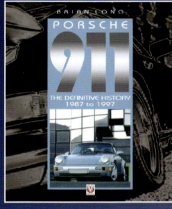

ISBN: 978-1-845844-59-2

• • • • • • • • • • •
Previous titles in the Definitive History series available as eBooks
• • • • • • • • • • •
Reprints coming soon as part of the *Veloce Classic Reprint* series - see the Veloce website for updates

Book 5 in the Definitive History series (1997-2005)
Enlarged and updated second edition
Full year-by-year coverage of production models; American and European markets, and limited editions covered in full with rare prototype photographs.

ISBN: 978-1-904788-42-3
Hardback • 208 pages
• 272 pictures

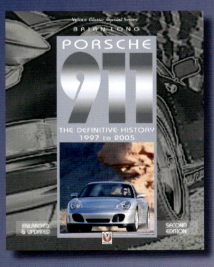

Book 6 in the series is the definitive history of the hugely successful 997-series, 1997-2005, provides in-depth detail on all the road cars sold around the world, as well as the 997's competition exploits.

ISBN: 978-1-845848-64-4
Hardback • 208 pages
• 363 pictures

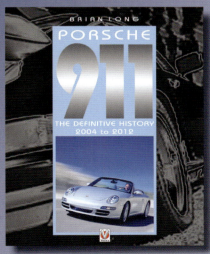

For more information or to order go to www.veloce.co.uk
• email: info@veloce.co.uk • Tel: +44(0)1305 260068

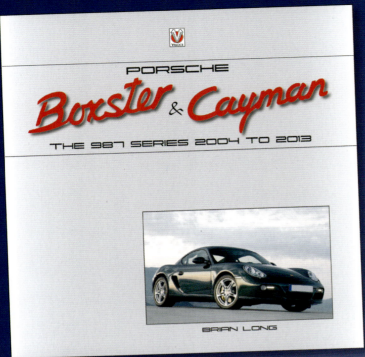

The definitive history of the Porsche 987 series Boxster and Cayman lines, including an overview of all the models sold in each of the world's major markets. Packed full of information and contemporary illustrations sourced from the factory, it provides the perfect guide for enthusiasts, historians and those looking for authenticity.

ISBN: 978-1-787110-81-6
Hardback • 25x25cm
• 180 pages • 288 pictures

The full history of Porsche's 981-type Boxster and Cayman lines, written with the help of the factory by an acknowledged marque expert.

ISBN: 978-1-787117-93-8
Hardback • 25x25cm
• 192 pages • 293 pictures

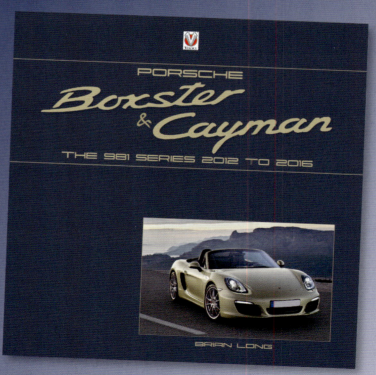

For more information or to order go to www.veloce.co.uk
• email: info@veloce.co.uk • Tel: +44(0)1305 260068

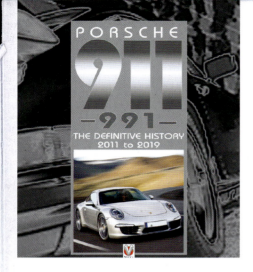

Index

Abu Dhabi Proton Racing 152
Achleitner, August 7, 8, 126, 202
ACO 183
ADAC 154, 197, 199, 205
AF Corse 152
Alegra Motorsports 182, 205
Alex Job Racing 119
Ammermüller, Michael 88, 107, 184, 185
Andlauer, Julien 198
Armbruster, Daniel 182
Aston Martin 75, 88, 199, 206
Aston Martin Racing 153
Attwood, Richard 177
Audi 8, 66, 91, 122, 136, 143, 150, 152, 181, 184, 197
Auto Express 163
Auto, Motor und Sport 38
Auto Union 10
Autocar 35, 75, 143, 176

Bachler, Klaus 183, 197
Bamber, Earl 107, 152, 183, 195, 197, 203, 204
Barker, Ben 107
Bathurst 107, 197, 205
Beijing Show 144
Bell, Derek 178
Bentley 8
Bergmeister, Jorg 68, 104, 152, 154, 196, 200, 201
Bernhard, Timo 68, 197
Black Swan Racing 152, 197
Blancpain 106, 121, 153, 183, 195, 197, 198, 205
Blume, Oliver 91, 136, 144, 160, 185, 190
BMC 13
BMW 8, 104, 120, 182, 183, 195
Bose 42
Boulle, Nicholas 203
Brumos 119, 199, 204
Bruni, Gianmaria 182, 198, 199, 206
Bugatti 8
Burmester 42

Cairoli, Matteo 155, 205

Cameron, David 150
Campbell, Matt 185, 198, 203, 205
Car 35, 118
Car & Driver 35, 59, 160, 181, 203
Catchpole, Henry 138
Chevrolet 120, 152, 183
Christensen, Michael 104, 106, 152, 196, 198-201, 206
Chung, Woosung 172
Circuit of the Americas 104, 120, 152, 182
Citroën 41
Coca-Cola 204
Competition Motorsports 183
CORE Autosport 102, 182
Craft-Bamboo Racing 197

Dalziel, Ryan 122
Davis, Andrew 104
Daytona 104, 106, 119, 120, 151-153, 182, 195, 203, 204
De Leener, Adrien 197
Dempsey, Patrick 104, 119
Dempsey Racing 104
Detroit 119, 152, 182
Detroit Show 43, 56, 57, 95, 96, 110, 113, 139, 159
Diess, Herbert 190
Dinamic Motorsport 205
Dodge 104, 119
Dumas, Romain 68, 88, 197
Dumbreck, Peter 122
Dürheimer, Wolfgang 8

EbiMotors 196, 197
Edwards, Sean 88
EFFORT Racing 122
Eng, Philipp 122, 123, 152
Estre, Kevin 152, 155, 182, 183, 188, 197-201, 206
Evo 27, 74, 203

Falken Motorsports 122
Farnbacher, Mario 152
Febbo, Michael 138

Ferrari 84, 88, 103, 104, 122, 150, 152, 153, 182, 183, 196, 199, 205, 206
FIA 69, 107, 119, 152, 183, 191, 195, 199
Fiat 8, 13
Ford 152, 182, 183, 198, 204
Frankfurt Show 6, 7, 10, 38, 76, 89, 124, 136, 138, 176
Fuchs 85, 134
Fuji Speedway 198, 200

Geneva Show 54, 69, 77, 95, 116, 144, 160, 185
Getrag 63
Giermaziak, Kuba 107
GMG Racing 183
Goodwood Festival of Speed 172, 206
GPX Racing 205
Grande America 195
Grove, Stephen 107
Guardian, The 190
Gulf Racing UK 121, 151, 152, 196

Haerter, Holger 8
Hargrove, Scott 196, 205
Harling, Bernd 55
Hatter, Tony 7
Hatz, Wolfgang 7, 8, 96, 138
Hedlund, Mike 153
Henzler, Wolf 105, 119, 122, 152, 153

Imola 153
Imperatori, Alexandre 122
IMSA 88, 102, 104, 152, 181-183, 185, 191, 195, 198, 203-205
IMSA Performance (Matmut) 153
Indianapolis 104
ItalDesign 8

Jaguar 16, 38, 75, 116
Jahn, David 155
Jaminet, Mathieu 197, 199, 205
JMW Motorsport 153

223

Kable, Greg 35, 85
Karmann 8
KCMG 152
Kern, Lars 164, 184, 188, 205
Klohs, Otto 205
Kulla, Matthias 7
KÜS 154, 197
Kyalami 143, 205

Lagaay, Harm 7
Laguna Seca 55, 104, 119, 120, 152, 183, 184, 196, 197, 203, 205
Lamborghini 8, 203
Larson, Greg 95
Le Mans 88, 89, 101, 119, 150, 151, 182, 190, 198-200, 202, 203
Lewis, Michael 153
Lieb, Marc 68, 88, 119, 183, 197
Lietz, Richard 68, 88, 119, 120, 152, 198, 199, 206
Lime Rock 119, 152, 182, 183, 196, 203
Lindsay, Patrick 119, 120, 196, 200, 201, 203
Long, Patrick 104, 106, 152-154, 183, 196, 203, 205
Long Beach 104, 105, 119, 152, 182, 195, 203
Los Angeles Show 55, 75, 89, 93, 179, 193, 194

Macau 153
Macht, Michael 8
Mader, Thomas 185
Magnus Racing 104
Maier, Bernhard 96
Makowiecki, Fred 152, 182, 184, 195-197
Manthey, Olaf 103, 150
Manthey Racing 103, 153, 154, 181, 197, 198, 205
Martini 100, 101
Mauer, Michael 7, 9, 18
May, Theresa 150
McLaren 84, 143
Mercedes-Benz 7, 19, 38, 138, 154, 197, 204
Merkel, Angela 136
Meschke, Lutz 136
Mezger, Hans 8
Michelin 204
Mid-Ohio 195, 196, 203, 204
Morbitzer, Ulrich 63
Mössle, Erhard 150
Motegi 154
Motor Trend 35, 59, 84, 138, 189
Müller, Matthias 7, 8, 56, 96, 124, 136, 190
Müller, Sven 123, 154, 155, 205

Needell, Tiff 99
Neubauer, Alfred 19
New York Auto Show 74, 75, 77, 101, 176, 203
Nielsen, Christina 196
Nissan 59, 74
Nürburgring 35, 74, 78, 82, 106, 107, 116, 118, 119, 122, 152, 154, 163, 164, 172, 183, 188, 205

Obama, Barack 159
Olsen, Dennis 185, 203, 205

Ontario 104, 119, 121, 152, 183, 196, 203, 204
Opel 8

Paris Salon 11, 63, 191, 192
Park Place Motorsports 152, 183, 196, 203, 205
PCA 113
Perfetti, Egidio 200, 201
Peugeot 89
Piech, Ferdinand 66
Piech, Ursula 66
Pilet, Patrick 68, 103, 119-121, 152, 182, 183, 195, 196, 203, 204
Pirelli 153, 183, 196, 205
Porsche, Butzi 10
Porsche, Ferdinand 10, 66, 91
Porsche, Ferry 7, 10, 54, 76, 91
Porsche, Wolfgang 7, 91, 167
Porsche Design 10, 170, 171, 203
Porsche GT Team 181, 182
Potsch, Hans-Dieter 8
Precote Herberth Motorsport 198
Preuninger, Andreas 163
Prosser, Dan 163
Proton Competition 121, 153, 183, 196, 197
Proton Racing (Dempsey-) 152, 181, 198- 200, 204
Pumpelly, Spencer 119, 120

Qatar Holding LLC 8

Raeder Automotive 103
Ragginger, Martin 122
Renauer, Robert 153, 198, 199
Rennsport Reunion 55, 192
Riberas, Alex 152
Ried, Christian 198
Road & Track 35, 159
Road America (Elkhart Lake) 104, 120, 152, 183, 195, 196
Road Atlanta 106, 120, 121, 153, 183, 195-197, 203
Robichon, Zach 203, 204
Roda, Giorgio 205
Rolls-Royce 93, 99
Rothmans 198
Rover 13
ROWE Racing 205
RUF 94

Saab 7
Scania 8
SCCA 107, 122, 153, 183
Schein, Michael 154
SEAT 8
Sebring 104, 106, 119, 152, 182, 195, 198, 203, 204
Sellers, Bryan 105, 119
Sepang 153, 184
Shanghai 103, 198
Shanghai Motor Show 77, 105
Sharapova, Maria 93
Silverstone 121, 154, 198

Skoda 8
Snow, Madison 120
Snow Racing 104
Sochi 107
Sofronas, James 183
Spa-Francorchamps 88, 183, 184, 197-199, 205
SRO 153, 195, 205
Steiner, Michael 136, 138
Streather, Adrian 154
Sutcliffe, Steve 75
Suzuka 197, 205
Suzuki 61, 172

Tandy, Nick 119, 120, 152, 177, 195, 196, 203-205
Team Falken Tire 104-106, 119
Team Manthey 69
Team Project 1 200, 201
Thiim, Nicki 88, 90, 107
Tokyo Motor Show 62, 89, 150, 179
Top Gear 148, 165, 176, 181
Tour de France Automobile 144
Toyota 150, 181, 185, 198
Trump, Donald 159
Tudor 102, 104, 152

USAC 183

Vanthoor, Laurens 182, 183, 195, 197, 200, 203, 204
Varga, Peter 13, 77, 186
VDA 139, 154, 165
Virginia 104, 120, 152, 183, 196, 203
Volkswagen 6-8, 10, 13 35, 54, 66, 91, 136, 144, 150, 190
Von Platen, Detlev 136, 193

Walkinshaw Racing 183
Walliser, Frank-Steffen 202
Walther, Jens 182
Watkins Glen 104, 106, 119, 152, 182, 196, 203, 204
WeatherTech 152, 182
Webber, Mark 160
Werner, Dirk 182, 183, 197, 205
What Car? 84
Which Car? 195
Wiedeking, Wendelin 6-8
Winterkorn, Martin 8, 136
Wright Motorsports 119, 183, 196, 197, 205

Yamano, Naoya 154
Yas Marina 88, 90

Zellmer, Klaus 148
ZF 28

The Porsche company, along with its subsidiaries and products, are mentioned throughout this book.